Holding Together

Christopher Cocksworth is the Bishop of Coventry, having been Principal of Ridley Hall, Cambridge, and Director of the Southern Theological Education and Training Scheme. He is the author of a number of books, including *Evangelical Eucharistic Thought in the Church of England* (Cambridge University Press, 1993) and *Holy, Holy, Holy: Worshipping the Trinitarian God* (Darton, Longman & Todd, 1997) and (with Rosalind Brown) *Being a Priest Today* (Canterbury Press, 2000 and 2006), now in its fifth printing. Christopher is married with five children.

Also by the same author and available from Canterbury Press

Being a Priest Today: Exploring Priestly Identity

Christopher Cocksworth and Rosalind Brown

'This well-crafted book on being a priest feeds the heart, mind and soul. Drawing deeply from the wells of scripture and tradition, it will inspire those considering a call to ordination, renew the vocations of those long ordained, and enlarge the vision of all God's people. In challenging times for the Church's ministry, that's a great gift.'

> *The Rt Revd Graham James, Bishop of Norwich and Chair of the Ministry Division of the Church of England*

'Here is wisdom, knowledge and experience . . . a rich source of inspiration.'

> *The Reader*

'This welcome book offers a picture of priesthood that is strongly focused and yet reflects a Church in which old ideological demarcations are dissolving in a new meeting of minds.'

> *Theology*

www.canterburypress.co.uk

Holding Together: Gospel, Church and Spirit

The Essentials of Christian Identity

Christopher Cocksworth

CANTERBURY
PRESS

Norwich

© Christopher Cocksworth 2008

First published in 2008 by the Canterbury Press Norwich
(a publishing imprint of Hymns Ancient & Modern Limited,
a registered charity)
13–17 Long Lane, London EC1A 9PN

www.scm-canterburypress.co.uk

Scripture quotations are mostly from the Revised Standard Version
of the Bible, copyright 1946, 1952 and 1971 by the Division of
Christian Education of the National Council of the Churches of
Christ in the USA. Used by permission. All rights reserved.

Some scripture quotations are from the New Revised Standard
Version of the Bible, copyright 1989 by the Division of Christian
Education of the National Council of the Churches of Christ in the
USA. Used by permission. All rights reserved.

British Library Cataloguing in Publication data

A catalogue record for this book is available
from the British Library

ISBN 978-1-85311-839-5

Typeset by Regent Typesetting, London
Printed in the UK by CPI William Clowes
Beccles NR34 7TL

Dedicated
to my mother and father,
to my mother- and father-in-law,
and to all my mothers and fathers
in the faith.

Contents

Preface

This is a book about Christian identity – a form of being and living as a follower of Christ that holds the gospel together with the life of the church and the life of the Spirit for life in the world. More specifically, it is about *evangelical* identity. It is written by someone who found the grace of God – or rather who was found by the grace of God – through the teaching and witness of evangelicals. Hence I will be for ever indebted to evangelicalism, eternally grateful to those who were compelled to share the love of Christ with me and from whom I discovered the power of the scriptures. The aim of this book is not in any way to go beyond the simple gospel of salvation and the conviction that the Bible is the inspired word of God that I learnt from my spiritual fathers and mothers. It is to go deeper into the scriptural gospel, to mine more of its depths, to receive more fully of its fullness, to grasp more of what it means to be a gospel person, an evangelical.

This book was written in an evangelical Anglican theological college while I was its Principal. Much of what it says has been on my heart for many years, but during my time at Ridley Hall I was much encouraged by the life and teaching of an evangelical leader of a generation long since passed: Handley Moule, the first Principal of the college. I find Moule inspiring because of his capacity to hold together those things which Christians, evangelicals included, sometimes allow to be unnecessarily forced apart. In the terms of his day he was an evangelical churchman, who was also, rarely for his time, a Keswick man. That means that he was a convinced evangelical who was at the same time committed to the continuous, visible, historical expression of Christ's people – embodied, for him, in the Church of England. So he described himself as a church evangelical. At the same time, he had discovered the dynamic, life-transforming power of the Holy Spirit as taught in the Keswick Movement of his day. Biblical gospel, catholic church, powerful Spirit: Moule held these fundamental realities of Christian existence together in his teaching, writing and ministering. In so doing, he presented a vision of an ecclesial form of evangelical life, enlivened by the Spirit.

Moule was satisfied with nothing less than the 'unsearchable riches of Christ' (Ephesians 3.8, RSV) and would frequently exhort his students and readers to seek the presence of Christ and search out the extraordinary goodness and graciousness of Christ's work in all its depth and breadth. Following his lead, Chapter 1 begins with some biblical study on the one in whom 'all things hold together' (Colossians 1.17) before moving on to make the central claim of all that follows, that there is no gospel without the church, and no church without the gospel, and that both are bound to the Spirit.

Chapters 2–8 consider some of the areas where evangelical Christians with their instinctive feel for the gospel, and catholic Christians with their instinctive feel for the church, have often found themselves in sharp disagreement. Chapter 2 looks at the relationship between scripture and tradition. Chapter 3 examines different understandings of justification. Chapter 4 focuses on the place of the church in God's purposes. Chapter 5 considers Mary as a way of rounding off this set of chapters on word, salvation and church, and testing out some of its conclusions. Chapters 6–8 form a different sequence, though still dealing with themes where evangelicals and catholics have seldom seen eye to eye: worship in Chapter 6, liturgy and baptism in Chapter 7 and the Eucharist in Chapter 8. Chapter 9 is on mission, the point at which Christians are under a very specific mandate to unite in order that the world may believe.

In different ways, each chapter attempts to hold the gospel together with the church, and to hold the gospel and the church together with the Spirit. In some chapters (for example,

Chapters 2, 3 and 7) this is done in what might be called a dialectical way very much in the spirit of Charles Simeon, often said to be the founder of modern Anglican evangelicalism, who believed that 'as wheels in a complicated machine may move in opposite directions and yet subserve one common end, so may truths [of scripture] *apparently opposite* be perfectly reconcilable with each other, and equally subserve the purposes of God in the accomplishment of our salvation'.[1] Here, often sharply contrasting positions in evangelical and catholic theology are made to face each other so that they can listen to each other *in the Spirit*. Amos Yong, a leading Asian Pentecostal theologian, argues persuasively that 'a vital pneumatology is indispensable for a truly healthy dialectic in that it drives the to-and-fro movement necessary to sustain both poles'.[2] As well as sustaining the debate between its two ends, the perspective of the Spirit often shifts its angle just enough to allow both sides to see each other's positions in a new light and to reveal their underlying complementarity.

In other chapters (for example, Chapters 6, 4 and 9) the approach is more dialogical than dialectical. Here the emphases that begin with the gospel are placed alongside those that begin with the church or with the Spirit. They are then allowed to converse with each other so that they are able to feed and enlarge our understanding of, for example, our calling to belong to God's people (Chapter 4), to worship God together (Chapter 6) and to proclaim the coming of God's kingdom (Chapter 9). In Chapters 5 (on Mary) and 8 (on the Eucharist) the method is more deliberately integrative. In these chapters, which form the conclusion to two sequences of studies (the first on word, salvation and church; the second on matters relating to worship), the three overarching themes of the book are held together by being used together in a common project, as a loom weaves different threads into one garment.

Three points of clarification are needed. First, these three methods are not quite as self-contained as they sound. Dialectic involves dialogue and implies some form of positive interaction, if not integration itself. Nevertheless, their different starting points make them suitable for different tasks within an overall theological purpose. This is why different methods are sometimes used in the same chapter. Second, more importantly, gospel, church and Spirit are most definitely not self-contained categories. The co-inherence of these theological categories is, in fact, a basic assumption of the book and the reason why it also proposes a certain co-inherence of the traditions of the church. On the one hand the delineation of the categories is simply an organizational device. Sometimes it can help to isolate individual theological concerns simply in order to see how they properly relate to the wider theological picture. On the other hand, though, there is a good deal of evidence in the life of God's people – including those of us who call ourselves evangelicals – of a tendency to so emphasize one aspect of God's grace that we neglect others, especially perhaps when we see them being over-emphasized elsewhere.[3]

Third – and consequently – readers will soon find that the easy equation of the theological themes and church traditions (i.e. of gospel–church–Spirit with evangelical–catholic–charismatic) is potentially confusing. For example, when proposing that evangelicals recover a more self-consciously catholic and charismatic identity, I am not suggesting that they become Roman Catholics or Pentecostals. As I hope will be clear in Chapter 2, my challenge to myself and other evangelicals is that we follow through the ecclesiological and pneumatological implications of the gospel, developing therefore what might be called a form of catholic evangelicalism in the Spirit. Generally in theological discussion, the association of the word 'catholic' with the Roman Catholic Church or the Anglo-Catholic tradition lends itself to particular confusions. These I have been unable to avoid. For example, I often draw on Roman Catholic or Anglo-Catholic theology to explore the ecclesiological depths of the gospel. I have done so because I have found that these theological traditions often work harder than my own at the 'being with others' that the gospel involves and that lies at the heart of what it means to be catholic. Sometimes I have found that the catholic theological tradition has informed my understanding of the corporate realities of the gospel. At other times I have felt that it has over-egged the pudding and, as it were, solidified the very gospel that forms the church and which 'the one, holy, catholic and apostolic church' (as the Nicene Creed puts it) is called to proclaim. You will notice that in these two sentences, as elsewhere in the book, I am using the word 'catholic' first in the sense of the ecclesial and theological tradition identified with the Roman Catholic, Anglo-Catholic, and, in some ways, Eastern Orthodox traditions, and second, in the sense of the ecclesial identity of all those who are made members of Christ. Again, I hope that Chapter 2, particularly with its semantic analysis of catholic (as well as evangelical and charismatic) will help to keep matters clear and show how to distinguish between the two uses in the rest of the book.

As this short summary of its contents has shown, this book does not directly address the holding together of the Anglican Communion during its present disputes. My sights are set on older – and, I would say, deeper, more fundamental – tensions and controversies than those that immediately confront much of the church today, Anglican or otherwise. Nevertheless, I hope that aspects of the book's method may be of value in the present situation: for unless followers of Christ can listen attentively to each other in the Spirit and according to the scriptures to discern what is of the gospel in the other's position, we have little to offer each other, let alone the world.

In addition to my eternal debt to those who first shared the gospel with me, I owe a great deal to those who helped me complete this piece of writing about the gospel and the church to which it gives rise, and the Spirit who gives life to both. Stephen Sykes' invitation to give the 2004 Michael Vasey Memorial Lecture kick-started the project some time ago. Believers in Egypt, Syria and India provided generous hospitality and much inspiration for it.[4] Colleagues at Ridley Hall modelled much of what I write about in their teaching, preaching and living. A group of research-active students at Ridley, first convened by Philip Hobday, gave up the chance to present their work to each other in favour of a few evenings discussing mine, much to my benefit. Philip later read the whole type-script and made invaluable stylistic, structural and theological suggestions. Another member of the group, Peter Sanlon, gave up some of his research time to introduce me to a computer program that much improved my endnotes. John Colwell of Spurgeon's College also read and commented on the manu-script, as did my good friend, Jeremy Begbie. My son, Ashley, spent many hours chasing up references that his father failed to record properly, and also pointed me to some new and valu-able sources, proving in the process to be a reliable theological guide in his own right. Although they cannot be held responsi-ble in any way for what follows, I am deeply grateful to all of them for their careful thought and kind support. I would also like to record my thanks to Kate Nix, my former secretary, for much help with the final stages of the typescript, to Christine Smith of Canterbury Press whose beguiling combination of patience and persuasion makes her my favourite publisher, and to Charlotte, my wife, and all of our sons, upon whom I have depended in this endeavour – as in every aspect of life – more than they can know. Finally, I should like to express my thanks to my mother and father, to my mother- and father-in-law, and to all my mothers and fathers in the faith whose influence lies behind this book by dedicating it to them.

Holding Together

'Therefore, what God has joined together, let no one separate.'
Jesus of Nazareth

Jesus Christ, God's own Son, is the heart of the gospel and the cause of the scriptures. Knowing Jesus Christ, being in personal relationship with him, is the essence of evangelical Christianity. Jesus – and all that he brings – is the good news of the kingdom of God. So in a book about evangelical Christian identity, which seeks to hold together the great themes of gospel, church and Spirit, the proper place in which to start is with the confession of Christ as the one 'in whom all things hold together' in the great hymn of redemption in Colossians 1.15–19.

Christ and the gospel, church and Spirit

The letter to the Colossians was written round about 60–61 CE.[1] The hymn in chapter 1, or at least some of it, may well have been circulating around the churches of the day before Paul made use of it in the letter.[2] It may even have had pre-Christian origins in first-century Jewish worship. Paul may well have added to it and adapted it to serve his particular theological purposes, how much we are not quite sure. But the important point to note is that the extraordinary claims it makes for Jesus Christ were being made only 30 years or so after he had hung on the cross, executed under Roman law as a criminal in a death considered by Jewish law to be accursed. He was now being acclaimed in the churches as the 'image of the invisible God' (1.15) in whom 'all the fullness of God was pleased to dwell' (1.19), as the one in whom and for whom 'all things

. . . were created' (1.16), and as the one through whom God 'reconcile(d) to himself all things' (1.20) through his death. The historical figure, still vivid in the memories of those who had met him, was actually the embodiment of God in human form. Although he was known as the son of Mary and Joseph who grew up in Galilee, in reality, he was – and is – the principle and purpose of the whole creative activity of God. The death he died in apparent defeat was, in fact, the action of decisive cosmic significance by which the record of our sins was erased and the forces of evil defeated. Here are the fundamental Christological claims of our faith which lead to the great doctrines of the Trinity, the incarnation, the atonement and the church. Through the eternal Word, God has created the world. The Word, God's own Son, became flesh. He died for the world on the cross and he was raised to life as the 'firstborn from the dead' (1.18), the head of the new community of the kingdom, his church. This is the 'mystery that has been hidden throughout the ages and generations but has now been revealed to his saints' (1.26).

Verses 17 and 18 of the hymn act as a pivot between the first stanza, which concentrates on creation, and the second, which focuses on redemption:

He himself is before all things and in him all things hold together (*sunestēken*). He is the head of the body, his church.

The verb *sunestēkenai* was used in Platonic and Stoic philosophy of the time to denote the unity of the entire world, a unity which was believed to be found in the divine Logos (God's self-expression) who was the unifying bond holding everything together. Jewish philosophers readily adopted the idea of God's Word being the creative presence or activity of God. Philo, for example, described God's Word as 'the bond of all things, the one who holds them together indissolubly and binds them fast, when in themselves they are dissoluble'.[3] The staggering claim of this early Christian hymn is that Jesus (the recently crucified messianic figure) is, as J. B. Lightfoot says in his commentary, 'the principle of cohesion in the universe [who] impresses upon creation that unity which makes it a cosmos rather than a chaos'.[4] He is 'the sustainer of the universe and the unifying principle of its life [without whose] *continuous* sustaining activity all would disintegrate', as Peter O'Brien's more modern commentary puts it.[5]

Where verse 17 sums up the claim of the first stanza of the hymn that Jesus is the mediator of the creative activity of God, verse 18 introduces the second stanza which confesses Christ as the one through whose death God's redeeming activity in and for the world is achieved. Jesus is the 'head of the body, the church', the new community which embodies the reconciling purposes of God. Christ's capacity to hold together the whole of creation is the basis of his redemptive ministry to bring together sinful, estranged humanity (1.21) and the God of grace (1.2). In these few verses Jesus Christ holds together the invisible God and the visible world, the uncreated and the created, the fullness of divinity and the life of a human being, the eternal reality of God and the contingent events of human history, all the spiritual powers and all material things, the holy God and redeemed humanity.

This is a breathtaking panorama of God's relationship with the world, at each point concentrated in the person of Jesus Christ. It provides the platform for the rest of Paul's letter to the church of Colossae. Paul commends the Christians of Colossae for their 'faith in Christ' and their 'love ... for all the saints' (1.4). He tells them how he continually gives thanks in his prayers for their grasp of the 'grace of God in truth' (1.6) and their 'love in the Spirit' (1.8). At the same time he is concerned about a danger hanging over their faith and life in Christ. An insidiously threatening teaching was probably widespread throughout the three cities of Lycus valley of which Colossae was one, and perhaps even beginning to make itself felt within the Colossian church. It was poised to prey on the unsuspecting Christians of the city (2.8) and, if allowed to take its course, would gradually dismember the Colossians' faith. Paul's letter is an exhortation to stand firm and to press on towards maturity in the faith (1.11, 23; 4.12).

Although biblical scholars are reticent about attempting to define precisely this false teaching, there is general agreement that it represented a form of Jewish faith heavily influenced both by mystical tendencies within Jewish religion and by contemporary pagan speculations about the soul's ascent through the heavenly realms. The former developed into *merkabah* mysticism with is complex exercises and rituals designed to lead to the sort of vision of the heavenly chariot (*merkabah*) experienced by the prophet Ezekiel.[6] The latter developed into sophisticated gnostic religious systems of spiritual spheres separating the material world from the divine life, through which the soul must navigate itself in order to find its way to the fullness of God's light.

Left unchecked, this teaching risked undoing everything. Although it was quite capable of high-sounding statements about Jesus Christ and his place in the order of intermediaries between God and the world, and on the importance of obeying his ethical instructions, this incipient form of Jewish–Christian gnosticism displaced Christ from the centre of God's purposes and denied the efficacy of his work on the cross. As F. F. Bruce puts it in his commentary on Colossians, Paul's strategy was to confront 'the false *gnōsis* and worldly *askēsis* taught at Colossae with the true *gnōsis* and spiritual *askēsis* of Christ'.[7] In other words, rather than advanced form of knowledge (*gnōsis*) and a complex systems of religious observance and abstinence (*askēsis*), which would assist the believer to orientate a route for the soul's redemption in the fullness of God, Paul reiterates 'the grace of God in truth' (1.6) – namely, that in Jesus Christ the fullness of deity dwells bodily. Christ is the Lord of all that exists. He has disempowered all the hostile spiritual forces with their claims against us. Forgiveness of sins has been achieved through his decisive death and powerful resurrection. The only form of *gnōsis* and *askēsis* needed for redemption is faith in Christ and participation in his life:

As you therefore have received Christ Jesus the Lord, continue to live your lives in him, rooted and built up in him and established in the faith, just as you were taught, abounding in thanksgiving (2.6–7).

It is worth pausing to note that Paul's campaign against the embryonic Colossian heresy reflects several features of the classic evangelical critique of catholic and charismatic forms of spirituality. Often with considerable justification, evangelicals have accused catholic theology of constructing 'human traditions' (2.8) which bind people to unnecessary religious practices and obscure the unique mediatorial work of Christ. My wife was brought up in South America and is not short of stories about a debased form of Christianity, in which the perfectly respectable practice of spiritual discipline, or a quite proper belief in the communion of saints, have been turned into superstitious systems of religious manipulation. The gospel of 'the grace of God in truth' – where Christ is the agent of creation, the mediator between heaven and earth and the reconciler of all things to God who offers us forgiveness of sin, freedom from all the powers of evil and fullness of life in the fullness of God – has been eclipsed through the accretions of human traditions, requiring forms of abasement or encouraging forms of invocation of the saints which look suspiciously close to all that Paul castigates in Colossae (2.16–18).

Some evangelicals have claimed – not always without reason – that charismatic devotion too easily lures believers into preoccupations with exotic religious experiences (2.18) and speculation about the hierarchies of angels and demons (2.20), diverting them away from simple faith in Christ and the demands of patient, faithful discipleship (1.11; 4.12). 'Why do we spend time bothering with a "word which someone feels might be from the Lord" rather than giving much more time to the preaching of scripture, which we know is *the word of the Lord*?', an ordinand asked me after (in his view at least) a particularly unconvincing sharing of 'pictures' and 'words' in a college chapel service. Whatever you think about the way God communicates his word, you do not need to have spent much time in charismatic circles before picking up the message that there seems to be just one more experience you need to have, one more gift you need to find, or one more new spiritual perspective you need to acquire if you are to keep up with the work of God.

The trouble with an over-emphasis on certain aspects of the faith is the over-reaction it causes, often leading to a form of the faith that distorts its proper contours by denying or neglecting that which is good, right and thoroughly scriptural. It is a travesty to equate catholic Christianity with 'human traditions' (2.8) or charismatic Christianity with preoccupations with 'visions' (2.18) and powers (2.15), just as it is very unfair to define evangelical Christianity as a loveless legalism and unthinking biblicism, as its strongest critics often do. Catholic Christianity is about belonging to Christ's body (1.24) and sharing fully in the process of being 'nourished and knit together' (2.19) by Christ. Charismatic Christianity is about living the life of God's 'love in the Spirit' (1.8). Later we will explore how, rather than being antithetical to being evangelical, being catholic and charismatic are necessary to evangelical faith and life. This is for the simple reason that, according to scripture, the church and the Spirit belong to the gospel.

We return to Paul's remedy for the Colossians. He preaches Christ to them as the incarnate mediator of God's creative and redemptive purposes for the world. One of the rallying cries of the Reformation – *Christ alone* – fits well with Paul's passion in the pages of this letter. Everything in the cosmos, material and spiritual, is created through Christ (1.16). The fullness of God dwells in him (1.9; 2.9). He has done all that is necessary to free us from evil (2.15), to put us right with God (2.13) and to give us fullness of life in him (2.10). Therefore, says Paul, hold fast to him (2.19). Stay bound to him, do not allow other practices or philosophies to bind you (1.8). Keep your faith in him as Saviour and Lord. This is the *gospel life* – life in Christ. It is the new life of the gospel made possible by receiving the gospel – by receiving Christ (2.6). At the same time, it is *catholic life*, life lived out in the community of Christ's disciples; and it is *charismatic life*, life lived out in the Spirit. Paul never isolates belief in Christ from membership of the church and empowerment by the Spirit. Indeed, a great deal of the letter is encouragement for the Colossian Christians to live the gospel that they have received in the fellowship of the church by the work of the Holy Spirit.

There are three further points that need to be made about the letter as a whole. They build upon and reinforce what we have already said. The first is to underline the importance Paul places on the church in the letter. As we have seen, the church is the body of which Christ is the head. Believers are *together* 'to put on' the virtues of the gospel – the characteristics of Christ (3.12–14) – so that they may be bound together 'in perfect harmony' (3.14). They are to build each other up through the word of Christ by mutual teaching and corporate worship (3.16). They are to express the rule of Christ in the ordinary human relationships of marriage, family and household (3.18–4.1). So intimate is the relationship between Christ and his people, and so intrinsic is membership of the church to Christian identity, that Paul talks about 'completing', through his own sufferings for the cause of the gospel, 'what is lacking in Christ's afflictions for the sake of his body, that is the church' (1.24). Paul does not mean, of course, that his or any one else's suffering contributes to the atoning work of Christ. The word he uses for 'sufferings' (*thlipseon*) does not have the least of a hint of a sacrificial act in the atoning sense. But, in the sense of encouraging or edifying the life of the church, it is, in the words of Lightfoot,

> a simple matter of fact that the afflictions of every saint and martyr do supplement the afflictions of Christ. The Church is built up by repeated acts of self-denial in successive individuals and successive generations. They continue the work which Christ began. They bear their part in the sufferings of Christ. (2 Corinthians 1.7; Philippians 3.10)[8]

Paul says that Christ's sufferings are incomplete, not in any sense to imply that the redemptive capacity of Christ is somehow lacking (the whole of his letter is designed to prove that it is sufficient), but because he believes in the literal participation of Christians in the life of Christ. The suffering of an individual member of the church for the sake of the gospel is a Christological and ecclesiological event. It involves Christ because the church is his body and it involves every member of the church because each is bound to the other in the one body.

Second, although Paul says less directly about the Spirit than he does about the church in the letter, his specific references to the Spirit count for a great deal. In 1.8 he commends the Colossians for their 'love in the Spirit'. In 1.9 he tells them about his prayer that they will be filled with 'spiritual wisdom', wisdom that comes as the Spirit's gift (see 1 Corinthians 2.10–16). In 3.16 he encourages them to sing 'spiritual songs', to worship in the Spirit (see Ephesians 5.18–20). Loving in the Spirit, thinking and acting in the Spirit, worshipping in the Spirit: these are the cornerstones of life lived in and through the presence and power of the Spirit.

These relatively few direct references to the Spirit are enough in themselves to build a strong doctrine of the importance of the life of the Spirit, but they can also be supplemented by Paul's many references to the ongoing presence and activity of the ascended Christ among his people, for we know that in Pauline thought 'the Spirit conveys what Christ bestows'.[9] Theoretically Paul could distinguish the indwelling Christ from the indwelling Spirit, but practically he and his converts knew that they could never be separated because 'the exalted Christ imparts his life and power to them through the Spirit'.[10] Hence, Paul's Christological emphasis in the letter to the Colossians is at the same time an implicitly pneumatological emphasis. We cannot live in Christ without living in and by his Spirit.

Third, in a book on the theme of *holding together*, it is worth noting again how Paul manages to hold so much together in this letter. We have already discussed the breathtaking claims made in the hymn in chapter 1 for Christ's capacity to hold all things together, even God and humanity. We have just underlined Paul's conviction about the intimate relationship between Christ and the church and we have seen that for Paul, Christ and the Spirit are inseparable – even, in terms of everyday experience, indistinguishable. But Paul makes other connections in his letter between, for example, baptism and faith (2.11–12), faith and love (1.4; 2.2–3; 2.6–7), faith and works (3.5; 3.12), Greek and Jew (3.9); word and worship (3.16), the spiritual life and the ordinary realities of human living and relating in family and economic life (3.18–4.1). He refuses to divide what he believes God has joined together.

Terms and purpose

As this short study of Colossians has reminded us (and we could have chosen other books to demonstrate the same thing), gospel, church and Spirit belong inseparably together. We are reconciled to God by the all-sufficient work of Christ, the incarnate image of God, and we live out our new life in Christ within his body, the church, and in the Holy Spirit, God's gift of life. Etymologically evangelicalism emphasizes the gospel – the *euangelion* in Greek or *evangelium* in Latin. Historically the adjective 'evangelical' was used first simply to describe what pertained to the gospel. As the sixteenth century progressed, it began to be applied to those who sought to make a stand for certain truths of the gospel, *evangelical* truths. During the eighteenth-century revival in the United Kingdom, 'evangelical', often with a capital 'E', became increasingly applied to supporters of the revival with their passion for the gospel and their desire to see scripture preached and lived in the church. Theologically, evangelicals have placed primary emphasis on the scriptural gospel, making it the controlling category in their theology, recognizing that it has been a continual temptation for the church to turn its back on 'the grace of Christ' and to try to dismantle the authentic gospel and construct, futilely, a 'different gospel' (Galatians 1.6–7).

Applying the etymological method to the catholic and charismatic traditions is also enlightening. The word 'catholic' is derived from two Greek words: *kata*, meaning 'with' or 'according to', and *holos*, meaning 'whole'. For many believers, 'being with other Christians', in the sense of sharing in the faith of the one church, being part of the life of the whole church and following the teaching believed by other Christians, is the starting point for Christian identity. The instinct for catholicity is born out of the profound recognition that there is only one body of Christ with Christ as its head. Similarly, 'charismatic' comes from the Greek *charismata*, referring to the gifts of the Holy Spirit. Charismatic movements have sprung up at various points in the church's history, often at times when God's people seemed to have neglected the dynamic, gift-giving presence of the Spirit in the life of the church. Theologically, charismatics stress the present availability of gifts such as healing, tongues and prophecy, and press for the renewal of the church as a Spirit-filled and Spirit-led community.

I want to describe a form of evangelicalism that takes seriously the life of the church and the life of the Spirit and sees them as intrinsic to the life of the gospel. I do so as an Anglican evangelical who has found that Anglican identity contributes something very significant to evangelical identity in a way that considerably helps this task. Anglican evangelicals belong to the reforming movement that swept across Europe in the sixteenth century as many Christians rediscovered the grace of the gospel and the power of God's word in scripture. It is a movement that has proved to be extremely effective in a variety of cultures and periods since then, including our own. At the same time Anglican evangelicals can trace a clear connection in all sorts of visible and tangible ways to the beginnings of Christian faith in Britain. Through our creeds, liturgies and orders of ministry, we are connected in some way to other churches that also claim an ancient origin and an unbroken continuation: Roman Catholicism, Greek and Oriental Orthodoxy. Furthermore, the movement of the Spirit in periods of evangelical revival, the historic Anglican interest in the Spirit (at least in its liturgical and theological theory if not always in practice), and the deep influence of charismatic theology and spirituality upon many contemporary evangelicals, brings Anglican evangelicals into close contact with the extraordinarily vibrant Pentecostal movements, the fastest growing form of Christian life in today's world.

The location of Anglican evangelicalism at a meeting point between the great Reformation, Catholic and Pentecostal traditions does not of itself produce a form of evangelicalism that successfully holds church and Spirit together with gospel. Because of the tendency we all have to concentrate on one set of truths to the neglect of the other, and because of the legacies of history, which often institutionalize legitimate theological concerns into exclusive ecclesiastical cultures, a self-conscious attempt to describe and develop what might be called a *catholic form of evangelicalism in the Spirit* is required.

I realize that I am taking a risk in talking about catholic evangelicalism. Christians formed in the catholic tradition of the church may accuse me of commandeering their name and claiming to represent the fullness of catholic faith. To them I say that I believe in the enduring need for a distinctively catholic tradition and that I want always to have the privilege of learning from others more deeply immersed in it than I am. Equally, I hope that in what I will say shortly, they will see why it is important, indeed essential, for evangelicals to reclaim their catholic identity.

Christians shaped in the evangelical tradition, especially those used to defining themselves in distinction from 'catholicism', may be horrified by any attempt to link the two together. To them I say that I am doing nothing that is *unevangelical* either in a theological or historical sense. Quite the contrary, in fact, because to be an evangelical one must be *with* (*kata*) the whole (*holos*) of the church (that is, one must be a *katholikos*). 'No gospel without the church; no church without the gospel' is my rallying cry. This is what the Reformers, according to Paul Avis' classic study of the Reformers' ecclesiology, believed: 'where the gospel is found Christ is present, and where he is present the church must truly exist'.[11] And here they were simply amplifying Ignatius' dictum from the second century: 'where Jesus Christ is, there is the universal (the catholic) church'.[12] When Jesus comes to us through the gospel he comes to us *with* his people to unite us with himself and *with* his people.

The form of evangelicalism I am proposing is one that is also authentically *charismatic* – one that rejoices in and reaches out for the dynamic empowerment of the Holy Spirit. In fact, just as we might say that the term 'catholic evangelicalism' is, strictly speaking, tautologous – for there is no gospel without the church, and no church without the gospel – so we might say the same for 'charismatic evangelicalism'. There is no gospel without the Spirit. Christ and his gospel come to us by the Spirit. And, of course, there is no church without the Spirit. Ignatius' Christological definition of the church needs to be held together with Irenaeus' pneumatological version – 'where the Spirit of God is, there is the church and all grace'.[13]

Precedents: sixteenth to twenty-first centuries

A strong doctrine of the church, which sees full participation in the life of the church as necessary for Christian existence and which is committed to the continuing, visible life of the universal church, is not alien to the historical origins of evangelicalism. In fact it lies at its heart. In a very revealing exchange between Cardinal Sadoleto and John Calvin in the 1530s (to which we shall refer on several occasions later), Calvin defines the church as 'the society of all the saints, a society which, spread over the whole world, and existing in all ages, yet bound together by the one doctrine and the one Spirit of Christ, cultivates and observes unity of faith and brotherly concord'.[14] He goes on to tell Sadoleto, 'With this Church we deny that we have any disagreement. Nay, rather, as we revere her as our mother, so we desire to remain in her bosom.'[15] In some places in Europe, such as England, the leading Reformers were bishops who were quite clear that they were not creating a new Protestant church but simply reforming the existing Catholic church of which they were the leading pastors and whose office gave them the responsibility and authority to teach the true faith and to maintain its purity. For example, Archbishop Thomas Cranmer called his presentation of a reformed view of the Eucharist *A Defence of the True and Catholic Doctrine of the Sacrament*. He would have considered any idea of his liturgical reforms as a departure for the catholic faith as a great insult. The whole point of his liturgical programme was to return the worship of the church to its true catholic character.

In other parts of Europe the Reformers found themselves in a more complex situation that required hard and, to many, regrettable choices. Heinrich Bornkamm vividly describes the dilemma faced by Martin Luther and other continental Reformers.

> Luther was excluded from his church because of his criticism of the theology and the ecclesiastical condition of his time. It was *his* church from which we was excluded, for it was no other church that he uttered his fervent pleadings and prayers, and his painful laments and angry indictments. Everything he did and said and wrote was not against it, but for it, for its sake, not in order to establish a new church. It was because it was *his* church, the Roman church of that time, that excluded him that an inner reform, which had often taken place before, became something new, outside the existing church.[16]

Even then it must be remembered that in much of continental Europe the creation of Reformation churches was territorial. The usual pattern was for cities or princedoms to join the Reformation. Hence the whole church in that area would re-form itself according to Protestant principles, creating a re-formed church rather than a new church. The chief Protestant principle, of course, was scripture on the grounds that the Bible is the word of God that holds – and holds before the church – 'the word of truth, the gospel' (Colossians 1.5), the word by which the church is formed. The Reformers, therefore, were not anti-catholic, and Protestantism was not an alternative to catholic faith. *Protestari*, the Latin word from which 'Protestant' is derived, means 'to witness, or testify', 'to make a solemn declaration'. The Reformers were trying to call the church back to its scripture and its gospel. Evangelicalism, which is true to their vision, will see itself as speaking within the catholic faith of the church, persuading the church to keep attentive to the dynamic of the gospel and, therefore, to the heart of catholic faith.

Even in the highly polemicized days of the seventeenth century, William Perkins, a leading Puritan, described himself as a 'Reformed Catholic'.[17] This he defined, in his important book with the same title, as 'any one that holds the same necessary heades of religion with the Roman Church, yet so, as he pares off and rejects all errors in doctrine whereby the said religion is corrupted'.[18] He went on to argue that the Roman church had added erroneously to the catechism of the church that had been 'agreed upon ever since the days of the Apostles by all Churches'.[19] Hence, rather than arguing on classic Protestant grounds that the Roman church had departed from scripture, he based his claim on a classic catholic foundation: it had failed to preserve the universal, catholic tradition of the church of which it claimed to be the custodian and interpreter.

John and Charles Wesley will appear at various points in the coming chapters. At this point, I simply want to note two marks of their ministry. The first is their enjoyment of the ordered, sacramental and liturgical life of the historic, continuing church (in a very real sense, they remained 'high-church Anglicans'). The second is their commitment to 'a catholic spirit'. Like other leaders of the eighteenth-century evangelical revival like George Whitefield, and, a little later, John Newton, the Wesleys were avowedly *catholic* in their attitudes to other Christians. They wanted to embrace other Christians wherever they were to be found. For the Wesleys at least, this involved a genuine attempt to be generous towards Roman Catholics as well as Protestant Dissenters, seeking to acknowledge points of agreement over the essentials of Christian faith rather than to focus on differences over less fundamental matters. In his open 'Letter to a Roman Catholic' (where he says that his reader 'deserves the tenderest regard I can show'), and in his celebrated sermon 'Catholic Spirit' (where he calls for 'catholic or universal love'), John Wesley carefully identifies the *catholic core of doctrine* and *catholic principles of Christian practice*, while at the same time allowing differences of genuinely held 'opinions' over secondary theological matters and in practical expressions of the faith.[20]

The rise of the Oxford Movement in the nineteenth century, and the ritualist movement that followed in its wake, caused evangelicals in the Church of England to be at best cautious and at worst antagonistic about anything resembling Roman Catholic thought and practice. Nevertheless, they maintained a strong view – perhaps a stronger view because of the renewed 'catholic threat' – of the Church of England as the rightful and historic church of the land, bearing its authentic liturgy, sacramental system and pattern of ministry. It is clear that relationships between English evangelicals and followers of the Oxford Movement (often called Tractarians) were very strained for most of the nineteenth century. But it should not be overlooked that a group of second-generation Tractarians displayed a remarkable combination of convictions about evangelical conversion on the one hand and catholic principles of church life on the other. George Wilkinson was the most well known and respected member of this small but very significant movement. Often described as a 'Church Methodist',[21] his teaching was thoroughly evangelical, with a strong emphasis on personal commitment to Christ, disciplined life of discipleship and strategies for church growth. Increasingly he was able to integrate these evangelical emphases with a strong view of Christ's presence through the actions of the church in a way that, according to Henry Scott Holland, a distinguished Tractarian, 'held together his Evangelical Gospel and Catholic Creed'.[22]

Although the rise of the Oxford Movement in the nineteenth century, and the fears that it evoked of 'ritualism' and

'Romanism', caused a hardening of English evangelical arteries against things perceived as 'catholic', movements on the world stage during the twentieth century led to a significant softening of attitudes and created opportunities for genuine engagement. The Second Vatican Council in the 1960s initiated a reform of the Roman church that generally took evangelicals by surprise. With clear similarities to many of the Reformation concerns of the sixteenth century, it created a new climate and a new language for theological dialogue. The rapid rise of Pentecostalism and the charismatic experiences of many evangelicals – which they shared with Christians from other traditions across the church – led to a greater humility among evangelicals and a readiness to work with and learn from others. Evangelicals were forced to recognize that the Holy Spirit could not be confined within the bounds of evangelicalism. Increasing contact with Eastern Orthodoxy opened the eyes of evangelicals to swathes of Christianity which, although very different from evangelicalism, provided many points of connection, not least a similar historic suspicion of elements of traditional Roman Catholic belief and practice. Evangelicals discovered that they often had more in common with Eastern Orthodoxy, Pentecostalism and modern Roman Catholicism than with Liberal Protestantism. Although sometimes cautious about involvement in official church dialogues, evangelicals have been engaged in various private initiatives with Roman Catholics and Orthodox which have led to some significant publications, such as *Evangelicals and Catholics Together* and *Reclaiming the Great Tradition: Evangelicals, Catholics and Orthodox in Dialogue*.[23]

James Cutsinger, the evangelical editor of *Reclaiming the Great Tradition*, shows that far from being just a piece of polite ecumenical politics, its aim is to: 'Test whether an ecumenical Orthodoxy, solidly based on the classical Christian faith as expressed in the scriptures and ecumenical councils, could become the foundation for a unified and transformative witness to the present age.'[24] The project in which he and others were engaged reflects a wider movement within some branches of American evangelicalism where an interest in the ancient church is gathering pace with determined attempts to retrieve the inheritance of the church of the first four to six centuries – the Great Tradition of the undivided, ecumenical church. Prominent here has been Robert Webber, who has written extensively about this renaissance of interest in the ancient church among evangelicals and has been engaged in a systematic attempt to relate the doctrine and practice of the ancient church to the contemporary missionary situation of the church in the West. He holds that our present culture bears striking similarities to the culture in which the church first evolved and that the theological method and ecclesiological practice of the patristic church has much to teach us. The closing words of his book, *Ancient-Future Faith: Rethinking Evangelicalism for a Postmodern World*, are worth quoting in full. They chime closely with the basic contention of this book that we need expressions of the Christian faith that hold together gospel, church and Spirit in the way that the church of the first few centuries managed to do so successfully.

> My argument has been that the evangelicals will do well to affirm a Christianity that has a deep kinship with the faith of the early church. What I sense is that many contemporary Christians who have been affected by cultural change toward a more integrated and dynamic view of life are in search of a faith that corresponds with their experience in general. For this reason an increasing amount of dissatisfaction is being expressed over rationalistic and divided Christianity. The challenge for us is to return to the Christian tradition. For here is a faith that, like a tapestry, weaves everything in and out of the main thread – Christ. My own experience with this rediscovered tapestry is a renewed and enriched faith. And I have talked with countless others who have experienced the same sense of newness in commitment through the insights of the early Christian tradition. Here, I believe, is a faith for our time, a faith that finds in the ancient Christian tradition a power to speak to a postmodern world.[25]

Chapel windows and Raphael's fresco

Webber's challenge to weave 'everything in and out the main thread – Christ' is exactly what Paul does in Colossians.[26] It is the distinctively *Christian* theological method. I think that it is 'anneal[ed] in glass', as the poet-priest George Herbert would say, in a fascinating set of stained-glass windows in the chapel of Ridley Hall where I have done much of my praying.[27] On one side of the chapel there is a set of windows picturing the Fathers of the universal tradition of the church, West and East, stretching from Irenaeus to Anselm, with James the Apostle, said to be the first Bishop of Jerusalem, heading up the line. Opposite them, on the other side of the chapel, is a sequence of Reformers of the church, beginning with Tyndale and concluding, somewhat surprisingly but very significantly, with George Herbert. Stephen, the first Christian martyr, who was stoned to death by representatives of the unreformed church of Israel, stands at their head. At the west end of the chapel is a group of pastors and missionaries who took this late-nineteenth-century chapel into the present day of its time with a window of the scholar-bishop Joseph Lightfoot, whose classic commentary on Colossians we made use of earlier, and who was a friend and mentor of Handley Moule, the first Principal of the college.

Most of the east end is made up of a magnificent single window depicting the risen Christ striding along the road to Emmaus to declare the gospel to the world. He is flanked by Peter, Matthew, John and Paul representing the great theological traditions of the New Testament church. Here is the scriptural Christ, surrounded by the authoritative apostolic witnesses. Behind and above him is the shape of the cross, subtly portrayed by the emblems of his passion. At the apex of the window is the Spirit, hovering over Gabriel the angel, and Mary, Jesus' mother, as the news of God's gift is announced and her obedient response is made. At the same time, the Spirit is also brooding over the cross, with its unimaginable suffering, empowering the resurrection ministry of Christ and overseeing the apostles' telling of his story to the world. It was as if the designers of the pattern of windows were saying: as you stand, sit and kneel here, at the west end of the chapel in your contemporary situation, recognize that you are part of an unbroken theological community. Keep one eye on the inherited catholic tradition of the church and the other eye on the continuing need to ensure that the church remains faithful to the gospel at the heart of its tradition. With dual vision, look up, look forwards and keep your eyes fixed on the scriptural Christ sent by the Father through the power of the Spirit to live and to die for the world. This Christ is powerfully risen from the dead and he calls you to follow him into the world to proclaim his risen life with all the energy of the Holy Spirit that he breathes upon you.

It is a Christological vision of theology, rooted in worship and proved in costly discipleship and mission. Charles Wesley captures something of this sort of theology in his poem 'Catholic Love', which his brother John published alongside his sermon on the 'Catholic Spirit':

Weary of all this wordy strife,
These notions, forms and modes and names,
To Thee, the Way, the Truth, the Life,
Whose love my simple heart inflames,
Divinely taught, at last I fly,
With Thee, and Thine to live, and die.[28]

It is also a charismatic vision of theology. It recognizes that it is the Holy Spirit who reveals to us the deep things of God and guides us into all truth (John 16.13). In another British theological college at about the same time, Charles Spurgeon was inspiring his students with a similar understanding of the role of the Spirit in theological understanding:

The Spirit of God is peculiarly precious to us because [the Spirit] especially instructs us as to the person and work of our Lord Jesus Christ . . . He takes of the things *of Christ*, and shows them unto us.[29]

Finally it gives a vision for a distinctively catholic–evangelical form of theology. It recognizes the interdependence of church and gospel. It celebrates the gift of the gospel to the church and receives all the good things that God gives through the continuing life of the church, while at the same time remaining vigilant to the church's capacity to obscure the gospel, and the need always to direct the church to the Christ revealed to us in the scriptures through the ministry of the Spirit. In his magisterial study, *The Gospel and the Catholic Church*, which had similar aims to this book but which approached the issues the other way round, from a catholic rather than an evangelical perspective, Michael Ramsey acknowledged that the great themes of the Reformation – '"The Word of God", "sola fide", "sola gratia", "soli Deo Gloria" . . . are Catholicism's own themes, and out of them it was born.' 'But', he went on to confess, 'they are learnt and re-learnt in humility, and Catholicism always stands before the church door at Wittenberg to read the truth by which she is created and by which she is judged.'[30] That seems to me to capture something of the spirit of the windows and the challenge of a catholic evangelical theology in the Spirit.

The theological method proposed by the windows in this small nineteenth-century evangelical chapel reminds me of a much grander project designed and executed by the Renaissance painter Raphael in the early years of the sixteenth century in the Stanza della Segnatura, the palatial rooms of the formidable Pope Julius II in Rome. At one end of the Pope's large private library Raphael created a massive scene of the church in theological dispute. *La Disputa* depicts the church on earth in a passionate theological discussion, with bishops, priests, monks and people, young and old, men and women thrashing out the finer points of eucharistic doctrine. Above them is the heavenly church, with the Holy Trinity at the centre of the picture, directly above the holy table. At the heart of the Trinity is the ascended Christ, bearing the marks of his death. Gathered around the heavenly Christ and mirroring the church below is a collection of biblical figures and saints of the church, in deep conversation with each other. In the earthly scene in the lower half of the wall, one wise-looking figure, dressed in blue, the colour of heaven, fixes his powerful eyes on the Fathers of the church and points with the index finger of his right hand to the risen Christ in the heavens. Like the designers of the chapel windows, Raphael appears to be saying 'The answer to all your theological questions is to be found in the living Christ, witnessed to by the biblical writers and the faithful theological tradition – look to him.' Interestingly, Raphael places the Spirit between Christ and the church rather than between the Father and the Son, as more normal in the classic Western 'Throne of Grace' rendition of the Trinity. This allows Raphael to show that we do our theology in the Spirit and that through the Spirit's ministry we receive the life and truth of the scriptural Christ.

It is fitting that one of these settings should be a chapel and the other a library. Chapels are places where Christ's people, his *church*, gather in the present as others have in the past, to hear and to celebrate scripture's *gospel* and to pray and praise *in the Spirit*. Libraries are places where we are drawn into the minds of brothers and sisters in the *church* over the centuries, listening in to their attempts to grapple with the *gospel* of the Christ of scripture, discerning how they have been led by the *Spirit* more deeply into Christ's truth and life. It is also fitting that one should be a chapel in the evangelical tradition and one in the catholic tradition, showing that what I am proposing in this book is not new to evangelicalism – others have sought to do same thing – and that the theological instincts of evangelicals and catholics, insofar as they are led by the Spirit, are united in their common quest to know and to love Jesus Christ, in whom 'all things hold together'.

2

Hearing the Word

For I handed on to you as of first importance what I in turn
had received: that Christ died for our sins in accordance with
the scriptures, and that he was raised on the third day in
accordance with the scriptures, and that he appeared to
Cephas and then to the twelve.
St Paul

Introduction

In 2 Corinthians 2, Paul tells us that the Holy Spirit leads us,
Christ's people, the church, into the mind of Christ. The task
of this chapter is to consider how the Spirit does this, what
means and ways the Spirit uses to do what Jesus promised that
the *Pareklētos*, the Advocate would do – take what is Christ's
(which is also, we are told, the Father's) and declare it to God's
people (John 16.14–15).

A fundamental conviction of the Christian church has been
that scripture is the primary way by which the Holy Spirit performs this ministry. 'The Fathers, scholastics, and reformers',
David Yeago, the Lutheran scholar, tells us, 'believed that when
we conform our thinking to the pattern of judgements imbed-
ded in the prophetic and apostolic scriptures, our understanding is illumined by the divine light (Psalm 36.9) and so we come
to share the *nous Christou*, the mind of Christ (1 Corinthians
2.16).[1] Elsewhere he makes the critical point that immersion in
the Old Testament – the 'prophetic scriptures' – enables us to do
this in a very concrete and tangible way, because Jesus' mind 'is
always certainly the mind of a Jew'.[2] The mind of Jesus the Jew
was formed by scripture. He was a member of a scripturally
shaped community that lived within the story of creation and

redemption told by its sacred writings and which received them as God's word to his people. Through the reading of scripture in the synagogue, the learning of scripture in school, the recitation of the *Shema* in the home, the praying of the psalms with others and alone, the Spirit taught Jesus about his unique place in the saving purposes of God. Jesus' Spirit-led ministry, whether doing battle with Satan in the desert, teaching the people through parables on the hillside, or offering himself as a ransom for many on the cross, was forged through a sustained engagement with scripture by which he interpreted his calling and found inspiration for his work.

We will not be able to get to the mind of Jesus unless we allow ourselves to be led through the door of his scriptures as he understood them. This is why the New Testament, in turn, plays a vital, life-giving part in the Spirit's work of declaring Christ to the church and the world. The 'apostolic scriptures' provide the Spirit's teaching about Jesus Christ (John 14.26). Luke tells us that he wrote his 'orderly account' so that Theophilus 'may know the truth' about Jesus Christ (Luke 1.1–4). John composed his Gospel so that we 'may come to believe that Jesus is the Messiah, the Son of God, and that through believing we may have life in his name' (John 20.31). Paul laboured over his letters to communicate 'God's wisdom, secret and hidden' that the crucified Christ is the 'Lord of glory' (1 Corinthians 2.7–8). They all, certainly, knew the sweat and toil of writing. Luke's historical labours, John's economic but elegant prose, Paul's failing eyesight and constant pressure of church leadership, leave us in no doubt that the normal constraints and conditions of literary composition were very much in place. But they also knew that they were caught up in the sort of spiritual process which Jesus had promised – a dynamic of recollection and revelation to the writers, declaration to the church, conviction to the world and glorification in the heavens (John 14—16) that involved the raising of human language into the form of divine speech: 'we speak of these things in words not taught by human wisdom but taught by the Spirit, interpreting spiritual things to those who are spiritual' (1 Corinthians 2.13).

So far, so good. Evangelical and catholic traditions both rejoice in the gift of scripture as the Spirit's primary means of teaching the church. Historically, however, there has been serious disagreement over how this common recognition works out in practice. What happened, for example, before the emergence of scripture as we know it? How was the Spirit communicating the gospel and teaching the faith *before* the apostolic writings were written and circulated, quite apart from when they were formally gathered into a recognized collection and bound together with the Jewish scriptures to form the Christian canon? What part did the church play in the formation of that scripture? How did the church, for example, recognize the authority of these particular writings and distinguish them from other, apparently inferior, documents? Once scripture had been commonly accepted and officially defined, how were Christians to be sure that they were interpreting it correctly, and how were decisions to be made about proper and improper interpretations? How do we handle theological discussions about major matters of faith where scripture provides a lot of data but does not make all the connections, where it leads us in certain directions but does not take us right to the end of the theological journey? And what do we do with questions of church practice and human living that are not directly addressed or decided by scripture and which take many different forms in the cultural diversity of the church's history?

The debate has often revolved around the relationship between *scripture*, recognized by catholic and evangelical traditions alike to be the word of God in written form, and the ongoing *tradition* of the church. A particularly sharp example of very different approaches to these questions can be found in the sixteenth-century exchange between Cardinal Sadoleto and John Calvin already mentioned. Sadoleto, a warm-hearted and eirenic cardinal of the church, wrote to the Genevan elders to persuade them to return to what he understood to be the 'catholic church'. He argued that the Reformers' determination to 'pull down what was ancient and argue against the Church' involved them in a direct confrontation with the Holy

Spirit, because the Spirit guides the church.[3] The church cannot err because the Spirit does not err. He sought to convince the Genevan elders to suspend their theological dispute with Rome and simply to trust as true what the church teaches. The church, he went on to say, only teaches now what has always been taught and believed. Their salvation would be on much safer ground if they just accepted what the church taught.

Calvin was appalled at Sadoleto's theological reasoning. 'You've remembered the Spirit but forgotten the word', was the essence of his reply: 'The Spirit goes before the Church, to enlighten her in understanding the Word, while the Word itself is like the Lydian stone, by which she tests all doctrines.'[4] In other words, the Spirit leads the church into all truth by teaching the word. Spirit and word are interdependent. Their ministries co-inhere. Calvin also refused to allow Sadoleto to claim that *Roman* teaching represents *catholic* teaching. He was adamant that the (Roman) church's teaching in his day was a corruption of the teaching of the ancient church, and by that he meant not simply the church of the New Testament but the church of 'Chyrostom and Basil . . . Cyprian, Ambrose, and Augustine'. 'All we have attempted', he said, 'has been to renew that ancient form of the Church.'[5]

However polemicized, Calvin's configuration of Spirit and word in the life of the church (with his implicit affirmation of a living tradition that is faithful to the Spirit's teaching ministry) provides some clear co-ordinates for the expression of an evangelical doctrine of scripture that takes seriously the responsibility of the church and the continuing activity of the Spirit. This chapter explores such an approach, identifying some basic principles of gospel and church, before moving on to relate their insights with the help of some biblical study on Revelation chapter 1. It concludes with a suggestion for the enrichment of evangelical life arising from the discussion.

Gospel principles: God's speech

God is the revealer and we are entirely dependent upon God's revelation; God is the saviour and we are entirely dependent on God's saving work.

The next two sections draw on two robust presentations of the importance of scripture in the life of the church: *Holy Scripture* by John Webster and *Scripture and the Authority of God* by Tom Wright.[6]

John Webster's 'dogmatic sketch' of holy scripture is based on the thesis that 'revelation is the self-presentation of the triune God, the free work of sovereign mercy in which God wills, establishes and perfects saving fellowship with himself in which humankind comes to know, love and fear him above all things'.[7] In a manner reminiscent of Karl Barth, Webster explains how God is the *content* of revelation (God is presented in revelation), the *agent* of revelation (God presents himself) and the *subject* of revelation (revelation involves the presence of God establishing 'saving fellowship' or reconciliation).

Although Webster makes little direct use of the biblical text itself, his argument is consistent with the God described in scripture. For example, a prophecy from Isaiah 52 shows how the sort of divine activity Webster defines in his theological prose was played out in the realities of Israel's relationship with God: 'Therefore my people shall know my name, therefore on that day they shall know that it is I who speak: here am I' (Isaiah 52.6). God's people are lost. They live in exile, in a land where the name of the Lord is despised. Their only hope lies in the revelation of God's name. The saving revelation of God involves the self-speaking of God which is at the same time the self-presentation, or the coming of God. And as we read on into the great Servant Song that follows, we discover that the saving speech and presence of God is intimately and ultimately identified with the words and works of the suffering servant who comes on the day of the Lord.

Although Tom Wright's book is different in many ways from

John Webster's, attending more closely to the actual story and text of scripture, his thesis is similar. He begins with the God described in scripture: the sovereign creator of the world who is working powerfully to renew the creation and establish his kingdom. God is the saving God who is committed to a pro-gramme of redemption that will result in a healed and restored world. This is the authority of God – the authority to estab-lish the kingdom of his just rule – and it is an authority that is exercised through his word. In his sovereign activity God demonstrates his divine identity as the Lord of creation and God of grace. This dynamic understanding of God's word as God's saving will and action lay at the heart of Israel's faith. Wright fittingly concludes his book with Isaiah's vision of the new creation shown by God's own speech.

> For as the rain and the snow come down from heaven,
> and do not return here until they have watered the earth,
> making it bring forth and sprout,
> giving seed to the sower and bread to the eater,
> so shall my word that goes out from my mouth;
> it shall not return to me empty,
> but it shall accomplish that which I purpose,
> and succeed in the thing for which I sent it.
> (Isaiah 55.10–11)

The revealing God uses scripture to transmit his revelation (to speak to his people).

The saving God uses scripture to effect his purposes, to equip his people for his missions.

Webster defines revelation as the saving self-presentation of God. This means scripture therefore cannot be *equated* with revelation, as though all that were involved in revelation were the fixing of a text, rather than the self-manifestation of God's saving presence and activity – the coming of God. Neither does it mean, however, that revelation can be separated from scripture because 'the biblical texts are creaturely realities set apart by the triune God to serve his self-presence'.[8] They are 'sanctified by divine use'.[9] They are words that have been inspired in order to become 'fitting vessels of the treasure of the gospel'.[10] Webster's notion of the *creaturely reality* of scripture allows him to affirm the fully human processes involved in both the formation of the Bible as we know it and in the continuing use of the Bible in the life of the church. At the same time, his understanding of the sanctified and inspired character of scripture allows him to affirm its *divine origin* ('those moved by the Holy Spirit spoke from God', 2 Peter 1.21) and its divine function ('useful for teaching, for reproof, for correction, for training in righteousness', 2 Timothy 3.16).[11]

> In sum: the biblical text is Scripture; its being is defined, not simply by its membership of the class of texts, but by the fact that it is *this* text – sanctified, that is, Spirit-generated and preserved – in *this* field of action – the communicative economy of God's merciful fellowship with his lost creatures.[12]

Webster's careful geometry can be seen sketched across the canvas of God's creative and re-creative activity by Wright's complementary picture of scripture's function in the purposes of God. As we have seen, Wright's defining category is redemption rather than revelation, but, just as for Webster revelation involves redemption, so for him redemption requires revelation. It requires the revelation of God's redemptive purposes and the formation of an obedient people to serve those purposes by following the true God. This is the function of scripture. It is 'the vehicle of God's kingdom coming to birth in the world'.[13] Through scripture God equips Israel, forms Jesus as the Messiah, the one who incarnates the word of grace for the world of which scripture speaks, and leads the church to proclaim the kingdom which is the culmination of scripture's story. This is what is meant by the authority of scripture:

. . . the shorthand phrase 'the authority of scripture', when unpacked, offers a picture of God's sovereign and saving plan for the entire cosmos, dramatically inaugurated by Jesus himself, and now to be implemented through the Spirit-led life of the church *precisely as the scripture-reading community*.[14]

If all this sounds a little bit remote, listen to these words from Weka Musuku, a Zaireian Christian rejoicing in the translation of the Bible into Ngbaka, his mother tongue: 'Now we have the Bible in Ngbaka, God speaks clearly and directly to our hearts! It is like Christ himself has come to visit us.'[15] God speaks, Christ visits. That is the heart of the evangelical doctrine of scripture. Sometimes the evangelical attitude to scripture is parodied as purely propositional, as if it is simply a set of sayings to be lifted off the page and uncritically applied to contemporary situations. In reality the evangelical approach to scripture is much more dynamic. Fundamentally, scripture is *positional*. It positions us before God. Through scripture God occupies his place and puts us in our place – the place in which to be addressed by God, the place in which to hear God, the place in which to meet God, the place in which to serve God by proclaiming him to the world. Here, in this position, God indeed *proposes* truth about himself, ourselves and our world and then *proves* himself to us as the faithful God about whom scripture speaks as we follow him, committed to his mission. 'We will only be happy in our reading of the Bible', claimed Dietrich Bonhoeffer, 'when we dare to approach it as the means by which God really speaks to us.'[16]

The church is founded on the prophets and the apostles and is, therefore, 'under scripture'.

Although John Calvin was very happy to call the church our mother and while he recognized that 'it is a proper office of the church to distinguish genuine from spurious Scripture', he was also clear that the church is birthed by the prophetic and apostolic word enshrined in scripture, and that the church, therefore, does not 'stand over' scripture as its judge but 'sits under' scripture as its servant.[17] In fact, he was not saying anything new or radical. In the fourth century, Hilary of Poitiers introduces his great work on the Trinity with this prayer:

> We, of course, in our helplessness shall pray for those things that we need, and shall apply ourselves with tireless zeal to the study of the words of your prophets and apostles and shall knock at all the doors of wisdom that are closed to us, but it is for you to grant our prayer, to be present when we seek, to open when we knock ... We hope, therefore, that ... you will summon us to share in the prophetic and apostolic spirit, in order that we may understand their words in no other sense than that in which they spoke them, and that we may explain the proper meaning of the words in accordance with the realities they signify. We shall speak of subjects which they have announced in the mystery ... grant that what we believe we may also speak, namely, that, while we recognize you as the only God the Father and the Lord Jesus Christ from the prophets and apostles, we may now succeed against the denials of the heretics in honouring you as God in such a manner that you are not alone, and proclaiming him as God in such a matter that he may not be false.[18]

Hilary was writing at a critical point in the church's life. The Council of Nicea in 325 had proclaimed the full divinity of Christ by using a definition that does not actually appear in scripture: '*homoousion* [sharing one being] with the Father'. By no means everyone accepted the creed. Many objected to it on the grounds of its use of a non-biblical word and its apparent contradiction of the plain meaning of other scriptural statements such as 'the Father is greater than I' (John 14.28). As well as being theologically unfashionable in much of the church, support for the creed was politically dangerous at the time. The Roman Emperor Constantius II had sided with the Arians against Nicea. Hilary himself had been exiled from his diocese. Nicea, moreover, with its minimalist 'We believe in the Holy Spirit' had unleashed a theological battle over whether the Spirit, like the Son, shares in the same divine being as the Father.

Hilary believed that the trinitarian understanding and experience of God lay at the heart of the Christian faith. He was also honest enough to admit that the doctrine does not leap off the surface of scripture. But at no point did he appeal to an authority higher than scripture, or to an esoteric method of interpreting scripture available only to the especially initiated or authorized, or even to a line of development which, though logically connected to its source, is at such a theological distance from it as to be unrecognizable. Instead, he asked for a *'share in the prophetic and apostolic spirit*, in order that we may understand their words in no other sense than that in which they spoke them, and that we may explain the proper meaning of the words in accordance with the realities they signify'.[19] Even though he was convinced that the liturgical life of the church pointed inexorably to the Trinity, he refused to play off the church's tradition against scripture. Even though he was sure that God was at work at Nicea, he did not fall back on the voice of the church rather than God's word. Even though he had suffered at the hands of those who, for reasons of theological misunderstanding or political expediency, were dismantling the church's Spirit-inspired confession of the Lordship of Christ, he based his case on the 'Word of God, together with the very power of its own truth which we received'[20] from the biblical writers rather than on any other authority.

Scripture is 'sufficient for salvation'.

The Church of England's Ordinal, in both its sixteenth-century and its contemporary form, asks prospective deacons, priests and bishops: 'Do you accept the holy scriptures as revealing all things necessary for eternal salvation through faith in Jesus Christ?'[21] During the revision process that led to the present *Common Worship* rite, moves were made to change this language. It was said that it was anachronistic, too rooted in the controversies and compromises of former days. Wisely, revision was resisted and the careful sixteenth-century balance was retained. Scripture is sufficient to tell us all we need to know about who God is and how God has saved us and what we are to do in order to participate in God's saving revelation. That is its function in the economy of God's grace. As Athanasius said, 'The Scriptures are really sufficient for our instruction', or, as Calvin said, they are God's 'special gift . . . to instruct the church'.[22] Athanasius and Calvin are both echoing 2 Timothy, which tells us that 'the sacred writings are able *to instruct us for salvation* through faith in Jesus Christ', or, as Tyndale's translation has it, 'to make us wise unto salvation'.

Two important points follow from this. Richard Hooker, the late-sixteenth-century Anglican theologian, will help us to explore them. It is important to be able to recognize the points at which scripture limits what the church can say with authority about God and God's saving purposes. We need to be able to distinguish that which is 'expressly contained in the word of God, or else manifestly collected out of the same' from that which is not.[23] Hooker recognized that discerning the truth of scripture is not an entirely simple process. Some of God's truth is 'expressly contained' in scripture and, as it were, hits us in the face. Some of God's truth, though, as Hilary very much knew, needs to be 'collected out of' scripture, searched out by our eyes and gathered in our hands of faith. Nevertheless, scripture is able to put certain boundaries around the church's teaching. It is able to say, 'There is no need to go there, better to stay here.' It is the difference between open-cast and deep-shaft mining. Rather than pushing out wider, scripture invites us to go deeper.

A corollary of this is that scripture sets certain limits on itself. Although Hooker was committed to the sufficiency of scripture he was clear that scripture does not claim to be sufficient *in all things*, just to be sufficient in what it is meant to be – the means by which God speaks of who he is and what he has done and how we can know God and be part of what God is doing with the world. Scripture is there to make us 'wise unto salvation' and trained for the good work of proclaiming God's salvation in Christ to the nations (2 Timothy 3.16; 1 Peter 2.9). There are certain matters which the church must decide for itself in ways that are congruent with the God revealed in scripture and the pattern of his saving purposes for the world.

Having identified some basic *gospel principles* about scripture, we can now move on to consider some that arise from the church's place in the construction and use of scripture.

Church principles: reception and responsibility

Truth and salvation preceded scripture.

People were hearing about Jesus Christ and calling on his name for salvation long before Paul's or Mark's pen touched papyrus. Many had encountered Jesus in the flesh, others through the teaching of his followers, and some through both. The good news of Jesus Christ and all that it means for human life was the *paradosis*, the tradition (1 Corinthians 11.2; 2 Thessalonians 3.6 – literally, 'that which is handed over'). And the gospel was communicated by passing on, handing over this tradition – literally by *traditioning* the gospel (the verb form of *paradosis* is *paradidōmi*). Paul tells the Corinthians that he '*handed on* to [them] as of first importance what [he] in turn had received' and then gives a brief summary of the gospel story – 'that Christ died for our sins in accordance with the scriptures, and that he was buried on the third day in accordance with the scriptures, and that he appeared to Cephas and to the twelve' (1 Corinthians 15.3–4). The *mysterion*, the deep truth and purpose of God's grace, previously hidden but now made known in Christ, was being entrusted to the 'servants of Christ' and 'stewards of God's mysteries' and handed on by their preaching (2 Timothy 1.12; 1 Corinthians 4.1), received by faith across the Middle East and lived out in the community of the church (Philippians 4.9) years before it was committed to what we now know as the New Testament.

The good news that Paul and the other apostles proclaimed and which the Corinthians and others believed (1 Corinthians 15.11), the tradition which was handed over, was more than a message. Although Paul also uses *paradidōmi* when recounting the institution of the Lord's Supper ('For I received from the Lord what I also handed on to you'), the actual content of the tradition is not simply the account of the Last Supper. It is the reality of sharing in the body and blood of Christ (1 Corinthians 10.16). It is the saving encounter with Jesus Christ and participation in his life. This takes us back to where we began – with Colossians – when Paul reminds the Colossian church that they have been not merely given knowledge about God's *mysterion*, they have been given 'Christ himself' (Colossians 2.2):

> *As you therefore have received Christ Jesus the Lord*, continue to live your lives in him, rooted and built up in him and established in the faith, just as you were taught, abounding in thanksgiving. (Colossians 2.6)

This dynamic definition of tradition as the passing on of the gospel of Christ, of making him available and accessible, of handing over the news of his work, and, in so doing, offering his full personal reality to those who would receive him, is reinforced by W. H. Vanstone's subtle and illuminating study of what we usually, though perhaps misleadingly, call 'the betrayal of Christ'.[24] Vanstone shows that rather than using *prodidōmi*, with its explicit associations of treachery and malice, the gospel writers almost invariably use *paradidōmi*, the much more neutral and functional word used elsewhere in the New Testament to describe the process of handing over the gospel. The point the writers seem to be underlining is that the good news of Jesus as the redeemer announced in the ministry of the church is historically rooted in the grim reality of Jesus being *handed over to die for us*. Vanstone goes on to note how Paul uses *paradidōmi* when describing his deepest experience and defending his most cherished convictions about the grace of the gospel:

For through the law I died to the law, so that I might live to God. I have been crucified with Christ; and it is no longer I who live, but it is Christ who lives in me. And the life I now live in the flesh I live by faith in the Son of God who loved me and gave [*paradontos*] himself for me. (Galatians 2.20)

Whether handed over to death by Judas, or proclaimed in the preaching and sacraments of the church *as the one who allows himself to be handed over*, it is Jesus himself who is placed into the hands of others. He is the *paradosis*, the tradition, the gift of the gospel.

The readers of Peter's first letter were told that 'the word of the Lord' which, according to the prophet Isaiah (40.4–9), 'endures for ever', is 'the good news that was announced to [them]' (1 Peter 1.24–25). Here is further evidence that truth and salvation preceded scripture as we know it, and yet, at the same time, proof that far from being in competition, the fundamental tradition of the church and the church's scriptures are, in fact, inseparable.[25] The tradition is the original and abiding proclamation of Jesus Christ as Son of God and Saviour of the world. The New Testament is the written and amplified form of this basic tradition which provides historical data, theological explanation, practical application in a variety of contexts and prophetic interpretation. The Old Testament – 'Peter's scriptures' – provided the story, the words and the theological grammar to begin to make sense of all that God had done in and through Jesus Christ. Luke's record of the first Christian sermon shows Peter grappling with the scriptural text, this time Psalm 16, in an attempt to set the extraordinary events of Easter and Pentecost in the context of God's revealed will and purpose. Athanasius, writing in the fourth century, gives a very helpful précis of Peter's argument.

Now David and all the prophets have died, and the tombs of all of them are here in our midst; *but the resurrection that has now taken place* has shown that the things that were written pertain to Jesus.[26]

The resurrection and the ensuing outpouring of the Spirit had made all the difference experientially and exegetically. Jesus was alive, present and active by the Spirit, and the Jewish scriptures – in the light of these events and experiences – became the tool for their interpretation. The apostolic tradition which Paul hands on 'as of first importance' is *'in accordance with the scriptures'*. It is not contrary to the scriptures. It has not been cultured in a test-tube of esoteric religion. It has been constructed within a textually formed and scripturally shaped community. It is not a new genetic phenomenon: it is the proper development of the genetic code of Jewish scripture. It is not a human invention: it is the living reality of the Lord present by the Spirit in the community of the church making sense of scripture. And it is the same hermeneutic used by Jesus himself:

> If you believed Moses, you would believe me, for he wrote about me. (John 5.46)

> Then beginning with Moses and all the prophets he interpreted to them the things about himself in all the scriptures. (Luke 24.27)

Scripture needs to be received faithfully and interpreted correctly.

Scripture, like all God's gifts, needs to be received. The church's calling to receive scripture begins with writers with whom the Spirit chooses to work, people with the right set of skills and the proper spiritual disposition to be used by God for the mind-stretching demands of 'sacred writing'. It then involves the church as the Spirit-endowed and Spirit-ordered community perceiving scripture, discerning the hand of the Spirit on the words of the writers, acknowledging the apostolic authority of certain texts and accepting their authority in the same way the church acknowledged the apostolic founders of the church and accepted their teaching. Furthermore, the full reception of scripture involves Christ's followers understanding what scripture means, hearing Christ's word through its words, and then obeying his word, witnessing to his resurrection, proclaiming him to the nations and participating in the work of his kingdom.

Hilary knew full well that 'scripture is not in the reading, but in the understanding'.[27] Interpretation, therefore, is necessary. Scripture itself, however, warns us that 'no prophecy of scripture is a matter of one's own interpretation' (2 Peter 1.20). The prophetic word recorded in scripture is a word from God, spoken by people 'moved by the Holy Spirit' (2 Peter 1.21). Hence, as Basil said, 'the judge of the words ought to start with the same preparation as the author . . . And I see that in the utterances of the Spirit it is also impossible for everyone to undertake the scrutiny of his word, but only for them who have the Spirit which grants the discernment.'[28] This is the same condition that we saw Hilary laying down. It is the ancient principle of hermeneutics that was affirmed by the Second Vatican Council: 'Holy Scripture must be interpreted according to the same Spirit by whom it was written.'[29] Although received by individuals, the Spirit is not the possession of individual believers. The Spirit is Christ's gift to the church. As 2 Peter 1.19–21 tells us, the prophetic truth-revealing work of the Spirit operates through the corporate life of the church. It is worth exploring this in a little more depth to make sure that we have the perspectives right.

In his detailed and eirenic study of the relationship between scripture and tradition written before the Second Vatican Council, George Tavard, a Roman Catholic scholar, wrote:

In her essence, the Church is not a power of interpretation: she is a power of reception. She receives the Word which God speaks to her in the Scriptures. It is this Word by her received which is authoritative for her members. Thus Scripture and Church are mutually inherent. To Scripture is attached an ontological priority; and to the Church a historical one because it is only in her receptivity that [people] are made aware of the Word.[30]

Of course scripture must be 'rightly divided', as the evangelical and catholic traditions have always agreed. This necessarily involves the responsible task of unfolding its meaning and uncovering its truth – a demanding exercise that necessarily includes interpretation and is a proper office of the church as a whole, not simply of individual preachers. Nevertheless, Tavard's words remind us that the *power* of interpretation lies with the Spirit and that the church is the *instrument* of the Spirit's interpretation. In this sense there is a 'mutual inherence' between the church and the Bible, an inter-animating relationship in which the church is the 'pillar and bulwark of the truth' (1 Timothy 3.15). The Spirit who inspired scripture within the life of the church guides the church into the interpretation of scripture. Luther said, 'The word of God cannot be without the people of God, and the people of God cannot be without the word of God.'[31] Calvin and Zwingli spoke of the Church as 'mother' from whom we receive the scriptural gospel. The Church of England Articles of Religion call the church 'the witness and keeper of holy Writ' (Article 20). The Reformers were most definitely committed to freeing scripture from erroneous interpretations and fought for mechanisms by which the deformed could be reformed, but they had no intention of removing scripture from the interpretive context of the church. The evangelical theologian Donald Bloesch puts it well when he says, 'When the Reformers spoke of *sola Scriptura*, they meant the Bible illuminated by the Spirit in the matrix of the church. *Sola Scriptura* is not *nuda Scriptura* (bare Scripture).'[32]

This is a position strongly asserted in 2002 by the evangelical members (which include Timothy George, James Packer and Charles Colson) of the 'Evangelicals and Catholics Together Project' in the USA:

We who are Evangelicals recognise the need to address the widespread misunderstanding in our community that *sola scriptura* (Scripture alone) means *nuda scriptura* (literally, Scripture unclothed, that is denuded of and abstracted from

its churchly context). The phrase *sola scriptura* refers to the
primacy and sufficiency of Scripture as the theological norm
– the only infallible rule of faith and practice – over all tradition rather than the mere rejection of tradition itself. The
isolation of Scripture study from the believing community
of faith (*nuda scriptura*) disregards the Holy Spirit's work in
guiding the witness of the people of God to scriptural truths,
and leaves the interpretation of that truth vulnerable to un-
fettered subjectivism.[33]

There is a proper circularity to this position. Scripture is interpreted within the scripture-reading community. We have seen
that this is how scripture – or at least the New Testament –
was written. The papyrus, in one sense, was not blank. The
scrolls of the law, the prophets and the writings lay beneath
its surface, their story etched on the minds of the writers. As
we read scripture today we join a universal, a *catholic* tradition of interpretation that stretches deep historically and wide
geographically.

Scripture needs the church's creeds.

Athanasius, Hilary and other Nicene Fathers in the fourth
century knew to their cost that Arius could quote scripture
profusely to argue that Jesus is not fully divine. The mainline reformers had to contend with the Socinian *Racovian
Catechism*, with its systematic scriptural case for Unitarianism.
A good deal of orthodox energy since the nineteenth century
has been taken up with defending the central doctrines of the
faith from, on the one side, attacks by Christian sects which
deny them on apparently scriptural grounds, and, on the other,
from the reductionism of theological methods which claim
that the credal faith of the church is a distortion of the semitic
gospel of the scriptures (or, at least, of the texts and experience
that lay behind the final form of the New Testament writings
which have been themselves hopelessly hellenized). The truth
which Hooker said is to be 'manifestly collected out of' scrip-

ture has not been manifest to everyone. Not all of those who have claimed the Christian name have believed, or, for that matter, believe today, that God is eternally Father, Son and Holy Spirit, that the Son became incarnate in Jesus Christ, that he died and was raised for our salvation, or that baptism is for the forgiveness of sins and that the life of the world to come entails the resurrection of the body.

In the third century Irenaeus was exasperated by the way the Gnostics handled scripture. He used an analogy to make his point. Imagine, he said, some precious stones skilfully arranged by an artist into a beautiful image of a royal figure. Then imagine someone else who picks up the gems and makes a different pattern – a dog or fox, for instance, and then says that this is really the original picture. Irenaeus says that we must not be fooled. The stones may be the same but the design is different. This, argued Irenaeus, was how the Gnostics were treating scripture. They were taking the words and putting them into another picture, to tell another story. They have disrupted 'the order and connection' of scripture and so 'dismembered the truth'.[34] Many centuries later, B. B. Warfield (whose doctrine of scriptural inspiration has been of enormous influence among evangelicals) defended the doctrine of the Trinity – including the non-scriptural word 'Trinity' itself – with another analogy. 'The doctrine of the Trinity', Warfield suggested, 'lies in scripture in solution; when it is crystallized from its solvent it does not cease to be scriptural, but only comes into clearer view.'[35] Crystallization of scriptural truth is the calling of the church. The creeds are the evidence of the church faithfully fulfilling its calling under the guidance of the Spirit. They are the framework for the gospel of grace. They are what Irenaeus liked to call the 'rule' or 'canon of faith'. They are a fuller answer to Jesus' question to the world – 'Who do you say I am?' – than Peter's immediate response, but they preserve and promote his inspired reply. They provide the necessary co-ordinates of the 'scriptural Christ'. They do not add to scripture, they crystallize it.

Scripture is read with others.

Scripture itself tells us that it is to be read with others. 'Give attention to the public reading of scripture' (1 Timothy 4.13), Timothy is told. 'Blessed is the one who reads *aloud* the words of the prophecy' (Revelation 1.3), John tells the seven churches of Asia. The original place for the reading of scripture was in the public gatherings of the church to worship the God who speaks to his people through scripture, and it remains the normative context to be addressed by God through scripture. The spiritual dynamic involved in Ezra's reading of the law to the returned exiles, surrounded as it was by worship and preaching, is an abiding reality in the life of God's people (Nehemiah 8), even if this is not fully appreciated or realized in the worship of the churches. This is not to undermine in any way the value of reading the Bible by oneself. The technology and theology of the Reformation placed scripture into individual hands, freeing it from the practical and ecclesiastical constraints of earlier periods. But it is to say that even when reading and studying the Bible alone, the believer is a *believer*, a confessor of Christ, a bearer of the Spirit, a worshipper of God. If we are to read scripture aright we need to be what Handley Moule liked to call a 'worshipping student of the Scriptures'.[36] We need to be bound to the worship of the scriptural Christ and, therefore, *bound to others* who have known and loved the Christ of scripture. As we shall explore more fully at the conclusion of the chapter, we read scripture as participants in what Alister McGrath has described as the Great Tradition of Christian interpretation of scripture. We read the Bible with those throughout the centuries who have 'testified to the word of God and to the testimony of Jesus' (Revelation 1.2). In this sense, as the Orthodox theologian Georges Florovsky says, we learn *in tradition* not just *from tradition* and, in so doing, we develop what he calls 'the Scriptural mind'.[37]

Principles of the Spirit's communicative work: lessons from the book of Revelation

With the help of the book of Revelation, and especially the first chapter, I now want to draw together these gospel and church principles into an integrated account of the work of the Spirit that takes seriously the gospel and church principles already described.

God's word is enfleshed in Jesus Christ.

The book of Revelation uncovers some of the deepest truths about the divine. It is perhaps the most profound example of the spiritual dynamic Paul described in 1 Corinthians 2 of the Spirit searching out the depths of God and revealing them to the spiritual. It is certainly a fulfilment of Jesus' promise that, as well as reminding his followers of all that he had said to them, the Spirit would also declare 'the things that are to come' (John 16.13) in the deepest sense of revealing how God will be seen to be when his kingdom finally and fully comes. It tells us that Jesus is the 'Word of God', the complete revelation of God in human form (19.13). In Spirit-inspired visions and prophetic words, John is shown that 'the Alpha and Omega', 'the Lord God, who is and who was and who is to come, the Almighty' has come to us in Jesus Christ (22.13). Jesus is the *handing over of God* within and to the created order. Jesus is the *self-presentation of God* to the world. He is the primary *paradosis* who came to the world to live and die for us, who reigns over the world as the risen one who continues to speak, and who will come again to establish the new world of the new heaven and the new earth.

God's word is entrusted to the church.

'The revelation of Jesus Christ', the truth of God which he brings to the world, is 'made known' by the ascended Christ through the work of the Spirit 'by sending his angel to his servant John' (Revelation 1.1). The revelation of the purposes of God in Jesus Christ is entrusted to the church – first to John and then to those to whom the prophecy is read. As we have just suggested, what is going on here is far more profound than the passing on of uninterpreted information about the '*things that are to come*'. It is the revelation of the true identity and activity of '*the one who is to come*'. Here, in John's prophecy, is the manifestation and glorification of Christ by the Spirit promised in John's Gospel. And here also is the fulfilment of Jesus' high-priestly prayer that all his followers – the disciples and those 'who will believe in [him] through their word' (John 17.20) – will be sanctified, consecrated in the truth and will live within the relationship of love between the Father and the Son.

The Spirit shows John that Jesus, the historical figure who lived and died, and whom he knows so intimately, belongs to the very being of God. This means that as well as being entrusted with the revelation of God – the truth that the word of God is enfleshed in Jesus – the church is entrusted with the Word himself. As those who belong to Jesus, the church is the community in which God's Word is embodied among his people. It is the body of Christ of which he is the head. Jesus lives in his followers and they live in him. He is formed in them as they are formed in him. They are his body. They are his witnesses, called to 'patiently endure' (1.9) for the sake of the kingdom that he brings and faithfully to pass on the Word with which they have been entrusted.

The reality that they are the body in whom Christ dwells means that Christ's followers are a people in whom, to whom and through whom Christ speaks. Equally, they are a people in whom Christ is developing the capacity to hear what he is saying to them by the Spirit and then to speak it faithfully to others. They are a word-receiving and word-telling people. As a word-receiving, a prophecy-discerning people, they must not only hear what the Spirit is saying to their particular situation but also what is being said to all the churches, the whole church. The Laodicians hear what is said to the Smyrnans, and the Sardisians hear what is being said to the Thyatirans, and so on. The word is contextualized and congregational but it is also permanent and catholic.

God's word entrusted to the church is committed to script through the Spirit, enscripted in the sacred writings; it is enscripturated, made scripture.

'Write in a book what you see and hear and send it to the seven churches' (1.10) John was told when he was in the Spirit on the Lord's day. The revelation of the true identity and final purposes of God made known in Jesus Christ is not given for John's mystical enjoyment. The *paradosis* (which, as we have seen, is consistent with and the fulfilment of the inherited text of scripture) is given to the church for the edification and empowerment of the church. It is to be committed to a new text so that its truth can be read, recognized and received by the churches. The text that transmits the *paradosis* is so important that it must not be added to or taken away from (22.18–19). It is sacred. It has entered into the realm of 'sacred writing' breathed by the Spirit (2 Timothy 3.16).[38] It is *holy* scripture, given by the *Holy* Spirit. It is the *sacramental expression* of the word of truth. It mediates the saving grace of Christ. Like other sacramental gifts to the church, its material, creaturely reality remains. Fully human processes were involved in its compilation and canonization, just as they are in its interpretation and application. But these processes have been sanctified by the Spirit: the 'Write this' of the Lord meets the 'Yes' of the Spirit's response in the life of the church (14.13).

Scripture is not the word of God in the same way that Jesus is the Word of God, just as the consecrated bread and wine are not the presence of Christ in the way that he is in his 'natural body', as the reformers would have put it. But scripture is the *sacramental form of God's word*. It is the appointed and consecrated means by which God's word is communicated. Emphasis on the *communication* of God's word through scripture is important. Like the bread of the Eucharist, 'it is not ordained of

Christ to be gazed upon, or to be carried about but that we should duly use it'.[39] It is to be used for the purpose for which it was written – 'so that [the world] may come to believe that Jesus is the Messiah, the Son of God, and that through believing [we] may have life in his name' (John 20.31; 3.16). Scripture is holy because the Holy Spirit, 'the Lord and giver of life', uses scripture to bring life under the Lordship of Christ, the Word made flesh. It is a sacramental sign of God's Lordship exercised through the Son by the Spirit and, therefore, it is *an effectual means* by which the triune God establishes his kingdom rule and brings life to those who would live under it. This leads us to our final stage in Revelation 1's integrative framework.

God's word is enacted by the church.

'Blessed is the one who reads aloud the words of the prophecy, and blessed are those who hear and who keep what is written in it; for the time is near' (1.3; see 22.7). By the work of the Spirit, Jesus is revealed as the definitive revelation of God, as the Word enfleshed. This revelation, entrusted to the church by the Spirit and enscripturated in its canon, is enacted by the church in the sense of being *re-told* through the public reading of scripture and in the sense of being *lived out* in the continuing life of the church as the followers of Jesus honour him in worship, obey him in faithful discipleship and speak of him to the world in mission. In the Middle Ages many theologians, Bonaventure in particular, liked to talk of the *Verbum increatum, incarnatum and inspiritum* – the uncreated word, the incarnate word and the inspirited word. This is the sort of pattern I am describing. The eternal word of God becomes incarnate in Jesus Christ who is 'inspired into us by the Spirit when we read the Scriptures that concern him', and when we inhabit and enact the scriptural story, when we live in it and speak of it.[40]

As we have seen, the handing of the *paradosis* of the self-presentation of the saving God is a dynamic process, an event in the life of the Spirit. Revelation's meaning is by no means entirely clear. We need the Spirit of prophecy, who first showed it to John, to unlock its treasures for us. And the key the Spirit gives to us is the Spirit-inspired *paradosis* (the tradition) of Christ and the Spirit-led *paradoseis* (traditions[41]) of following him in an inhospitable world. If we lose our love of Jesus Christ, fail to worship him as the Lamb who sits on the throne of God (7.10) and give up on the 'patient endurance' (1.9) of faithfully testifying to him in word and deed, the Bible will cease to function as *holy scripture*, God's word to us in written form, and will become a text that we manipulate into confused and misleading patterns.

'Patient endurance' is a recurring theme in the book of Revelation. John tells his readers that because he shares with them 'in Jesus', he also shares with them in 'the persecution and the kingdom and the *patient endurance*' (1.9). The churches in Ephesus, Thyatira and Philadelphia (2.2, 3, 19; 3.10) are all commended for their 'patient endurance' in times of false teaching within and persecution without. The church in Pergamum is praised for 'holding fast to [Christ's] name' (2.13) even though they live 'where Satan's throne is' (2.13) in the midst of massive temples of Aesclepius, Athena, Zeus and even the Emperor Augustus. The Smyrnan Christians are called to 'be faithful' (2.10) in the face of a wave of persecution that is bound to involve death. The Sardisians and Laodicians are exhorted 'to conquer' (3.5, 21) their own corruption and complacency. After John's visions of cosmic battles between the forces of good and evil being fought out in the daily living of the churches, he prophesies to all of them: 'Here is a call for the endurance of the saints, those who keep the commandments of God and hold fast to the faith of Jesus' (14.12; 13.10).

Revelation's recurring theme of 'patient endurance' in an inhospitable world is echoed in Jesus' interpretation of the parable of the sower, as told by Luke: 'But as for [the seeds] in the good soil, these are the ones who, when they hear the word, hold fast in an honest and good heart, and bear fruit with *patient endurance*' (Luke 8.15). The agricultural imagery of Jesus' parable may be more soothing than the terrifying scenes of John's visions, but the underlying realities are the same. Just as Jesus' parable shows that the quality of the soil determines the strength and productivity of the seed, the Spirit's prophecy through John addresses the conditions of the churches in order to ensure that they provide the best sorts of environments for the sustained growth and self-propagation of the churches. Neither imply that there is anything automatic. The right conditions do not take the pain and the struggle out of growth. 'Patient endurance' as a continuous act of commitment remains necessary. But they do give growth a chance. They allow the roots to grow deep and the stem to be firm.

The question this raises, of course, is how these conditions are most effectively put in place in our churches. How is the good soil nurtured? How is 'an honest and good heart' cultivated in a believer and a church community so that the word of God can be heard and faithfully lived out in an inhospitable world? What are the practices, traditions (*paradoseis*) that have been handed on, 'by word of mouth and by letter', as Paul puts it (2 Thessalonians 2.15) which will engender the sort of attention, repentance and perseverance to which the Spirit is calling the followers of the *paradosis* of the gospel and hearers of the word? Which of these are found in scripture and which have been passed on through the continuing life of the church, some of them perhaps stemming from the apostles' oral instruction, and so have been sanctified by use, even if not inspired in origin? And what new *paradoseis* are being commended by the the Spirit to the churches today?

The list of questions could go on, with each one generating its own set of questions quite beyond the scope of this chapter. Some of them will be addressed in later chapters, and the final section of this one, which calls for a greater sense of *living in the tradition*, relates to them in a general sort of way. Before moving on to this, though, there is one issue (and one that underlies these various questions) that we have not yet tackled face on – whether the Spirit speaks in ways other than scripture.

The Spirit's voice outside scripture

Sola scriptura does not mean that scripture is the only way God speaks. It is simply the claim that we are bound to the deep truths of scripture, that in matters of salvation there is no truth beyond these deep truths, and, therefore, no need to look for it. As we said earlier, this does not mean that scripture says everything about everything. The sufficiency of scripture is not, in this sense, *self*-sufficiency. Nevertheless, what the Spirit says about salvation in scripture enfolds, in some way, the whole of life, and, therefore, it is proper to test any claim to truth by the deep truths of scripture. In this way, scripture serves a normative function in the Spirit's work, providing the benchmarks for the church's continuing responsibility to hear the Spirit's voice amidst the complexities of life in the world in different contexts and centuries. Steven Land puts it well, 'The Spirit is the Spirit of Christ who speaks scripturally but also has more to say than Scripture.'[42] The awe-inspiring words at the end of Revelation do not put an end to prophecy in the church (22.18–19). They only say that *this* prophecy is permanent and cannot be changed or contradicted by other prophecies. Indeed, part of its function is to form the sort of word-hearing and prophecy-discerning community of which we have just spoken.

It is entirely scriptural to expect the Spirit to speak through the contemplation of nature, individual conscience, the counsel of others, prophetic visions and words, symbolic and sacramental actions, synods and counsels of the church, as well as through the study and preaching of the scriptures. Furthermore, as the Spirit of the Word through whom all things are created, and as the Spirit of the cosmic Christ, the Spirit is not bound to the church. Therefore we also expect to find and hear the Spirit speaking in the vitalities of the world. However, discernment of the words of conscience, counsel, church and world is necessary if we are truly to hear God speak in our own time. Spiritual discernment, discernment in the Spirit, involves a Spirit-led process by which all claims for truth are sifted through what we know of God and God's ways in the Spirit-given truth of scripture. The wisdom to see whether these words are 'scriptural' (consistent with the pattern of salvation and the saved life) and therefore 'spiritual' (of the Spirit), calls, as Steven Land rightly says, 'for a body of people who are formed by the whole counsel of God',[43] among whom there will be those anointed and appointed to guard the faith, and, as Anglicanism puts it, to 'proclaim afresh in each generation'.[44]

One of the most famous accounts of God speaking in ways other than scripture is the story of Augustine's conversion in the fourth century. What is really fascinating in the story is the way in which the church's tradition of reading and enacting scripture, and the Spirit's capacity to speak in ways that are both unmediated and mediated by scripture, all play their part.

God had been working on Augustine for some time. He was not far from the kingdom of heaven. His mother had been praying for him for many years. He was intellectually convinced of the truth of Christianity but he was not yet ready to follow Christ and to turn his back on his 'chain of sexual desire . . . and from [his] slavery of worldly affairs' (he was still praying his famous 'Grant me chastity and continence, but not yet').[45] For reasons more to do with business than religion, a Christian named Ponticianus called on Augustine and his friend Alypius. After expressing surprise when he saw that the only book the great teacher of rhetoric had open on his desk was a Pauline epistle, Ponticianus moved the conversation on to the Egyptian monk Antony. Augustine and Alypius knew nothing about Antony and the extraordinary movement of the Spirit that began only a century or so before in the Egyptian desert. They listened with 'rapt silence' as Ponticianus went on to tell them about two of his friends who happened to find a copy of Athanasius' *Life of Antony* one day when they had some time to spare while the emperor, for whom they were worked, was watching the circus in Trier (they were 'agents in the special branch'). Ponticianus told them how one of his friends picked the book up and was soon 'amazed and set on fire'. 'Filled with holy love and sobering shame', he decided there and then to become a monk. The other friend did the same.[46]

The story threw Augustine into a 'burning struggle with himself'.[47] He yearned to follow Christ but could not move his will to make the step: 'I was deeply disturbed in spirit, angry with indignation and distress that I was not entering into my pact and covenant with you, my God, when all my bones were crying out that I should enter into it.'[48] Alypius sat with Augustine in a garden, silent, as his friend 'struggled with himself against himself', frozen in the 'agony of hesitation'. Eventually, Augustine left Alypius to try to find some solitude for himself. Now alone, 'weeping in the inner agony of his heart', he heard a child calling out, *'Tolle lege, tolle lege'*, 'Pick up and read, pick up and read.'[49] The voice arrested him. He knew it was 'a divine command'. He also remembered how Antony was fully converted to God when he walked into a church and heard the Gospel reading. Augustine knew he was being told to read the Bible. He ran back to Alypius, picked up his Bible, still open at Romans chapter 13 from his earlier struggles, and read: 'Not in riots and drunken parties, not in eroticism and indecencies, not in strife and rivalry, but put on the Lord Jesus Christ and make no provision of the flesh in its lusts' (13–14). 'At once', he recalls, 'it was if the light of relief from all anxiety flooded into my heart. All shadows were dispelled.'[50]

The Spirit had spoken through Ponticianus as he told the story of two people who were prepared to endure everything for the joy of knowing Christ to whom scripture testifies. The Spirit spoke directly through the child and sent Augustine to read the scriptures again. Now the scriptures, which Augustine had read many times before, took on a new light, the light of the Holy Spirit who told him 'to put on the Lord Jesus Christ and make no provision for the flesh'.[51] No longer did Augustine have to summon all the religious energy he could find to try to move his will. God had moved it by the grace of the gospel by the work of the Spirit through the scripture, within the tradition and with the help of a child's voice.[52]

An implication for evangelicalism: to inhabit a living tradition

D. H. Williams, an American evangelical Baptist who is proud to call himself a 'true son of the Protestant Reformation', has written a book with its aim encapsulated in its title: *Retrieving the Tradition and Renewing Evangelicalism*. He defines tradition in this way:

> In the final analysis, then, the Tradition denotes the acceptance and handing over of God's Word, Jesus Christ (*tradere Christum*), and how this took concrete forms in the apostles' preaching (*kerygma*), in the Christ-centred reading of the Old Testament, in the celebration of baptism and the Lord's Supper, and in the doxological and creedal forms by which the declaration of the mystery of God Incarnate was revealed for our salvation. In both *act* and *substance*, the Tradition represents a living history which, throughout the earliest centuries, was constituted by the church and also constituted what was the church.[53]

As the title of his book suggests, Williams is convinced that 'the path to the renewal of evangelicalism must happen through an intentional recovery of its authentic roots in the church's early spirituality and theology'.[54] I agree. Evangelicalism is truest to itself when it allows itself to connect with the original dynamic of the gospel presented, preserved and passed on in the faithful witness of the ancient church to others who, in turn, have done the same. This does not mean accepting everything that the Fathers said or the canons of the ancient councils (as opposed to their creeds) decreed. Indeed, we continue to test everything by scripture because we have learnt from them to trust the 'Word of God, together with the very power of its own truth which we received' from the biblical writers.[55] But it does mean finding gospel ways of consciously inhabiting the tradition of which we are part, thanks to their faithfulness in passing on 'the word of truth' (Colossians 1.5). Conscious of the risk of over-simplification, I offer the following 'ABC' as a way of helping evangelicals to reconnect with the Great Tradition.

We need to *acknowledge* the unique position of the ancient church in relation to the reception of scripture and the constitution of the church's scriptural doctrine and life. This is not a plea for nostalgia or romanticism. There is no way we can return to the ancient church, and we should not try to re-create it. It was by no means perfect, and God is always leading his people forward. Nevertheless, the road along which God is taking us into the future is the same road on which he first set us in the past.

> Thus says the Lord:
> stand at the crossroads, and look
> and ask for the ancient paths,
> where the good way lies; and walk in it,
> and find rest for your souls. (Jeremiah 6.16)

Eduardo Chillida, the famous twentieth-century sculptor and great admirer of Bach, said, 'I have written somewhere concerning Bach: *morderno como las olas. Antiguo como el mar*, modern like the waves, old like the sea.'[56] It is only as we inhabit the work of the Spirit in the life of the church, and appreciate the foundational work completed in its early centuries, that we can move with the movement of the Spirit in our time.

We need to *befriend* the Fathers as interpreters of scripture so that we may learn from them and from those who have continued to interpret scripture according to the gospel and led by the Holy Spirit. The Fathers have inspired a community of readers, a *union of scripture readers*, through whom the Spirit has been layering wisdom upon wisdom. John Wesley was one of them. He considered the Fathers to be 'the most authentic commentators on scripture, as being nearest to the Fountain and eminently endued with the Spirit by whom "all scripture was given"'.[57] The catholic tradition which they began is now, of course, deep and wide, extending historically and geographically. Reading scripture within this community of interpretation allows us to engage with cross-cultural and trans-historical perspectives on scripture so that we might better hear what the Spirit is saying to the churches in our day and in our place.[58]

We should *celebrate* that we belong to a living witness to the gospel with these shapers of the church *and* with those who have followed them in the tradition *and* with those who continue to do so. It is a living tradition of fellowship which is defined by scripture, summarized in the creeds, dramatized through worship, symbolized in all sorts of material, tangible, visible ways, expressed in consistent patterns of living, and embodied in people who pass on the faith from one generation to another. By celebrating our part in this continuing communion of saints, and by receiving all that the Spirit of truth and fellowship gives to us through it, we will be fulfilling Paul's prayer that we 'may have the power to comprehend, *with all the saints*, what is the breadth and length and height and depth, and to know the love of Christ that surpasses knowledge, so that [we] may be filled with the fullness of God' (Ephesians 3.18–19). And we will be following the advice of Heiko Oberman, a distinguished evangelical theologian, who made his 'first and most basic' assumption that 'an evangelical theology properly so called is executed in obedience to Holy Scripture, in communion with the Fathers, and in responsibility with the Brethren'.[59]

3

Being Saved

For the beginning is faith and the end is love.
Ignatius

Introduction

The doctrine of justification by faith lies at the heart of evangelical theology, spirituality and identity. It was the answer to Luther's anguished search for a gracious God and the source of the Reformation protests about the theology and practices of the church in the sixteenth century. It was the solution to John Wesley's quest for a holiness that would make him acceptable to God, and the theological trigger that led to the Revival that swept through Britain in the eighteenth century. In the minds of many evangelicals today it is, as it was for Luther, the 'first and chief article of faith on which the church stands or falls', and remains, as it did for Richard Hooker in the seventeenth century, 'the grand question which hangeth yet in the controversy between us and the Church of Rome'.[1] Therefore any consideration of the matter of salvation from an evangelical perspective – and certainly one which is seeking to be, at the same time, authentically *catholic* and *of the Spirit* – must focus on the place of faith and the manner of our justification before God.

Of course, justification is only, as Wesley said, 'one branch' of God's total saving activity.[2] We are called 'to proclaim the mighty acts' (1 Peter 2.9) of God which stretch from God's creation of the world to the consummation of his purposes in the new heaven and the new earth, and which include the reconstruction of human beings and human society in his image through the incarnation of his Son by the transformative work of his Spirit. The justification of sinners before a holy God is fundamental to this cosmic plan of salvation, just as secure foundations are essential to a building, but it would be a mistake to miss the splendour of the building because of a preoccupation with its base. The edifice of salvation is different from and bigger than the event of justification. Nevertheless, because of the foundational character of the doctrine of justification and because it has been a longstanding area of dispute between evangelical and catholic theology, this chapter will focus on it. We begin by listening in again on the debate between Calvin and Sadoleto in the sixteenth century. We then examine the issues in more detail, drawing particularly on the twentieth-century dialogue between Lutherans and Roman Catholics. After this analysis we move on to consider John Wesley, whose strong doctrine of the Spirit helped him to resolve some of the tensions in the classic debate. Continuing with Wesley and with the theme of the Spirit, we explore his understanding of sanctification and the Spirit's work in transforming us into the likeness of Christ in anticipation of the eschatological fulfilment of our salvation. Finally, we show how, both for Wesley in the eighteenth century and for many Pauline scholars today, our justification and sanctification are inexorably bound to the life and ministry of the church.

Calvin and Sadoleto in the sixteenth century

In his letter to the Genevans, Cardinal Sadoleto said that 'we obtain this blessing of complete and perpetual salvation by faith alone in God and in Jesus Christ'.[3] What could be more uncontentious, evangelically speaking? Salvation is God's gift to us in Jesus Christ. God causes our salvation. We are saved by his grace. It is God's work for us. It is appropriated by faith, and by faith alone. Moreover, God's gracious salvation comes to our receiving faith 'complete and perpetual'. We can be assured that God is faithful, confident that he fulfils his promises. *Grace alone! Christ alone! Faith alone!* Are these not the great themes of the Reformation and the life-blood of evangelicalism? What then was all the fuss about at the Reformation? Why was Martin Luther condemned by other cardinals of the church, and why did John Calvin spend a good deal of his reply to Sadoleto setting this cardinal's doctrine of salvation straight? It was because the Reformers' exegesis of scripture led them to a precise understanding of the place of justification in the process of salvation and of the place of faith in relation to justification.

The exchange between Sadoleto and Calvin illustrates the point. 'I am persuaded that in the cross of and blood of Christ all my faults are unknown', Sadoleto confessed, '*but*' – a 'but' so crucial as to divide the church – he went on to say, this faith 'is not enough' by itself. It must include 'the hope and desire of obeying God, together with love'.[4] 'When we say, then', Sadoleto went on to argue, 'that we can be saved by faith alone in God and Jesus Christ, we hold that in this very faith, *love is essentially comprehended as the chief and primary cause of our salvation.*'[5]

Calvin was not impressed: 'I was amazed when I read your assertion, that love is the first and chief cause of our salvation. O, Sadoleto, who could ever have expected such a saying from you?'[6] To Sadoleto's claim that faith has 'a larger signification', that includes hope and love, Calvin responded with a double-edged exegesis, sharpened on one side by an exact definition of justification and on the other by an exact definition of faith:

> I answer, if you would attend to the true meaning of *justifying* in Scripture . . . it does not refer to a man's own righteousness, but to the mercy of God, which contrary to the sinner's deserts, accepts of a righteousness for him, and that by not imputing his unrighteousness. Our righteousness, I say, is that which is described by Paul (2 Corinthians 5.19) that God has reconciled us to Himself in Jesus Christ.
>
> Whenever [Paul] attributes to [faith] the power of justifying, he at the same time restricts it to a gratuitous promise of the divine favour, and keeps it far removed from all respect to works.[7]

Hence (in language coined by the Reformers in their debates with the Rome) the formal cause of our justification is faith and not love. Justification, in turn, is the formal cause of our salvation. God's mercy is expressed in his 'gratuitous justification', whereby he reconciles us to himself because of Jesus Christ.[8] We receive this mercy to us and accept this justification of us when we place our faith in Christ. For faith, according to Calvin's Genevan Catechism, is 'a sure and steadfast knowledge of the love of God toward us, according as He declares in His gospel that He is our Father and Saviour (through the mediation of Jesus Christ)'.[9]

Calvin was clear that salvation involves more than the forgiveness of sins and reconciliation with God through faith in the merits and mediation of Christ. It also involves our *regeneration* so that we become 'zealous of good works', and, in time, are sanctified by the Holy Spirit.[10] But he was equally clear that because our sanctification is a gradual and continuous process that will not be complete until we are eschatologically transformed in God's future kingdom, it is not the basis of our salvation or the ground on which we are judged. If it were so, it would let us down. Even regeneration is not formally the basis or ground of our salvation. The only basis and ground is Christ and his righteousness. It is this that justifies us before God because it is in and through Christ that God establishes his merciful righteousness, a righteousness demonstrated and defined in Jesus Christ as abundant grace and undeserved mercy. This is what Calvin means by 'gratuitous justification': God's merciful acceptance of us *on account of Christ, through our faith in him.* And this is why Calvin said to Sadoleto that 'justification by faith' is 'the first and keenest subject of controversy between us':[11] because faith, not love, is the formal cause of our justification, the only way we receive the unmerited goodness of God. We are saved by God's love, not by our love.

The issues examined in twentieth-century dialogue

The second half of the twentieth century witnessed a good deal of genuinely *theological* ecumenical endeavour in which ecclesial and theological traditions tried to listen to the other on the doctrine of justification, learn from the other's perspective and to explore ways in which the historic divides could be overcome. One of the most impressive examples was the dialogue between American Lutherans and Roman Catholics which led to the agreement of a *Common Statement* on justification by faith in 1983. It was an important staging post to the historic *Joint Declaration on the Doctrine of Justification* by the Lutheran World Federation and the Roman Catholic Church in 1999.[12] An important link between the two was the work of the Ecumenical Study Group convened after Pope John Paul II's visit to Germany in 1980, which drew Roman Catholic, Lutheran and Reformed theologians together to consider whether, with all theological integrity, the mutual condemnations of the sixteenth century could be lifted, at least as far as understandings of justification were concerned. Their report succinctly described the original concerns of both sides of the Reformation debate:

> In the sixteenth century, Catholic theology was afraid that the result of the Reformers' doctrine of justification could be summed up as: no freedom, no new being, no ethical endeavor, no reward, no church. Protestant theology was afraid that the result of the Catholic doctrine of justification could be summed up as: the triviality of sin, self-praise, a righteousness of works, purchasable salvation, a church intervening between God and human beings.[13]

'No freedom, no new being, no ethical endeavor, no reward, no church': these are the classic concerns of the catholic tradition over the Reformation doctrine of justification by faith. Catholic theology fears that the doctrine is fatalistic and determinist, that it teaches that human nature, even under the direct influence of the Holy Spirit, is incapable of choosing and doing good; that it is bound to do evil even when it has been bound to Christ through baptism and faith. It suspects the doctrine of disallowing the redemption of the human being – our new creation in Christ, that, though always prone to sin, we are yoked to Christ and bearers of his Spirit by whom we are being transformed. It worries that the encouragement to do good is swept away by beguiling assurances of salvation which, though properly confident about forgiveness, forget that we have been 'created in Christ Jesus for good works, which God prepared beforehand as our way of life' (Ephesians 2.10). It detects a 'canon within the canon' in which Paul's teaching on faith is exalted over Jesus' teaching on the rewards which come to the faithful in his kingdom, even that there is a canon within Paul which isolates his teaching on faith in Christ from his teaching on love in the Spirit. It can find no room in the picture for the church and for the ministry of Christ and his Spirit in the ordered actions of his people, and no answer to the person who says, 'I can be a Christian without going to church.'

'The triviality of sin, self-praise, a righteousness of works, purchasable salvation, a church intervening between God and human beings': these are the classic concerns of the Protestant tradition as it seeks to defend what it considers to be the clear teaching of the Bible on grace and faith. Protestant theology fears that Roman Catholic theology underestimates sin, seeing it as something on the surface of humanity, something that can be avoided with a little bit of help, rather than a deep strain of corruption which reaches to every part of the human being and human society and impresses upon it a predilection to evil which stains every human action, and which will not be completely overcome until, by the still unmerited mercy of God, we are totally transformed by his Spirit in our future resurrection. It warns of any attitude that encourages us to congratulate ourselves on our own moral efforts and tempts us into thinking that we should try to gain God's favour by our own works, as if God wanted us to prove ourselves to him rather than trust that he has proved himself faithful to us. It abhors the slightest implication that our salvation is anything other than the free gift of God that invalidates any form of religious activity that seeks to do something in order to acquire God's favour. It is always on the lookout for ecclesiastical devices which attempt to dispense the grace of God and broker God's blessings.

Elements of church life on both sides exacerbated the disagreement and made mutual understanding more difficult. Indulgences, sold to speed the progression of the soul through purgatory; a penitential system which appeared to make the forgiveness of God dependent upon the absolution of a priest and the performance of quantifiable duties to satisfy God's demands; the sacrifice of the Mass which seemed to undermine the finality and sufficiency of Christ's one sacrifice – all these concentrated the minds of the Reformers and made them determined to strike at the theological roots of the gospel-eroding practices of the church. On the other side, as the Reformation took its course, many of the original concerns about Luther's teaching seemed to be proved true as radicals within the Reformation movement (much, it has to be said, to Luther's consternation) began to give up on the sacraments completely, abandoned any notions of the church's authority, spiritualized Christian living (even to the extent of abandoning preaching and relying on the inner word in the heart) and became suspiciously lax ethically.

The combination of theological passion (some derived from new scholarship) and institutional policy (whether for the reform or the protection of the church), combined with complex political manoeuvring, created a climate that was bound to breed misunderstanding. There were two particular semantic confusions which muddied the waters then, and are liable to do so today unless care is taken to hear what is actually being said, rather than what is thought to be said. They concern the two key words of the debate – *justification* and *faith* – and we have already seen them in evidence between Sadoleto and Calvin. The Reformation rode on the Renaissance with its revival of the biblical languages, especially Greek. With Erasmus' Greek New Testament in their hands, the Reformers came to the view that *dikaioun*, the Greek word for righteousness, means 'to pronounce righteous', that is, to declare that we are considered or estimated to be righteous and that righteousness is *imputed* to us. This was very different from the received understanding which was dependent on the Latin vulgate translation of *dikaioun* by *iustificare*, which had the primary meaning of being *made* righteous, of having righteousness *imparted* to us so that it inheres within us.[14] Hence, whereas traditionally theologians had understood the righteousness which justifies us to be an actual righteousness that we possess and is inherent in us through God's work with us (a righteousness that is given to us by God and adheres to us), the Reformers spoke of an *imputed righteousness*, a righteousness that is not our own but resides outside us in Christ (an 'alien righteousness', as Luther called it) which, in the mercy of God, is counted or reckoned as ours when we receive it through God-given faith.

Although Augustine toyed with the declaratory, forensic interpretation of *iustificare*, in which we are counted, or reckoned as righteous by the forgiving mercy of God, he sided with the more natural meaning of the Latin: 'being made righteous' or transformed by the continuing activity of God.[15] Hence, for Augustine and for the medieval tradition that followed him, justification referred not only to an event in which God graciously claims us for his own, despite our sinful state, but also to a divinely aided process by which we are enabled to turn from sin and live righteously. Alister McGrath summarizes the 'characteristic medieval understanding of the nature of justification' in this way:

> Justification refers not merely to the beginning of Christian life, but also to its continuation and ultimate perfection, in which the Christian is made righteous in the sight of God and the sight of men through a fundamental change in his nature, and not merely his status. In effect, the distinction between justification (understood as an external pronouncement of God) and sanctification (understood as the subsequent process of inner renewal), characteristic of the Reformation period, is excluded from the outset.[16]

This has left a lasting legacy. Essentially, catholic talk of justification sounds to evangelical ears as though it is making our reconciliation with God dependent upon our own holiness (our sanctification), a state that despite the transformative work of the Spirit in us will not be complete this side of heaven. On the other hand, evangelical talk about justification sounds to catholic ears as though it neglects the promise of God to restore his image in us and conform us to the life of his Son. Ironically, each side accuses the other of a failure to face up to the full reality of divine holiness. Evangelicals insist (quite properly) that it is neither possible nor necessary to reach the standards of God's righteousness in order to gain his favour. Catholics say (again quite properly) that we should not imagine that God will remain content with anything less than our total re-creation as spiritual, moral and social beings. It is interesting that even the Evangelical Catholic Initiative among Roman Catholic Christians, which is thoroughly committed to evangelical principles of theology and spirituality, defines evangelicals as 'those whose lives have been transformed by the message of the Gospel'.[17]

The other major semantic confusion that dogged the sixteenth-century debate, and can easily do the same today, is over the meaning of faith. The Reformers' commitment to *faith alone* appeared to many in the church to be reducing Christian identity to intellectual belief, merely acknowledging the central truths around the doctrine of salvation. They appealed to Paul's notion of faith working though love (Galatians 5.6) and argued that it is not faith alone that justifies us but faith formed by love (*fides caritate formata* rather than *sola fide*). The Reformers, for their part, were just as antithetic to a purely intellectual belief. Their understanding of faith was dynamic and active, a 'living faith' as they called it. It was a faith that led to a new life – a faith that most certainly works through love. Nevertheless, largely because of the Reformers' definition of justification, they were determined to distinguish faith from love and to show that God accepts us because of his saving action *for us*, not because of a moral change *within us*. 'It is

therefore faith alone which justifies, and yet faith which justifies is not alone', was Calvin's way of distinguishing faith from
love, while simultaneously relating them together.[18]

Twentieth-century dialogues on the theme of justification
readily acknowledged that both sides of the sixteenth-century
debate were operating within very different patterns of thought,
each with its own logic, consistency and purpose. It was also
recognized how each was good at guarding against the weak-
nesses of the other, but less good at seeing the other's strengths.
This task is intrinsically difficult, then and now, especially
where each side defines itself against the other. Productive dialogue requires genuine engagement, a willingness to enter into
the thought form of the other. Each side must step into the
other's world and see how things look from there. This does
not mean that all the differences will be resolved. It does mean
trying to discern whether, behind the contrasting structures of
evangelical and catholic thought on justification, complementary truths may be found. This was very much the spirit of the
German Ecumenical Study Group charged with considering the
'Condemnations of the Reformation Era'. It committed itself to
laying 'bare the innermost centre of the interpretation of justification maintained on both sides and to recognize it unreserv-
edly in its Christian truth, *together with* the mutual tension of
the two understandings'.[19] So it concluded:

> According to Protestant interpretation, the faith that clings
> unconditionally to God's promise in Word and Sacrament is
> sufficient for righteousness before God, so that the renewal of
> the human being, without which there can be no faith, does
> not in itself make any contribution to justification. Catholic
> doctrine knows itself to be at one with the Protestant con-
> cern in emphasizing that the renewal of the human being
> does not 'contribute' to justification, and it is certainly not
> a contribution to which he could make any appeal before
> God. Nevertheless, it feels compelled to stress the renewal
> of the human being through justifying grace, for the sake of
> acknowledging God's newly creating power; although this

renewal in faith, hope, and love is certainly nothing but a response to God's unfathomable grace.[20]

As well as providing some encouragement for the next section in which we explore authentically evangelical ways of integrating the core catholic concerns into a doctrine of salvation, such an account also provides some signposts and parameters for the task. For example, it points to the place of new birth in the Spirit as a key in the scheme of salvation and it marks out the territory of the initiative of God and the responsive character of faith, hope and love through the Spirit, as the common ground on which Christians of different traditions can build their understanding of the saving God who justifies sinners.

John Wesley and justification

John Wesley, a convinced Protestant, was committed throughout his life to the Church of England's brand of Reformation theology expressed in its 39 Articles of Religion, Homilies and Book of Common Prayer. But he had also been formed in the High Church tradition of Anglicanism and was an avid reader of spiritual works from across the traditions. This gave him a deep regard for the catholic inheritance of the church, East as well as West. In many ways this dual commitment to the Reformation and to the catholic identity of the church had already become a mark of Anglicanism. It had been forged through the episcopally led reform of the church in the sixteenth century and shaped through a process of self-definition in debate with Roman Catholicism and Puritanism in the seventeenth century. In this sense Wesley was not unusual as an Anglican Christian. But his Aldersgate experience made him distinctive. While listening to Luther's preface to his commentary on Romans which was being read to the Moravian meeting on the evening of 24 May 1738 in Aldersgate, London, Wesley discovered the spiritual reality of his church's teaching on justification by faith, a doctrine which he accepted in theory, preached in practice but knew little of in his heart, until:

About a quarter to nine, while [Luther] was describing the change which God works in the heart through faith in Christ, I felt my heart strangely warmed. I felt I did trust in Christ, Christ alone for my salvation. And an assurance was given me, that he had taken away *my* sins, even *mine*, and saved *me* from the law of sin and death.[21]

This transformative experience reorientated his theological map and renewed his ministry. It certainly constituted him as an evangelical. It connected him more explicitly to the power of God's grace, thereby injecting a new confidence into his own spiritual life and a new capacity to communicate the saving grace of God to others. Most interesting, however, from our point of view, is the way his Protestant doctrine and evangelical experience did not override his pre-Aldersgate commitment to the renewal and transformation of the moral identity of the believer. The quest for holiness had been Wesley's driving spiritual motivation in his Oxford days, leading, among much else, to the formation of the Holy Club. It was why he accepted Peter Böhler's invitation to the Moravian meeting in May 1738.[22] Spreading scriptural holiness through the land was, in Wesley's mind, the rationale for the Revival and the calling to teach the reality of the 'renewal in love' (or 'entire sanctification') was, in his judgement, the particular charism of the Methodist movement. Indeed, we can see from his testimony that 'the *change which God works in the heart* through faith in Christ' was right at the centre of his Aldersgate experience. This dual commitment on Wesley's part – to justification by faith in the atoning death of Christ and to the complete renewal of the believer by the work of the Spirit in and through the life of the church – make him a particularly helpful source for our purposes.[23] Indeed, his words in his sermon 'On Working Out Our Own Salvation' represent an abiding challenge: 'Let us remember that God has joined these together in the experience of every believer; and therefore we must take care, not to imagine they are ever to be put asunder.'[24]

In the previous section we saw that there were two very different understandings of justification at work in the sixteenth century, leading to layers of mutual misunderstanding over the centuries. One of the great steps forward in the Roman Catholic–Lutheran dialogue was the mutual recognition of each side's essential exegetical principles, as we can see from these words of the high-level German Ecumenical Study Group.

> New Testament exegesis teaches us today that the Protestant way of talking about the righteousness which exists and is efficacious 'outside us' (*extra nos*) has a proper biblical foundation. God has made Christ himself righteousness for us (1 Corinthians 1.30). Consequently, a person is righteous in God's sight only if he is joined with Christ through faith and baptism, and has died with him to sin and to his own sinful self (cf. Romans. 6.6f.; 7.4).
>
> Yet the idea of grace 'poured into' the soul and 'adhering' to it (*adhaerens*) clearly also has a sound biblical basis. For the love of God which remains 'outside us' is nonetheless 'poured into our hearts' (Romans 5.5), being identical with the gift of the Holy Spirit (Galatians 3.2–5; 5.6; Romans 8.23; 2 Corinthians 5:5); and as such it unites with Christ, fills us with confidence and joy, and makes us capable of a new life, which we nonetheless never owe to ourselves in any way, since it is fellowship with Christ and the gift of the Spirit.[25]

In many ways, John Wesley had already reached this position in the eighteenth century. In his sermon on 'Salvation by Faith' he describes how the word '"justification" . . . taken in the largest sense, implies a deliverance from guilt and punishment and a deliverance from the power of sin, though Christ "formed in his heart"'.[26] Again in his sermon on 'Justification by Faith', Wesley allows that, on a few occasions at least, the scriptural definition of justification includes the process of sanctification. Here Wesley is very much in line with catholic instincts. He kept the end game very much in view – the refashioning of the moral character of the believer, the transformation of the child of God by the grace of God. However, Aldersgate had sharpened his sensitivities to the ordering of God's work. It made him clear about the beginning of the game and its rules of play. He drew a firm line between justification and sanctification. Justification is God's acceptance and forgiveness of sinners. It is God's pardon and reconciliation. It has nothing to do with our own worthiness. It is God's grace for the worthless. It is not acquired by our own works, even works aided by the Spirit. It is gained by the work of Christ dying our death for us, bearing God's judgement upon us, on our behalf. It is therefore received entirely by faith, our acknowledgement of God's acceptance of us. Furthermore, 'It is not being made actually just and righteous [for] this is *sanctification*; which is indeed in some degree the immediate *fruit* of justification, but nevertheless is a distinct gift of God, and of a totally different nature.'[27] Here Wesley is very much in line with fundamental Protestant concerns, that the gospel of grace is the good news that sinners are forgiven not on the basis of improvement in their lives but solely because of what God has done for us in Christ; that we are reconciled to God entirely through his mercy and not by our own effort.

Wesley and the new birth

The line that the Reformers drew between justification and sanctification was firm but fine. The declaration of righteousness through Christ led to a life of righteousness in and through him. Hence although, as Calvin said, justification is by faith alone, *faith is never alone*. Even though Wesley was completely convinced about the distinction between justification and sanctification, he was more explicit in explaining how, in the words of the *Homily on Salvation of Mankind*, which he liked to quote, 'faith giveth life to the soul'. He wanted to identify the hinge that held justification and sanctification together. He called it 'new birth' and described its connection to justification in this way.

Although . . . justification and the new birth are in point of time inseparable from each other, yet are they easily distinguishable . . . things of a widely different nature. Justification implies only a relative, the new birth a real, change. God in justifying us does something *for* us: in begetting us again he does the work *in* us. The former changes our outward relation to God, so that of enemies we become children; by the latter our inmost souls are changed, so that of sinners we become saints. The one restores us to the favour, the other the image of God. The one is the taking away the guilt, the other the taking away the power, of sin. So that although they are joined together in time, yet they are of wholly different natures.[28]

The new birth, for Wesley, was the 'gate' or 'entrance' into sanctification. It was the 'real change' of heart without which holy living is impossible. It was birth by the Spirit for life in the Spirit. It was the rebirth of the sinner, who had died to sin in Christ, into the new life of the saint by the Spirit. We will return to Wesley's teaching on sanctification, including his contentious claims about 'entire sanctification', later. For the moment I want to keep the focus on his doctrine of the new birth because it is this that represents his most helpful contribution to the classic debate on justification.

Wesley was not the first by any means to talk about the new birth. Luther, for example, had done so before him. Nevertheless, the way Wesley handles the theme of new birth is distinctive and very un-Lutheran. His definition of the new birth in terms of 'the renewing of our fallen nature', the changing of our 'inmost souls', and even the deliverance from the 'power of sin' meets the driving catholic concern for the reconstitution of the moral identity of believers, our re-creation after the image of God.[29] Wesley's strong doctrine of the Spirit and his continuing focus on the call to holiness left him dissatisfied with any account of salvation which did not explain how sinners are transformed from their sinful state into the dignity that God intends for them, the stature of Christ. At the same time, his commitment to and experience of justification by faith would not allow him to confuse the reconciling movement of God to us with the renewing action of God within us. It was vital, as far as Wesley was concerned, to distinguish them because the former was the basis of the latter. It is as God reconciles us to himself through Christ by sheer mercy in a movement of love that is totally undeserved by us, that, at the same time but in a distinct divine work, he re-creates us and makes it possible for us to live in his love and to be perfected by it.

The new birth is not the condition of our justification. God does not accept us because he has changed us. He accepts us because he loves us and in Christ has done all that is necessary for us to be forgiven. The new birth is the consequence of justification. It is what happens when sinners acknowledge and respond to the mercy of God. They are reborn by this mercy. As they put their faith in Christ's work *for them*, they receive, by his Spirit, Christ *in them* and they are made new by his life. This does not mean that the new birth brings complete sanctification, any more than natural birth brings adult maturity. But it is the creation of the capacities for good, it is 'a vast inward change, a change wrought in the soul by the operation of the Holy Ghost, a change in the whole manner of our existence; for from the moment we are "born of God" we live in quite another manner than we did before; we are, as it were, in another world'.[30]

Wesley's co-ordination of key Protestant and Catholic concerns was not dissimilar to the agreement reached at the Diet of Regensburg in 1541, though it was better. The Emperor Charles V called together official representatives from both sides of the Reformation divide in an attempt to hammer out their doctrinal differences.[31] Melanchthon and Bucer were among the Protestant delegates, Calvin was also present. The Diet eventually foundered on a number of doctrines but a text on justification was agreed. It proposed a form of 'two-fold righteousness' by which the sinner is both 'justified by living and efficacious faith, for through it we are pleasing and acceptable to God on account of Christ', and infused with the love 'which heals the will so that the healed will may fulfil the law'.[32] Hence, for Regensburg, 'living faith is that which both appropriates mercy in Christ, believing that the righteousness that is in Christ is freely imputed to it, and at the same time receives the promise of the Holy Spirit and love'.[33] In this way righteousness is imputed, and, at the same time, imparted to the believer, though the basis or cause justification lies with the former and not the latter, for 'we are justified by [Christ's] merits, not on account of our own worthiness or merits'.[34]

Luther dismissed the article on justification as a flawed attempt to 'glue together' opposing and irreconcilable conceptions. Calvin was more positive. He recognized that the article did not always use the language that the Reformers would choose, but he felt that the catholic side had made surprising concessions and had retained 'the substance of the true doctrine'.[35] These very different assessments are reflected in contemporary evangelical views on the success of Regensburg. Alister McGrath, for example, describes it as a 'scissors and paste job'; Anthony Lane suggests it was 'a giant leap for Christian theology'.[36] There is no doubt that the article has all the marks of committee and compromise. As a result, at several points it is confusing, leading to the suspicion that it is, in fact, confused throughout. Nevertheless, its present interest and value is that it seeks to hold the declaration of acceptance and reconciliation to God through the work of Christ *together with* the renewal of the person's moral and spiritual capacity by the activity of the Spirit, and to ensure that they are ordered in the right way. This is exactly what Wesley was attempting. The fact that some of the most prominent Reformers were able to sign up to it indicates that Wesley, far from developing a new departure in the theology of the Reformation, was simply bringing to the theological surface a dimension of the evangelical doctrine of God's saving grace that is all too easily missed in the heat of debate.

For a number of reasons, Wesley was more successful than Regensburg, at least at a theological level. First, of course, he was writing in a very different context and was able to apply a single mind to the task and so avoid many of the ambiguities of the article. Second, he was able to demonstrate a clearer distinction between, on the one hand, justification and the re-creation of the will, and, on the other, justification and the sanctifying process, and so protect against the sort of confusion to which Regensburg was prone. Third, he was able to do so by his doctrine of new birth. Wesley's understanding of the new birth was in terms of a regenerative event that establishes the possibility of righteous living. It is distinct both from justification (by which Christ's righteousness is imputed to us) and from sanctification (by which Christ's righteousness is imparted to us). It is the consequence of the one and the basis of the other.

Nearly 450 years after the failure of Regensburg, American Roman Catholic and Lutheran theologians produced the *Common Statement* on justification to which we have already referred. Crucially it asserts that 'our entire hope of justification and sanctification rests on Christ Jesus and on the gospel whereby the good news of God's merciful action in Christ is made known; we do not place our ultimate trust in anything other than God's promise and saving work in Christ'.[37] On the basis of this common affirmation of grace and building upon its detailed and empathetic study, the *Statement* declared that:

> We have encountered this gospel in our churches' sacraments and liturgies, in their preaching and teaching, in their doctrines and exhortations . . . We are grateful at this time to confess together what our Catholic and Lutheran ancestors tried to affirm as they responded in different ways to the biblical message of justification . . .We believe that we have reached . . . a fundamental consensus on the gospel.[38]

The mutual recognition of the validity of the intentions of their sixteenth-century forebears is particularly clear in one of the *Statement*'s key confessions:

> Justification, as a transition from disfavor and unrighteousness to favor and righteousness in God's sight, is totally

God's work. *By justification we are both declared and made righteous.* Justification, therefore, is not legal fiction. God, in justifying, effects what he promises; *he forgives sin and makes us truly righteous.*[39]

Should our reaction to this be the same as Luther's after Regensburg – 'so they were right, and so are we'; justification involves putting us right with God *and* making us right in ourselves? Was that not exactly the connection that Luther and the other Reformers were trying to avoid? To understand what the *Statement* meant by these words, we need to draw upon its argument about the power of the word. Earlier the *Statement* had come to an agreement about the *performative function* of God's word, that it 'effects the reality of which it speaks'.[40] Hence, when God declares to us that we are righteous in his sight, God, at the same time, transforms us. God's word is effectual, achieving what it says. It does not return to him empty (Isaiah 55.11). The most obvious way of interpreting this in Lutheran terms is from an eschatological perspective. God's justifying word to us today is an anticipation of his word to us on the last day. On that day God's word to us will be fully and finally transformative: it will make us fit for the eschatological life of God's perfect kingdom. God's declaration of our righteousness will be, therefore, a description of how we are, actually. The word that will be spoken to us then is spoken to us now, so that the gift of righteousness we shall eventually actually possess through Christ is both accounted to us now by our faith in Christ's eschatological work for us, and effective in us now through our faith in him. Interestingly, however, although the *Statement* makes use of the eschatological dynamics of justification, it places more emphasis on the renewal of God's image in us through the work of the Spirit in our justification. It draws on the Helsinki Assembly of the World Lutheran Federation in 1963 and quotes one address which argued, in a way reminiscent of Wesley, that 'The old alternative [between forensic and transformative notions] is begging the question', for God's action brings about 'rebirth'.

The *Common Statement* was an important milestone along the road to the *Joint Declaration on the Doctrine of Justification* issued by the Lutheran World Federation and the Roman Catholic Church which announced, with the full authority of the two Communions, that they had reached 'a consensus in basic truths of the doctrine of justification'.[41] Although it acknowledged that differences remained in 'language, theological elaboration, and emphasis', it affirmed that 'the Lutheran and the Catholic explications of justification are in their difference open to one another'.[42] The heart of the *Declaration* is the agreement that:

> When persons come by faith to share in Christ, God no longer imputes to them their sin and through the Holy Spirit effects in them an active love. These two aspects of God's gracious action are not to be separated, for persons are by faith united with Christ, who in his person is our righteousness (1 Corinthians 1.30): both the forgiveness of sin and the saving presence of God himself ... When Lutherans emphasize that the righteousness of Christ is our righteousness, their intention is above all to insist that the sinner is granted righteousness through the declaration of forgiveness and that *only in union with Christ is one's life renewed* ... When Catholics emphasize the renewal of the interior person through the reception of grace imparted as a gift to the believer, they wish to insist that God's forgiving grace *always brings with it the gift of new life*, which in the Holy Spirit becomes effective in active love.[43]

Clearly the *Joint Declaration* is operating with very similar intentions and methods to Wesley. It is seeking to relate different dimensions of God's saving activity: that we are forgiven by God, counted as righteous in his sight because of the work of Christ, and renewed by God so that, in the Spirit's power, we may live Christ's life of righteousness. It is a good example of holding together the deep truths of evangelical and catholic convictions by concentrating on the Christ who saves and in whom all things hold together: 'Justification and renewal are joined in Christ, who is present in faith.'[44]

It is worth adding, though, that a proper emphasis on the Spirit's work in our eschatological salvation helps to strengthen the case and further protect the fundamental concerns of both traditions by undergirding the *Declaration*'s Christological convictions. The Holy Spirit brings us into relationship with Christ, giving us a real share in Christ's own righteousness and sustains us in relationship with Christ and his messianic work, transforming us into his righteous image. Although a performative word of the Spirit that really does change us because of the participation in Christ and his life that it brings, it remains a *gracious word*. It is a word about the grace of God in Christ and our place in Christ. The righteousness of which it speaks is a righteousness that belongs to Christ and in which we share by grace, through the work of the Spirit. Hence, the righteousness established in us through the work of the Spirit is not a sufficient basis for God's justification of us. That can only be found in Christ's righteousness, which, one day – the day of the kingdom – will be found in us, through the grace of God. God's justifying word to us today spoken in the Spirit is an anticipation of his word to us on the last day, the day for which the Spirit yearns in us and throughout creation. On that day, God's eschatological purposes will be fulfilled in us because we will be like Christ (1 John 3.2). We continue this Spirit-perspective by exploring Wesley's particular understanding of the work of the Spirit both in the believers' sanctification and in the various ministries of the church.

Wesley and sanctification by the Spirit

Earlier we saw how for Wesley the new birth involves the Spirit 'taking away the power of sin'. It is a bold, perhaps unwise, claim to make for the new birth. A form of the expression certainly became a bone of contention within the Revival movement. One of the verses of Charles Wesley's great hymn,

'Love divine, all loves excelling' originally had the line 'take away the power of sinning'. Joseph Fletcher objected to it on the grounds that it was effectively asking God to take away our human nature by eradicating our ability and responsibility to make moral choices. Intriguingly, John decided that the whole verse should be omitted, suggesting that he would prefer to lose the whole thrust of the verse rather than qualify this particular line. Charles followed his brother's advice, though some hymn-books include a revision of the line to say, 'take away the *love* of sinning'. Actually, John Wesley said that the new birth takes away the power of *sin* rather than the power of *sinning*. His point was that God transfers us from darkness to light, from the old life to the new life, from the kingdom of this world to the kingdom of the world to come. Sin no longer rules us because we are *reborn* into the Lordship of Christ. It remains in us but it does not reign over us.[45] 'God be thanked', he said, 'that though ye were in the time past servants of sin, yet now – "being free from sin, ye are become servants of righteousness"' (Romans 6.18).[46] Similarly it can be found in the *Joint Declaration* in its discussion of the Lutheran principle that the Christian is 'at the same time righteous and sinner', where it states that 'the enslaving power of sin is broken on the basis of the merit of Christ. It is no longer a sin that "rules" the Christian for it is itself "ruled" by Christ with whom the justified are bound in faith.'[47]

Nevertheless, there is a very real sense in which Wesley thought that we could lose the *power of sinning*. Freedom from the 'power of sin' brings with it 'power over outward sin'[48] which may lead to such a reality and intimacy of relationship with God that, while the obedient disciple 'abideth in faith and love and in the spirit of prayer and thanksgiving, not only "doth not", but "cannot" commit sin'.[49] Wesley was realistic about the difficulty in reaching, and, more to the point, remaining in this relationship with God. But he was convinced that the state of 'entire sanctification' was possible this side of our final salvation in the kingdom of God. Although often called 'sinless perfection' by others, Wesley was clear that it did not involve the total absence of sin, only the absence of voluntary, or outward sin (sins of word and action). Neither did it involve perfection in any sort of permanent or completed state. Drawing on pseudo-Macarios and other Eastern writers, he had a dynamic understanding of continual growth in grace, a movement from glory to glory in which Christian perfection is seen not as a final arrival point but as a stage on our journey from which we may either return to sin or be further perfected (perfecting upon perfecting as it were).

Wesley's speculations on 'entire sanctification' soon die the death of a thousand qualifications. To his own caveats we may add emphases on the corporate nature of sin and its invasive influence on us, recalling how we are bound to the sin of others and how sin affects – even *infects* – every aspect of us. But there is a ring of scriptural truth in his recognition that there may be occasions when sin loses its appeal, when we see through the beguiling nature of temptation and when, just for a moment perhaps, we lose 'the love of sinning' and live in the victory of Christ over sin.[50] It also chimes with the experience of the great saints of the church.

Furthermore, Wesley's advice on how we may avoid 'the unquestionable progress from grace to sin'[51] is a profound delineation of the life of the Spirit that is worth heeding by all who want to live more obediently. First, he describes the discipline of loving attention to God: 'if the loving eye of the soul be steadily fixed on God, the temptation soon vanishes away'.[52] Evangelical faith, faith in the grace of God, works itself out in love of God (Galatians 5.6). As we hold to God in faith, so we are held by God and sustained in the love which overflows into obedient living. Second, Wesley shows how this intensive relational interplay, this 'life of God in the soul of the believer', involves 'the continual inspiration of God's Holy Spirit: God's breathing into the soul, and the soul's breathing back what it receives from God'.[53] The 'perpetual inspiration of the Spirit' had been taught by William Law, the Anglican divine whose writings were a great influence on Wesley.[54] Law, in turn, claimed to have learnt the doctrine from the Collects of the Book of Common Prayer, with their strong emphasis on the Spirit, without whom 'we are not able to please Thee'.[55] Wesley weaves together the action of the Spirit with the response of the person. The Spirit, who has renewed us in the new birth and made us capable of godly living, continually breathes life into us and draws breath and life from us. Third, this leads him to stress 'the absolute necessity of this re-action of the soul . . . in order to the continuance of the divine life therein'.[56] The 'unceasing presence of God' which is given to us, is to be met by 'an unceasing return of love, praise, and prayer, offering up all the thoughts of our hearts, all the words of our tongues, all the works of our hands, all our body, soul, and spirit, to be a holy sacrifice, acceptable unto God in Christ Jesus'.[57] Wesley was careful to maintain the strict priority of God's action for us that the Reformers felt had been obscured by much of the teaching and practice of the church for many years. But at the same time he was adamant that God calls for our co-operation – not in our justification, this can only be received by faith – but in the shaping of faithful lives. Hence, in these terms, he was quite happy to quote one of Augustine's principles that was dear to the heart of the catholic cause: 'He that made us without ourselves, will not save us without ourselves.'[58]

For Wesley, faith in the grace of God remains the essential undergirding of godly living. It is not something that begins our Christian identity only to give way to human effort once we have started on the journey. It is not like the ignition of a car that just gets the engine going. It is a continual, active trust in the grace of God to forgive and accept us regardless of the poverty of our thoughts, words and actions in which there is always a 'mixture of evil' and which do not have 'anything meritorious in them'.[59] Nevertheless, this faith in a forgiving God who restores us into relationship with him and renews our inner being will lead inexorably – if it is authentic faith – into good works and godly living. Faith will work itself out in love because faith forms love within us.[60] It does so because our faith is not in a proposition but in a person. It is faith in Christ who calls us to willingly follow him and to live in his way by his Spirit: '"Therefore, there is no condemnation to them that are in Christ Jesus", justified by him, provided that they "walk in him whom they have received", "not after the flesh but after the spirit".'[61]

Wesley and the ministries of the Spirit in the church

Although Wesley was deeply indebted to the Moravians, his relationship with them did not last. Within 14 months of his Aldersgate experience he had broken from the Fetter Lane Society because of their neglect – almost rejection – of the ministries of the Spirit in the church. They had taken the Reformation principle of *faith alone* to the extreme, and, like some of the radical groups of the sixteenth century, they had dispensed with the external practices of the church in favour of the practice of stillness in which people simply *wait* for the gift of justification and of sanctification. Any attempt to do otherwise, they argued, by means of personal or ecclesial activity, would imply that salvation is earned by our effort, not received by our faith. Every theological and spiritual bone in Wesley's body reacted against this. His revivalist ministry was based on preaching, and his spiritual life relied on the Eucharist. Throughout his sermons and writings he called his hearers and readers to make full use of the practices of the church – prayer, sermons, scripture, fasting and Lord's Supper, etc. They have been chosen by God as means or channels of his grace: 'By "means of grace", I understand outward signs, words, or actions, ordained of God, and appointed for this end, to be the ordinary channels whereby he might convey to man, preventing, justifying, or sanctifying grace.'[62]

Although Wesley could sing, 'But I of means have made my boast, of means an idol made',[63] he knew that disregarding them was contrary to the teaching of scripture, the witness of the church's tradition and his own experience. And so he could also sing, joyfully and gratefully:

Why did my dying Lord ordain
this dear memorial of His Love?
Might we not by faith obtain,
by faith the mountain sin remove,
enjoy the sense of sins forgiven,
and holiness, the taste of heaven?
It seem'd to my Redeemer good
that faith should *here* his coming wait.[64]

Even in his teaching on the new birth he did not to deny that people had been born again at their baptism but rather implored all those who did not display the marks of new birth to 'receive again what they have lost, even the "Spirit of adoption, crying in their hearts Abba, Father!"'.[65]

In most cases the place of the church in God's saving purposes did not figure very highly on the agenda of many of the twentieth-century ecumenical dialogues on justification. It was generally decided to concentrate on the theological issues which have caused the most difficulty. I have chosen to follow the same pattern in this chapter and to reserve the more obviously ecclesiological and sacramental questions to later chapters. However, the fact that Wesley found himself having to defend the external practices of the church against the Moravian interiorization of faith is an important reminder of the tendencies within Protestant faith and evangelical piety to detach God's justifying and sanctifying work from the life and activity of the church. Luther fought the same battle 200 years before.

If God were to bid you to pick up a straw or to pluck out a feather with the command, order, and promise that thereby you would have forgiveness of all sin, grace and eternal life, should you not accept this joyfully and gratefully, and cherish, praise, and esteem this straw and that feather as a higher and holier possession than heaven and earth? . . . Why then are we such disgraceful people that we do not regard the water of baptism, the bread and wine . . . the spoken

word, and the laying on of [person's] hands for the forgiveness of sins as such holy possessions, as we would the straw
and the feather, though in the former, as we hear and know,
God himself wishes to be effective and wants them to be his
water, word, hand, bread, and wine, by means of which he
wishes to sanctify and save you in Christ, who acquired this
for us and who gave us the Holy Spirit from the Father for
this work?[66]

Justification and the 'new perspective'

The intrinsic relationship between justification and the life
of the church has been reinforced over recent years by what
has become knows as 'the new perspective on Paul'. Although
this development in Pauline studies has confirmed Luther's
exegesis of Paul's definition of justification and faith (that we
are declared righteous on the basis of our faith in Christ), it
is critical of the perceived polarization of law and gospel in
Paul which Luther bequeathed to Protestant theology. The new
perspective claims that Luther superimposed his complaints
against medieval Catholicism – that it was a religion of merit
and achievement rather than grace and mercy – on to Jewish
religion. These projections led Luther away from the reality
that God's covenant with his people has always been based on
grace. The law, rather than being a means of gaining favour
with God, was God's gracious gift to his covenant community, and obedience to it brought the blessings of the covenant.
The 'works of the law' to which Paul refers are not, according
to Tom Wright, 'proto-Pelagian efforts to earn salvation, but
rather "sabbath [keeping], food-laws, circumcision"'.[67] They
are 'badges of national identity'. The thrust of Paul's preaching was not to call people to faith in Christ in place of obedience to God's fundamental law, but to proclaim that in Christ,
God had expanded the boundaries of the covenant people beyond the Jewish race to include all those who have faith in
Christ. The vocation of Israel to live faithfully, even to the ex-

treme point of bearing God's judgement on the unfaithfulness of the world by his death on the cross, had been fulfilled in Jesus. Faith in him, as the one in whom and through whom God's righteous will to restore and renew the whole creation is being worked out, is now the mark of membership of the covenant community. Justification is God's declaration that we are righteous because we belong to the covenant community of his grace by our faith in Christ, that we are members of the covenant because we are followers of Christ. Baptism is the obvious setting for God's declaration of membership of this reconstituted covenant community, and the life of discipleship, lived necessarily with other disciples, is the way we live the life of the covenant and maintain our status within it.

The new perspective has provoked a debate on Paul's attitude to the law and its relationship to faith in Christ. There is some way for the debate to go before it is clear exactly how far the new perspective on Paul should lead to a new perspective on justification. But it is clear at this point that while the new perspective has confirmed the traditional evangelical conviction in the grace of the God who declares us righteous by our faith in Christ, it is at the same time challenging evangelicalism to remember that we are justified by Christ's blood into his body, his church, for 'no one goes to heaven alone', as Wesley once heard someone say.[68] It is to Christ's people, his messianic community, the church of God, that we now turn as we explore the corporate nature of the salvation he brings to the world and the work that God effects through the church.

4

Living Together

*The task of evangelical theology is to describe the relation
between the gospel and the church.*
John Webster

So far, some strong claims have been made about the church. Chapter 1 proposed that there is 'no gospel without the church'. Chapter 2 asserted that the church receives and interprets God's word. Chapter 3 concluded with John Wesley's principle that 'no one goes to heaven alone' and acknowledged that the corporate realities of salvation are often understated in evangelical theology. Indeed, an aim of this book is to suggest ways in which evangelicalism may appropriate a fuller, more self-consciously *ecclesial* identity, one that celebrates and lives within the calling to be members of Christ's Spirit-filled community, his messianic community, and that rejoices that we are with (*kata*) the whole (*holos*) in 'the communion of the Holy Spirit' (2 Corinthians 13.13). It is now time to focus more directly on the church and to test out whether this sort of approach represents an authentic expression of evangelicalism.

Evangelicals and the church

It is often claimed that evangelicals are weak on ecclesiology. We have already implied that there is some truth in this, and we will be going on to acknowledge areas in which this might be addressed. But right at the outset we need to see that the situation is much more complex than is sometimes recognized by those who criticize evangelical attitudes to the church. *Practically*, evangelicalism has a very strong track record of commitment to the corporate dimension of the faith and to the building up of the life and health of the church. 'Fellowship' has always been a fundamental value of evangelicalism. At my own conversion, the necessity of being with others who shared the faith was made very clear – a coal that slipped out of the fire would soon cease to burn, I was told. Small groups have been a key component of evangelical strategy from Luther's call for gatherings of those who 'seek to be Christians in earnest', to Wesleyan class meetings and to the structure of the 'Alpha Course', 'Christianity Explored' and other evangelistic tools. Regular worship and full involvement in the life of a local church are basic assumptions of evangelical life. Daily reading of the Bible in common with others through some form of lectionary, perhaps accompanied by shared teaching notes, in order to create a union of scripture readers, is one of the traditional marks of evangelical spirituality. Growing the church and planting new churches is at the centre of evangelical missionary practice. Theologically, the roots of evangelicalism in the mainstream Reformers go deeply into the importance of the church in the purposes of God. 'So powerful is participation in the church', said John Calvin, 'that it keeps us in the society of God'.[1] Historically, the flowering of evangelicalism involved a remarkable ecclesial ease as Christians turned their backs on the religious wars fought on the basis of ecclesial difference ('there is a . . . horrid reproach to the Christian name . . . there is war between Christians', said Wesley) and embraced those from whatever church tradition in whom the same love of Christ could be found ('Is thine heart right, as my heart is with thy heart?', as Wesley said even more famously).[2]

The ecclesial richness of evangelicalism should be affirmed and celebrated. There is much in evangelical history that has renewed, deepened and extended the life of the church. Nevertheless, it is difficult to deny that some of the fears of those who opposed the principles of the sixteenth-century Reformation have been fulfilled. As we saw in Chapter 2, (Roman) Catholics were anxious about a perceived disconnection of the interpretation of scripture from the authority of the church. They feared that private interpretation of scripture would lead to privatization of the faith and of the church, in other words to heresy and schism. I have to admit that I have seen plenty of evidence of both. I have known individuals and groups distort and then deny fundamental doctrines of the church. I have witnessed division and fragmentation *within* evangelicalism, sometimes leading to the creation of new ecclesial communities. In Chapter 3 we heard the catholic complaint that the Protestant doctrine of justification by faith was bound to lead the individual to individualism. No longer dependent upon the life-changing and grace-giving actions of the church, believers were bound to become independent of the church. Again, we do not need to go far to see examples of the church being rendered tangential to Christian faith. Most evangelism in which I was involved for many years was theoretically committed to integrating converts into the life of the church, but its evangelistic message revealed a deep embarrassment with the church, almost an antipathy to it. 'Point people to Jesus and for heaven's sake (literally) get their eyes off the church', we were told.

Much self-analysis within the evangelical movement recognizes that 'individualism may be evangelicalism's Achilles heel'.[3] The historical connections between the rise of evangelicalism and the emergence of modernity, with its stress on the autonomous individual, run the risk that evangelicalism's 'stress on *personal* faith and piety easily becomes a purveyor of the strong strains of Enlightenment-spawned individualism'.[4] Furthermore, evangelicalism's missionary strategy of cultural adaptivity makes it particularly vulnerable to the corrosive forces of consumerism and fragmentation of postmodern society. Whether it is modernity's 'I think, therefore I am', or postmodernity's 'I choose, therefore I am' (or, as more likely, a powerful cocktail of the two), the deep biblical principle embedded in the South African word *ubantu* – which roughly translated means, 'I belong, therefore I am' – is not easy for evangelicalism to live out, despite its best intentions.

In recent years there have been some significant attempts both to *address* the cultural captivity which numbs evangelicalism to the ecclesial realities of the gospel and to *redress* evangelicalism's tendency to relegate ecclesiology to a low position in the list of theological priorities. John Stackhouse's collection of essays on evangelical ecclesiology aptly warns:

> When the church is confused about who it is and whose it is, it can become just another human institution, just another collective, just another voluntary society. So we need ecclesiology – the doctrine of the church – to clarify our minds, motivate our hearts, and direct our hands. We need an ecclesiology so that we can be who and whose we truly are.[5]

Knowing 'who we are and whose we are' so that we can 'be who and whose we truly are' is necessary for its own sake. It is also a vital missionary imperative for three reasons. First, despite the corrosive forces of some elements of the contemporary culture on a shared existence (one that is given and not merely chosen), other features of postmodern life challenge Christianity to recover its communal forms. In many ways the internet is the symbol of our age. Its universal interconnectivity epitomizes the movements in science, global economics and international politics which impact upon us in a million ways, from communication systems to supermarket shelves, and create both a sense of universal connectedness and a deep desire to re-create local and distinctive networks of relationships. In this age, with its distrust of the isolated individual and the edicts of pure rationality, people expect truth to be performed and proved in practice for it to be authenticated personally and communally. One result, neatly summarized by Robert Webber, is that 'the church is the new apologetic in the post-Christian era'.[6] Evangelicalism's affinity with modernity's confidence in the self-deciding, self-fulfilling individual served its evangelistic task effectively in the past. But postmodernity's recognition that the self is shaped by communication, context and community may leave evangelicalism marooned on a past cultural island, still inhabited by some but deserted by most, unless it reconnects with principles which lie at the heart of its biblical faith but which have been overshadowed by the cultural clouds under which it grew for a number of centuries.

Second, responding to these cultural realities, contemporary evangelism is experimenting with forms of ecclesial life that aim to be more attractive and accessible to postmodern society than many of the inherited patterns. Evangelicals are playing a leading part in these innovative missionary initiatives, creatively reimagining the shape and style of the church of today and tomorrow. The danger, however, is that without deep thought about the fundamental character of the church ('who we are and whose we are'), these 'new ways of being the church' or 'fresh expressions of the church' will be driven by pragmatic panic rather than by the ecclesiological principles of the gospel. In an age when we realize that the conversion of individuals requires the re-creation of Christian communities, the doctrine of the church is a *missionary priority*.

Third, there is serious leakage from the church. Research by Philip Richter and Leslie Francis published in 1998 found that despite all the efforts of the decade of evangelism, people were leaving faster through the back door of the church than they were joining through its front door.[7] Peter Brierley's findings confirm the seriousness of the situation. 'The country is littered with people who used to go to church but no longer do. We could bleed to death', he says, through 'a haemorrhage akin to a burst artery.'[8] Generally evangelical and charismatic churches have fared better than other traditions, often providing glimmers of hope amid generally depressing figures. To pretend, though, that evangelical churches are protected from these shifts would be foolish and inaccurate. Bob Jackson's research indicates worryingly low growth rates among large churches – many of them evangelical – and Alan Jamieson's findings among evangelical and charismatic churches reveal that people with longstanding involvement in the church, including responsibilities for leadership, are also finding their way out through the back door.[9] The most interesting aspect of Jamieson's research is that the majority of the leavers do not want to abandon the faith, they simply feel that they have outgrown the church and have decided to 'work out their salvation' without it. Their experience challenges evangelicalism to consider both whether its forms of church life are sufficiently nourishing for the long-term formation of people and communities into 'the full stature of Christ' (Ephesians 4.13), and whether its teaching on the church implicitly allows believers to conclude that they can do without its life and ministry.

The deep thought about the character of the church that is needed in our missionary age involves digging[10] beneath the surface forms of the church to uncover what the Second Vatican Council described as the 'inner nature' of the church.[11] Dietrich Bonhoeffer, in his seminal study, *Communion of Saints*, which we will draw upon on several occasions, defined this inner nature of the church as 'the life-principles of the new basic-relations of social existence'.[12] Daniel Hardy, the Anglican ecclesiologist, calls it the 'logic of the church', or its 'code'.[13] Somewhat similarly, Howard Snyder, in his various studies of evangelical ecclesiology, talks of the church's DNA, its consti-tutive genetic make-up.[14] C. S. Lewis almost called his spiritual classic *Deep Church* rather than *Mere Christianity*.[15] His aim was to search out the deep, underlying connections between evangelical and catholic visions of the church's faith and life. The place to begin is with the gospel and the catholic church, as Michael Ramsey shrewdly saw in his magisterial work of the same title.

The gospel and the church

The focus of the last chapter was particularly the disputed issue of justification. The gospel, though – as we acknowledged – embraces more than the individual's standing before God. The gospel is the story of God's relationship with the world – a story of boundless grace. It is the revelation of God's perfect, triune life of love overflowing outwards in the divine deci-sion to create the cosmos as the expression of God's nature.

It is the manifestation of God's covenant to perfect creation, to overcome whatever forces of rebellion that the freedom of creation's space gave rise to, and to bring the creation into fullness of relationship. It is the gift to humanity, made according to the likeness of God (Genesis 1.26), of participating in God's life through adoption as God's creaturely, reconciled child. This expansive work of God stretches from 'before the foundation of the world' (Ephesians 1.4) into the kingdom of the 'new heaven and new earth' (Revelation 21.1) which shall have no end. God's declaration of righteousness upon sinners on the basis of Christ's atoning work received by faith, and God's accompanying rebirth of the sinner through the gift of Christ's life in the Holy Spirit, thrusts believers into the renewed and perfected creation, even while they inhabit the conditions of the old order, with its disrupted and damaged sets of relationships.

Because God's intention has always been to gather his creation into communion with him, God's activity each step along the way has involved the gathering of a community to know and love him in and through their knowing and loving of each other:

So God created humankind in his image, in the image of God he created him; male and female he created them. (Genesis. 1.27)

The Lord your God has chosen you out of all the peoples of the earth to be his people, his treasured possession. (Deuteronomy 7.6)

As you, Father, are in me and I am in you, may they also be in us, so that the world may believe you sent me. (John 17.21)

The *ekklēsia*, the people that God gathers from the corners of the world, participate in God's new creation because, through the life, death and resurrection of Christ for others, we have been reconstituted as a people reconciled to God, to each other and to the whole of creation. The church is, therefore, a prophetic embodiment and demonstration of God's will and purpose.

> Of this gospel I have become a servant according to the gift of God's grace that was given to me . . . to bring to the Gentiles the news of the boundless riches of Christ, and to make everyone see what is the plan of the mystery hidden for ages in God who created all things; so that *through the church* the wisdom of God in its rich variety might be made known to the rulers and authorities in the heavenly places. This was in accordance with the eternal purpose that he has carried out in Christ Jesus our Lord, in whom we have access to God in boldness and confidence through faith in him. (Ephesians 3.7–12)

In its response to the Anglican–Roman Catholic International Commission's Report, *Salvation and the Church*, the Vatican's Congregation for the Defence of the Faith was at pains to make clear that, according to the teaching of the church enshrined in the Second Vatican Council, the church is a 'mystery of faith', and therefore necessary for salvation.[16] It not only witnesses to salvation but is able to make it present through its sacramental actions. It does not only point to salvation in Christ, it provides it, because the church is his body. Before we go on to consider these claims – which lie right at the heart of catholic ecclesiology – I would like us to hear them in a different key, hear them in a different sound, as it were. Henri de Lubac was a Roman Catholic theologian who not only wrote about what it means to be, in Origen's phrase, 'an ecclesial person' but also clearly lived and felt it. His book, *The Splendour of the Church*, written before Vatican II, had a significant influence on the Council itself and upon catholic ecclesiology since, both Roman and otherwise. Here is a long quotation and one of a number I will be using in this chapter. Although remote from evangelicals in terms of theological tradition, de Lubac's love of Christ,

passion for the gospel and commitment to the church with all
its failings, should not fail to command respect.

Let us look for a moment at the whole great panorama of
the twenty centuries [of the church's history]. It begins in
the wounded side of Christ on Calvary, goes through the
'tempering' of the Pentecostal fires and comes onward like
a burning flood to pass through each in his turn, so that
fresh living water springs up in us and new flames are lit.
By virtue of the divine power received from her Founder the
Church is an institution which endures; but even more than
an institution, she is a life that is passed on. All the members
of the great 'family of Christ' recognize one another and call
to one another . . . The voice of the one Spirit, speaking to
His Bride, finds an echo in the depths of each individual consciousness, and correspondingly, it is the same faith, hope
and charity everywhere; the outward expression of a unity
that goes down to the roots, and the blazing up of one single
flame.

From their first generation onwards Christ's followers,
however thrilled by the newness of Christianity, were also
aware . . . [that] the very word 'Church' . . . was the word
which, in the Greek translation of the Bible, was applied
in particular to the assembly of Israelites round Moses in
the far-off days of the Exodus . . . To be received into the
Church was thus to be introduced into this time-honoured
assembly and admitted to 'the dignity of an Israelite' . . .
This is the . . . fine flower of the 'remnant' spoken of by these
same Prophets, the remnant of the 'fewest of any people',
which Yahweh had promised to bring together again after
its scattering, and which had just been focused in its entirety,
in Christ.

If we are to survey all its dimensions . . . we have to look
beyond Moses and the covenant of Sinai and beyond the
promises made to 'our father Abraham' into the dawn of
time . . . But the idea of a prefiguring of the Church and
that of her effective commencement in Adam are neither of

them entirely adequate. For though Christ was not to appear in the humility of our flesh until long after these things, He is nonetheless 'the first-born of every creature', as St Paul teaches; so that whatever is true of Him is also true of His Bride the Church. . . . But all this does not bring our exploration to an end. Having looked deeper and deeper into the past, we now have to look deeper and deeper into the future, to the very end of time – 'from the time of Abel the just unto the last elect, from the beginning of the world to the end'. The definitive reality is that which comes first in the plan of God. As Clement of Alexandria said (and said superbly): 'Just as the will of God is an act and is called the world, so also His intention is the salvation of humanity and is called the Church': and we should say of the Church, as of Christ, that her kingdom 'shall be without end'.[17]

It is interesting to compare de Lubac's rich panorama of God's purposes for the church with Heinrich Bullinger's terse statement which was later incorporated into the Second Helvetic Confession of 1562:

Because God from the beginning would have humankind saved, and to come to know the knowledge of the truth (1 Timothy 2.4), it is altogether necessary that there always should have been, and should be now, and to the end of the world, a Church.[18]

The difference in style should not mask the substantial similarities. Both de Lubac and Bullinger regard the church as intrinsic to God's saving purposes. It performs a necessary instrumental function in communicating the gospel and provides a space in which, and the means by which, people can receive the ongoing grace of the gospel. There is a rich doctrine of the church, often under-appropriated in evangelical circles, built upon its unique function in God's economy. We will return to this later in this chapter and in subsequent chapters. Here, though, I want to home in on what appears to be at least one significant difference between de Lubac and Bullinger which emerges at the end of both quotations. Whereas de Lubac sees the church as a permanent reality in the eschatological fullness of God's purposes, Bullinger does not envisage it continuing into the future kingdom. It will have fulfilled its function. The gospel will have been made known to the ends of the earth. It will not be heard in the kingdom of heaven because the kingdom is the fulfilment of the promise of the gospel. For de Lubac, though, that is precisely why the church continues in, indeed *as*, the kingdom. An ecclesial mode of existence is the very form of human life into which the gospel brings us and which the kingdom will fulfil for us. It will not pass away in the kingdom, because this form of life is the purpose of the kingdom.

Of course, to be fair to Bullinger, he would not have denied that eschatological life is communal, but his definition of the church in terms of *activity* rather than *identity*, *utility* rather than *mutuality*, is indicative of inherent tendencies within evangelicalism over the place of the church in the purposes of God. In a telling analysis of the 1999 Global Consultation on Evangelical Missiology, George Hunsberger concluded that 'for the most part, "church" is an object to which the participants relate themselves, not the identity they wear'.[19] Ironically, despite evangelical reluctance to define the church in institutional terms, we often, by default, view the church as an *operational organization* with which individuals co-operate (or otherwise) rather than as a *dynamic organism* in which we live. De Lubac's poetic panorama, therefore, opens up a number of critical issues which need to be teased out. They are wound around three interconnected questions: 'Does the church belong to the gospel?'; 'Is the church an association of believers or an action of God?'; 'How is the church related to Christ?'.

Does the church belong to the gospel?

If the short résumé of the gospel a few pages ago is anything close to being faithful, there can be no real doubt that the church belongs to the gospel. 'Out of the plenitude and limitless perfection of his own self-originating life as Father, Son and Spirit, God determines to be *with his creatures*', as John Webster succinctly puts it.[20] The *announcement* of the gospel of fellowship with God necessarily gives rise to the *assembly* that experiences fellowship with God. Hence, we can affirm that 'The Christian faith is thus ecclesial because it is evangelical', with as much joy and confidence as we declare that Christian faith is personal because it is evangelical.[21] Indeed, the fuller the recognition of the ecclesial reality of evangelical life, the greater the realization of the personal dynamics of the gospel, for just as surely as Christ brings us into right relation with God, so he brings us into right relationship with each other. We are wrenched, as de Lubac says – entirely by grace – from our solitude and 'brought *together* into the heart of the life of the Trinity'.[22]

The inseparability of our relationship with Christ from those to whom Christ is also bound was a prominent and vivid theme in Luther's theology, particularly his eucharistic theology. Our communion is with Christ 'and all his saints'.[23] Our faith relationship with Christ establishes a love relationship with his people in which 'living not in ourselves, but in Christ and our neighbour', we share each other's strengths and bear each other's burdens to the point of being 'changed into one another through love'.[24] Here, incidentally, we see Luther's emphasis on justification by faith combined with his equally passionate belief in the transformation by love. The faith that justifies brings us into a set of relationships and responsibilities which, through the freedom and release that faith gives to love, becomes the anvil on which Christ shapes us into the pattern of his life for others.[25]

Very much in the Lutheran tradition, Bonhoeffer was insistent that 'When Christ comes "into" us through the Holy Spirit, the church comes "into" us.' Relationship with Christ, for Bonhoeffer, always involves relationship with the church because 'in Christ himself the church is already established'.[26] Therefore, Bonhoeffer is clear that the church 'is not merely a means to an end but also an end in itself. It is the present Christ himself. This is why "being in Christ" and "being in the church-community" is the same thing.'[27] Christ's vicarious representation for others on the basis of his life with others becomes for Bonhoeffer, as with Luther, the order of ecclesial life. Because we live in Christ, we live in his way, with and for others in the three great acts of love':[28] self-renouncing work where we 'give up happiness' for the other;[29] intercession where 'each one bears the other's burdens';[30] and forgiveness 'in God's name' where we take 'sin from the other's conscience' by 'laying it in turn on Christ'.[31] None of this for Bonhoeffer or for Luther undermines the individual's direct and personal relationship with God. The individual's dealings with God remain a matter of the utmost seriousness. In a very real sense the individual does 'face God singly and alone' but, at the same time, 'this individual still remains within the church-community, and in every situation and problem of life *the church community is with this individual*'.[32]

Luther's and Bonhoeffer's understanding of the connection between the church and the gospel depends upon prior convictions about the relationship between Christ and the church and about the role of the church in communicating the gospel. Hence we must move on to consider our second and third interconnected questions.

Is the church an association of Christians or an action of God: is it 'meeting' or 'mother'?

When I was told at my conversion to 'join a church', the implication was that church membership was a consequence of faith requiring my choice, my election, rather than a corollary of faith to be received as God's gift to me. The total membership of the whole church appeared to be the cumulative total of the various churches which, in turn, was made up of the cumulative total of all the believers who had chosen to join the churches. As a method of calculating the quantity of the church on earth at any one time, this statistical method is reasonable. It also has a sound biblical basis. The gospel writers often talk about the *number* of Jesus' followers, and Paul addresses his letters to the saints in, for example, Corinth or Ephesus who make up the church in those places (1 Corinthians 1.2; Ephesians 1.1). However, as a theological description of the church's *quality*, the cumulative definition is inadequate. It needs to be set within the New Testament's more corporeal images of the church which concentrate the many members of the churches into one collective reality: the body and bride of Christ, the people and household of God, the temple of the Holy Spirit and city of light, the holy nation and royal priesthood, the new humanity.

These biblical analogies of the church all rely on the multiplicity of real, actual human beings, but they envisage them as so closely connected and so integrally bound to each other that they form one organic whole which draws its life not from their combined energy but from a prior constitution in the purpose and power of God. This is why Luther (with the other mainline Reformers) and Bonhoeffer happily affirmed the teaching of the Fathers that the church is our *mother*:[33] 'Thus the church-community as the community of the saints carries its children like a mother, as its most sacred treasure. It can do this only by virtue of its "communal life"; if it were a "voluntary association" the act of baptism would be meaningless.'[34]

Bonhoeffer's reference to baptism is important. The New Testament regards baptism as intrinsic to Christian identity: 'those who welcomed [Peter's] message are baptized . . . and day by day the Lord added to their number those who were being saved' (Acts 2.41, 47). Baptism is a communal act performed by the church for the individual. I cannot baptize myself. Similarly the Lord's Supper is a communal act performed in and by the church. I cannot eat this meal alone. Our dependence on the sacramental action of the church for Christian status and sustenance also applies to other spheres of the life and practice of the church. This is why Friedrich Schleiermacher's neat distinction between Protestantism, which 'makes the individual's relation to the Church dependent on his relation to Christ', and Catholicism which 'makes the individual's relation to Christ dependent on his relation to the Church' is too neat.[35]

Christian faith has always been *ecclesially mediated*. It is the pattern of Pentecost (Acts 1.37–47). Without people to tell me about Christ, to show the difference that following him makes to life, to show me his word in the scriptures and to help me read the scriptures in the Spirit, to pray with me and for me – and unless others had done the same for them – I would never have heard and seen the gospel. 'Appropriately understood,' writes Miroslav Volf, 'the motherhood of church is a statement that the transmission of the faith occurs through interpersonal ecclesial interaction.'[36]

However, this does not mean that the church saves me. Although we cannot believe *without* the church, we do not believe *in* the church as the cause of our salvation. Thomas Aquinas in particular, and the catholic tradition generally, has always been clear that the credal affirmation of belief in the church is the expression of belief in Christ's presence and action in the Holy Spirit *through* the church. Whatever we say about the church as our mother must not be confused with what Anselm, Julian and others call the motherhood of Christ and what the New Testament describes as the birth-giving of the Spirit. This is why we must now move to the third of our interrelated questions.

How is the church related to Christ?

Bonhoeffer made a bold connection between Christ and the church:

> The body of Jesus Christ is identical with the new humanity which he has assumed. The body of Christ is his church-community. Jesus Christ at the same time is himself and his church-community (1 Corinthians 12.12). Since Pentecost Jesus Christ lives here on earth in the form of his body, the church-community . . . Through the Holy Spirit, the crucified and risen Christ exists as the church-community.[37]

'At the same time', however, Bonhoeffer also argued that 'the unity between Christ and his body, the church, demands that we recognise Christ's Lordship over his body.'[38]

The relationship between Christ and the church which Bonhoeffer describes – a relationship that is organic but differentiated and equal – is present in the Pauline images of the church. Perhaps it was first impressed on Paul's mind at his own conversion when he heard the risen Christ speaking to him as the one to whom the church belongs (and therefore as *beyond* the church) while being the one to whom the church belongs as his body (and therefore as *bound* to the church): 'Saul, Saul, why are your persecuting *me*?' (Acts 9.4). For Paul, the church is Christ's *body*, of which Christ, at least in his later development of the image, is also its *head*. Similarly, the church is the bride of Christ, to whom Christ is bound in *one flesh*, and whom he nourishes and cares for as his own body.

The *totus Christus*, the whole Christ, played a significant part in Augustine's theology. He spoke in very rich terms about the inseparability of the head and members of the one body of Christ: 'Jesus Christ is but one Man, who has head and body; the saviour of the body and the members of the body are both one single flesh, and one single voice, and one single passion, and – when sin shall pass away – one single rest.'[39] Nevertheless, because Christ remains 'the saviour of the body', the relationship between the head and the members is not an equal one. Therefore, in order to preserve the basis of the common life between Christ and his people, it is necessary to maintain a proper delineation between the head and members of the church, as Augustine does when he describes the worshipping life of the church.

> Christ prays for us, as our priest; Christ prays in us as our head; Christ is prayed to us, as our God. Let us recognize then our word in him, and his words in us.[40]

Hence, de Lubac's claim that 'whatever is true of [Christ] is also true of His Bride the Church' will not do as it stands. It fails to express the asymmetrical relationship between Christ and his church. Even as the 'teaching church' through which Christ speaks his word to the world, the church continues to be the 'hearing church', receiving Christ's word and being re-formed by it. We remain, even as members of Christ's body in whom he dwells, 'objects of his mercy'.[41] However, the more qualified, sacramental language of *Lumen Gentium* is more promising: 'By her relationship with Christ, the Church is a kind of sacrament of intimate union with God, and of the unity of all mankind . . . that is she is a sign and instrument of that union and unity.'[42] Partly through its own processes of refinement and partly in response to some Protestant misgiv-ings, contemporary Roman Catholic theology has been careful to distinguish between the primordial divine sacramentality of Christ and the derivatively participative sacramentality of the church. In Christ the Word became flesh – divinity embodied in the humanity of Christ, made visible and tangible, 'seen with eyes . . . looked at and touched with hands' (1 John 1.1). The space that the eternal Son occupies in relation to his eternal Father took shape in the creation in the incarnate Christ and his glory was seen (John 1.14). Jesus Christ, the sacrament of God, is proclaimed in the apostolic teaching and manifested in the fellowship of the church. 'We declare to you what we have seen and heard so that you may truly have fellowship with us; and truly our fellowship is with the Father and with his Son Jesus Christ' (1 John 1.3). The church is, in the words of the Protestant theologian Eberhard Jüngel, 'the great *sacra-mental sign* which represents Jesus Christ' and presents him to the world. Indeed the church is the 'self-presentation of Jesus Christ'.[43] As the sacrament of Christ, the church is the form in which, through the Spirit, Jesus presents and offers himself, makes himself available, gives visible shape and tangible bodily form to the space that he occupies in relation to God.

Bodily community with Christ was of fundamental concern to Bonhoeffer. 'The body of Jesus Christ is the ground of our faith and the source of its certainty; the body of Jesus Christ is the one and perfect gift through which we receive our salvation; the body of Jesus Christ is our new life.' Like the first disciples we must live 'in the bodily presence of and in community with Jesus'.[44] We do so through taking our place in the life of the church, entering the sacred space which he establishes in the church by speaking his word through his people, incorporating believers into his body through baptism and sustaining them in his life through his supper. With good reason, evangelical theology has been very cautious of talking of the church as the 'extension of the incarnation'. Without proper qualifications it too easily denies the differentiation between Christ and the church and risks 'overthrowing the nature of a sacrament' by subsuming the sign into the reality. But we can be assured, and we should celebrate, that Christ has so intimately covenanted himself to his community, that insofar as it is obedient to him, it is the space which he continues to occupy on earth: for where two or three are gathered, Christ is present among them (Matthew 18.20).

We conclude this section on the gospel and the church by affirming that the church is integral to the gospel while at the same time recognizing the derivation of the church from the gospel. Webster again:

> It is . . . an especial concern for evangelical ecclesiology to demonstrate not only that the church is a necessary implicate of the gospel but also that gospel and church exist in a strict and irreversible order, one in which the gospel precedes and the church follows. Much of the particular character of evangelical ecclesiology turns upon articulating the right way the relation-in-distinction between the gospel and the church – 'relation', because the gospel concerns fellowship between God and creatures; 'distinction', because that fellowship, even in its mutuality, is always a miracle of unilateral grace.[45]

The church, therefore, originates in the gracious calling of God. It is chosen not because of the strength of the people or the power of its organized life, but because 'the Lord set his heart on us and chose us' (Deuteronomy 7.7). It depends on the continual constitution of the Spirit who binds us to the life of Christ. Therefore, while we truly participate by the Spirit in Christ, we never possess him. Christ remains to the church the Father's gift in the Spirit. We do not own him. This *giftedness* of the church means that although we cannot separate the gospel from the church, we should not confuse them. The gospel generates the church: hence the balancing proposition to 'No gospel without the church' is 'No church without the gospel'. Actually, although catholic and evangelical practice may have different ways of judging at what point terminal deviation from the gospel is reached, catholic theology has no difficulty in agreeing that without the gospel individual church communities – and even the church as a whole – can give up any claim to being the body of Christ. Henri de Lubac again:

> For my own part I will go so far as to say that if the Church were not what she claims to be – if she did not, essentially, live by faith in Jesus Christ, the faith proclaimed by Peter on the road to Caesarea, I should not wait for her to deceive me at the human level before I separated from her. For in that case not all her benefits on the human level, not all her splendour, nor all the riches of her history, not all her promise for the future, would be able to make up for the dreadful void at the heart of her . . . If Christ is not her wealth, the Church is certainly destitute; if the Spirit of Christ does not flourish in her, she is certainly destitute.[46]

The gospel and the order of the church

We must now move on to consider whether this agreement between evangelical and catholic theology – that the church is integral to the gospel – can be extended to Michael Ramsey's claim that the order of the church arises out of the gospel and is a necessary expression of the gospel. In his *Gospel and the Catholic Church* Ramsey argues that the catholic order of the church 'is a development which grew in the Gospel and through the Gospel, and which expresses the Gospel and can be belittled only at the expense of the Gospel'.[47] The order of 'the Catholic Church' is, therefore, 'an utterance of the Gospel'. It is required by the gospel. It also 'proclaims the Gospel'. It manifests the gospel. Ramsey presents a particular challenge to the traditional evangelical position that the order of the church is a secondary issue on which churches are free to apply scriptural principles in whatever ways are applicable to their context and calling. Rather than arguing on the grounds of antiquity ('This is how the church of the Fathers did it') or universality ('This is how the whole church did it until its division, and how the churches which have preserved the undivided tradition do it'), Ramsey defended catholic order on evangelical grounds – *on the gospel.*

Is Ramsey correct? Does the gospel lead to the order of the church? The gospel certainly involves the reordering of the human being. The grace of the gospel reconstitutes the human self into a life that is lived with and for others – an ecclesial self – and, therefore, at the same time, reconstitutes human society. This reconstitution of humanity is forged in the humanity of Jesus Christ who takes our humanity with its orientation towards the satisfaction of the self, and reorientates it to God, to the messianic community that forms around him, and to the despised and rejected, the lonely and lost, the suffering and dying of the world. The reconstitution of the self that is established for us in Christ is applied to us through the fellowship of the Holy Spirit – through life lived in the Spirit, in the messianic community of Christ, the people who, in Bonhoeffer's words, 'participate in Christ's encounter with the world'.[48] The dynamic of this messianic life – the formation of the ecclesial, *missionary* self – necessarily requires the other. This self is shaped by the other. It can only find itself and be itself through fellowship with the other in the Holy Spirit. In this sense it receives itself *from* the other as a gift of the Spirit from the other.[49] Paul's picture of the new humanity of Christ's body where Jew and Gentile, male and female, slaves and free, share one flesh with Christ and where each member of the body is defined by the other and depends on the other, has a striking correspondence to the story of the original creation of humanity in Genesis, where Adam recognizes Eve as 'flesh of his flesh and bone of his bone' (Genesis 3.23) and where they share a common vocation, which they cannot fulfil apart, to 'be fruitful and multiply' (Genesis 1.28).

Christian identity is orientated to the other, both the other within the church and the other beyond the church: the other who is a brother or sister, the baptismal other, and the other who is a stranger, the missionary other. The other *within the church* includes both those we know personally and those we will never meet. Hence, our fellowship with the other extends from the local, to the regional, to the national and to the international church. Moreover, as well as the present, geographical community, the other with whom we are in fellowship embraces the past, historical community. I am who I am in Christ because of those who have gone before me in the faith. The other *beyond the church*, the missionary other, includes all those to whom Christ is sending us to prepare the way for him, to announce the salvation that he brings (Luke 1.76–77).[50]

In this sense we can affirm that the order of the church belongs to the gospel, that the gospel requires a certain order and that where this order is absent, the church is deficient. Certainly Paul spent much of his correspondence to the Corinthians trying to correct their desire to have their fellowship with others on the basis of religious preferences rather than on the basis of divine calling into the body of Christ, and their tendency to abuse their fellowship through immoral lifestyles, chaotic worship and divisive Eucharists. He reminds them of their rebirth by the one Spirit into one community (1 Corinthians 12.13) and the Spirit's gifting of each person for the common good (1 Corinthians 12.7). In this sense, Paul went to great lengths to maintain the godly order of the church as a manifestation of the Spirit. But can we go beyond these generalizations about the communal identity of Christian life and the interpersonal relationships of Christian living? Can we say that the order of the church involves a distribution of service to the other into a pattern of ministry which is universally applicable?

The various gifts which members of the New Testament churches were given by the Spirit to serve each other and to extend the mission of the church, clearly included identifiable ministries which co-ordinated the life of the churches by equipping and empowering, steering and leading others. Apostles and prophets in Paul's lists seem to have had pre-eminence (1 Corinthians 12.28; Ephesians 4.11). The church was built upon their foundation (Ephesians 2.20). Elsewhere in the New Testament the offices of bishops, presbyters and deacons emerge in the life of at least some of the churches. It has long been recognized, though, that attempts to uncover a clear blueprint for orders of ministry from the New Testament are doomed to failure. The information is too sparse and the situation too embryonic for us to be able to lift out of the New Testament a pattern that will fit all situations for all times. Ramsey, of course, does not attempt to build his case on the New Testament evidence alone. But he does argue that the gospel principles of the church's life revealed in the New Testament point inexorably towards the episcopate and, therefore, derivatively, to the presbyterate and the diaconate as structures of church life which belong to the structure of the gospel. To receive the apostolic faith into which the Spirit led the church, while at the same time rejecting the apostolic order, is to secularize the church and to remove its life from the sacred realm of the gospel, he argues.

On one level Ramsey's argument is persuasive. The gospel does mediate principles for the life and order of the church which belong to its essence. But do the principles of, for example, oversight, local leadership and costly service require embodiment in appointed persons to oversee (*episcopoi*), to teach and lead (*presbyteroi*) and to serve (*diakonoi*) in such a way that without them, we must say with Ignatius, that 'no group can be called a church'? Are these ways in which Christ has chosen to exercise his gentle rule (his kingly office), his representative leadership (his priestly office) and his prophetic service (his prophetic office)? Is this how the Spirit administers the church?

Miroslav Volf's theology of the church is developed from explicitly pneumatological principles and seeks to defend a consciously Free Church perspective in which 'the communal confession of faith' of the gathered community is 'the basis for ecclesiality' rather than the presence of particular office holders.[51] However, he recognizes that 'common responsibility' for the life of the church by all its members, each one of whom is endowed with and gifted by the Spirit, 'is compatible with the particular charismata of leadership ("office")'.[52] The task of leadership is first 'to animate all the members of the church to engage their pluriform charismatic activities, and then to coordinate these activities', and second, 'to be responsible for a mature church that is called to test every manifestation of the Spirit (1 Thessalonians 5.21)'.[53] He defines these offices as 'charismata focused on the entire local church' and regards them as indispensable for a local church's fulfilment of its calling 'over time'. Therefore, 'leaders, teachers and deacons' are 'a necessary part of ecclesial life'.[54] More formally, he is quite happy to agree with a 'threefold understanding of office . . . insofar as all important functions involving the local church as a whole can easily be subsumed under the titles *episcopoi* ('bishops'), *presbyteroi* ('presbyters'), and *diakonoi* ('deacons')'.[55] This does not mean that churches must include those ordained as bishop, presbyter and deacon, but that the leading, teaching and serving functions of these ministries need to be fulfilled in some way through the church's various office holders.

It is worth pausing to note both the considerable degree of agreement between Ramsey's catholic vision and Volf's evangelical and charismatic commitments, and the point at which they differ. They both root the church's identity in its reception of the gospel and in the Spirit's activity among all its members ordering them towards the other, endowing them with the gifts to serve each other. This Spirit-given gospel order of the church includes those who are orientated towards the life of the church as a whole, those who are called to steer, equip and inspire the church to fulfil its calling to be Christ's people, to be what it truly is – the presence, albeit provisional and broken, of the eschatological life of redeemed humanity in a reconciled creation. They also agree that these bearers of 'charismata focused on the entire local church' perform an episcopal, presbyteral and diaconal ministry, even if not so named.

Nevertheless, considerable differences between Ramsey and Volf remain over how the Spirit effects this order in practice. The difference centres on the ministry of bishops and particularly their view of the relationship of bishops to the apostolicity and catholicity of the church. For Ramsey the charismata and calling of bishops are *dually* focused on the local church *and* on the universal church. The bishop's responsibility for the well-being of those Christian communities in a given locality (a diocese) is exercised through a ministry which is personally connected to the church in its apostolic depth and catholic breadth, and which is charged by the Spirit to lead the local church towards the realization of its apostolicity and catholicity. For Volf, this responsibility is located in the Christ-confessing and Spirit-filled life of the local gathering of Christians. For Ramsey, bishops are more than local leaders: they are embodiments of the 'unity', 'continuity' and 'sentness' of the church. That is why they are necessary to the church; they embody essential characteristics of the gospel. For Volf, the episcopal function within the local church necessary for the good governance of the church is exercised by those who are equipped by the Spirit and recognized by the congregation to do so. Whereas Volf's bishops do the work of the bishop-presbyter of the New Testament churches, Ramsey's owe more to the ministry of the apostles and 'bear that essential relation to the Gospel which Apostles bore before him'.[56]

The danger with Ramsey's position is that apostolicity is seen as concentrated in the bishop rather than constituted by the Spirit in the whole church. Yves Congar, the Roman Catholic theologian who, like Volf, develops a pneumatological ecclesiology, is clear that apostolicity 'is fundamentally an apostolicity of faith'.[57] The Spirit 'keeps the church apostolic' by keeping 'the Church faithful to the faith of the Apostles'.[58] As we saw in Chapter 2, the Spirit does so through the proper

use of scripture in the life of the church. The apostolic teaching is enshrined in sacred text by the Spirit who also gives to
the church what Schleiermacher calls 'the sense for the truly
apostolic', so that it can authentically receive the teaching of
the apostles.[59] Nevertheless, the gift of scripture does not mean
that we need to conclude, as Calvin did, that certain ministries
operative in the New Testament churches have ceased to be
part of the Spirit's activity in the church. The church continues
to need, and the Spirit continues to inspire, apostolic ministries which express the unity and catholicity of the church (by
relating churches to each other), and express the holiness and
apostolicity of the church (by holding the church to its apostolic
faith and apostolic mission). This is what bishops are called to
be and to do. They are overseers who *see beyond* the present
horizons of the church both *back to* the originating, generating
dynamic of the gospel and *on to* the new opportunities for the
release of the gospel's grace and power outward through the
mission of the church for the sake of the world.

Therefore, in line with the conclusions of several ecumenical
dialogues, although faithfulness to the apostolic teaching and
mission cannot be *guaranteed* by the historic episcopate, it can
be *signified* in a living, tangible, embodied connection to the
apostolic figures of the early church. Where this sign receives
the charismata of the Spirit to function in truly apostolic ways,
it becomes an effectual sign of apostolicity, guarding the truth
of the faith and extending the reach of the faith by creating the
conditions for the health and growth of the church. In the third
century, Irenaeus was very confident that this would happen:
'Where, therefore, the *charismata* of the Lord have been depos-
ited there is it proper to learn the truth, namely from those who
have that succession of the Church which is from the Apostles
and who display a sound and blameless conduct and an un-
adulterated and incorrupt speech.'[60] Although the gospel does
not require us to rely on the succession of the gospel through
the succession of office holders, it does invite us to receive the
ministry of the Spirit through ministers of the gospel who stand
in a symbolic and functional relationship to those who first led

and shaped the church, and whose ministry is committed to connecting Christians in one time and space with the church in all its depth and breadth. As we shall see in Chapter 9, the health of the church in a missionary age may in practice depend upon the capacity of apostolic ministries to preserve and to promote the apostolicity of the church by sustaining the apostolic teaching, fellowship, worship and sacramental life, and by extending the messianic mission of the church. It may well be that the urgency of the missionary task renews a sense of the apostolicity of the bishop in evangelical theology as we learn from the dynamic ministries of missionary bishops and other apostolic figures gifted by the Spirit to create the conditions for the growth of the church through the proclamation of the kingdom.

5

Meeting Mary

As the embodiment of sola gratia *and* sola fide, *that is, the material and formal principles of the Reformation, Mary should be thus highly extolled in evangelical theology and worship.*
Timothy George

Introduction

In 2005 Pope John Paul II died. His funeral was an international event. Catholic, in an expansive sense of the world, it drew vast numbers of Roman Catholic and other Christians to the great city that has played such a part in the history of the Christian faith. It brought together Roman cardinals with Eastern patriarchs and representatives of the churches of the Reformation. It gathered leaders of the nations of the world and focused the world's media on a simple wooden coffin wherein lay the remains of someone who had confessed Christ with great courage in times of persecution and of power. Although speaking on a world stage, Joseph Ratzinger, soon to become John Paul II's successor, preached a tender and homely sermon which seemed to capture the respect and affection of millions of Christians of whatever persuasion, and unite them in a tide of common Christian grief and gratitude . . . until, that is, his final words. After explaining that 'Karol Wojtyla, who at an early age had lost his own mother, loved his divine mother all the more . . . And from the mother he learned to conform himself to Christ', Cardinal Ratzinger concluded his sermon by saying: 'We entrust your dear soul to the Mother of God, your Mother, who guided you each day and who will guide you now to the eternal glory of her son.'[1] These words of commendation epitomized the enigma that John Paul II represented to evangelical Christians.

On the one hand, his love for Christ was unquestionable, indeed it was almost palpable as he uttered the name of Jesus with a particular sweetness; and his desire for the world to know Christ and to live under his Lordship was full of the passion of the gospel. On the other hand, his affection for Mary and his encouragement of Marian devotion, despite a certain reticence and caution on the part of Vatican II, was bewildering. The only place it appeared on the evangelical radar was as an ominous bleep, warning of past excesses and present dangers.

Tragically, Mary the mother of Jesus, has become a focus of division between Christians. Evangelicals at their most polite are deeply suspicious of Marian tendencies in all forms of catholic piety, whether Roman, Orthodox, Anglican or other. Equally, catholic Christians are astonished by her near absence from evangelical theology and spirituality. Of course history has bequeathed layers of misunderstanding between evangelical and catholic over their respective assessments of Mary, with the centuries of polemic pushing the positions into extremes and making it even more difficult for each side to hear what may be of the gospel in the other's view. But it would be wrong to dismiss the differences as simply the effects of piety or polemics in overdrive. There are substantive issues involved. Indeed, when Mary is discussed, traditional differences between catholic and evangelical surface in the three theological themes we have so far explored – word, justification and church – as the following words by François-Xavier Durrwell, a Roman Catholic theologian, show:

There are 'extrinsicist' theologians in which the mystery of the incarnation is never accepted in the realism of its depth. In this case Mary is not recognized in all truth as *Theotokos*, as mother of the God-man; the Church is not truly regarded as the body of Christ, in communion with Christ in the work of salvation; the believer does not see himself or herself radically justified but simply overlaid by God's justice. Fundamentally, in this case one dare not believe that in Jesus Christ God became totally involved in humanity.[2]

Durrwell overstates his case. Evangelicals are thoroughly committed to the reality of the incarnation, to the church as the body of Christ and to the moral transformation of the believer. But he is right to imply that the tradition's affirmation of Mary as *Theotokos* ('the one who gives birth to God') at the Council of Ephesus in 431 CE is required by scripture's confession of the divinity of Christ, and that the role of Mary in the incarnation raises real issues both about human co-operation in the story of salvation, including the ministry of the church, and in the effects of grace upon human beings.

Therefore, the task of this chapter is to consider Mary from an evangelical perspective and, in so doing, to allow Mary to act as a test case for the sort of approach the last three chapters have developed for the relationship between scripture and tradition, justifying and transformative grace, and the church and the purposes of God.[3] As before, I am not attempting anything like a complete systematic study, neither am I seeking to address all of the issues of controversy between evangelicals and catholics over Mary. My sights are set on the main lines of a distinctively *catholic–evangelical* assessment of Mary which, I suggest, will have the following characteristics. First, it will *recognize* that, in the words of the Anglican–Roman Catholic International Commission statement on Mary, 'it is impossible to be faithful to scripture and not to take Mary seriously'.[4] Second, it will *repent* over a disrespect that evangelicals have often shown to Mary that we would not tolerate in speech about anyone else's mother. Third it will *rejoice* with Zwingli and the other Reformers in the part that God chose Mary to play in the life of his Son: 'The more honour and love for Christ, the more also the esteem and honour for Mary, since she has borne us such a great and at the same time merciful Lord and Redeemer.'[5] The human and historical fact is that 'one does not have Jesus Christ without Mary'.[6] The theological question is whether she, therefore, in some way presently belongs to the gospel. Devotionally, the issue is whether regard for Mary contributes to a greater appreciation and deeper experience of the grace of her son, Jesus.

Mary: model of the grace of God in action

Luke tells us that very soon after Mary was visited by the angel
Gabriel and told that by the action of the Holy Spirit she had
been chosen to 'conceive . . . and bear a son' who 'will be called
the Son of the Most High' to whom 'the Lord God will give
. . . the throne of his ancestor David' (Luke 1.32), she visited
her cousin Elizabeth. As soon as Mary entered the house and
called out her greeting, Elizabeth 'filled with the Holy Spirit
[she] exclaimed with a loud cry':

> Blessed are you among women, and blessed is the fruit of
> your womb.
> And why has this happened to me, that the mother of my
> Lord comes to me?
> For as soon as I heard the sound of your greeting, the child
> in my womb leapt for joy.
> And blessed is she who believed that there would be a
> fulfilment of what was spoken to her by the Lord. (Luke
> 1.42–45)

Mary, clearly also full of the Spirit, responded with her great
song of praise and prophecy:

> My soul magnifies the Lord,
> and my spirit rejoices in God my saviour,
> for he has looked with favour on the lowliness of his
> servant.
> Surely, from now on all generations will call me blessed;
> for the Mighty One has done great things for me,
> and holy is his name . . .
> He has helped his servant Israel,
> in remembrance of his mercy,
> according to the promise he made to our ancestors,
> to Abraham and to his descendants for ever. (Luke 1.46–49;
> 54–56)

The covenant promise made to Abraham and to his descendants was being fulfilled in and through Mary. Centuries before, Abraham, despite his old age and Sarah's infertility, had been told, 'As for your wife . . . *I will bless her*, and she shall be a mother of nations; kings of peoples shall come to her' (Genesis 17.15, 16). This was the cause of Elizabeth's greeting and Mary's song – that she, Mary, small and insignificant in the eyes of the world, symbol and spokeswoman of the *Anawim*, the poor of Israel, had been chosen by God to be the mother of Israel's Messiah and the world's Saviour. In his genealogy Matthew places Mary in a line of unlikely women, all of whom 'had an irregular or extraordinary marital union' (Tamar, Rahab, Ruth, Bathsheba) and whose sons played strategic parts in God's covenant purposes.[7] Though 'lowly' and 'hungry' in the world's eyes, she had become a servant of the 'Most High', included in his household, lifted above all of the rich and powerful masters of the world. This is why she is called *blessed* – because she has been blessed by the God of grace, chosen by God's mercy for God's purposes.

John Calvin commends Elizabeth for taking 'the middle way' which, he says, 'we should follow'. 'She honours the Virgin, in as much as Mary was honoured by God . . . But at the same time she does not stop at this point . . . she shows that the Virgin Mary has no dignity of herself but that rather everything hinges on God's wish to accept her.'[8] The theme of God's choice of Mary – her election by grace for grace – runs deeply throughout the theological tradition, in Catholic and Protestant form. Mary's election is rightly seen as a prototype, a model, of our own election in Christ, of the 'grace God has freely bestowed on us in the Beloved' (Ephesians 1.6).

However, as true as this is, it is important not to lose sight of the distinctiveness of her calling – that she was chosen, as the Collect of the Feast of the Blessed Virgin Mary in my own church prays, to be 'the mother of [God's] only Son'.[9] This is her 'unique vocation' as *Theotokos*.[10] In his classic study of 'The Virgin Mary in Evangelical Perspective' published in 1964, Heiko Oberman reminds us that 'the beginning of a historical reality, *kaine ktisis*, the new creation' took place within her.[11] The mind-stretching wonder of God's conception in human form, and the extraordinary implications it had both for God and for Mary, has mesmerized artists, composers and poets throughout the centuries. John Donne is among the most sublime:

> Loe, faithfull Virgin, [he] yields himself to lye
> In prison, in thy wombe; and though he there
> Can take no sinne, nor thou give, yet he'will weare
> Taken from thence, flesh, which deaths force may trie.
> Ere by the spheres time was created, thou
> Wast in his minde, who is thy Sonne, and Brother,
> Whom thou conceiv'st, conceiv'd; yea thou art now
> Thy makers maker, and thy Father's mother,
> Thou'hast light in darke; and shutst in little roome,
> *Immensity cloysterd in thy deare wombe.*[12]

Similarly, George Herbert puts it with striking simplicity as he plays on the spelling of Mary's name:

> How well her name *Army* doth present,
> In whom the *Lord of Hosts* did pitch his tent![13]

As Elizabeth said, Mary is blessed among women. Indeed, her 'unique vocation' as *Theotokos* makes her blessed among *all women, all people*, in that only she, by the grace of God, performed this work. Mary, therefore, according to scripture and the gospel, has a unique place among all the faithful because she was blessed with the particular calling of being chosen to bear the Son of God and to bear the conditions and consequences of fulfilling this calling faithfully.

We must consider more carefully what those conditions of Mary's faithful fulfilment of her calling were. Was she chosen because of her inherent holiness? In terms of the categories we were using in Chapter 3, was grace imparted to her to make her 'favourable' (Luke 1.28) to God, or was God's choice of her entirely independent of her own readiness to obey and moral capacity to mother the Son of God? There is no doubt that Gabriel's greeting to Mary as the 'favoured one' has been a singular source of controversy. The Latin vulgate translated the Greek *kecharitōmenē* as *gratia plena*, 'full of grace', implying that Mary was chosen because of her goodness. English translations of the Bible around the Reformation, and in the Protestant tradition since then, recognized that this was a mistranslation and preferred the translation 'favoured one' (sometimes 'highly favoured one'), with its greater stress on the elective grace of God. However, there is no need to accept a complete dichotomy on the contrasting theological emphases let loose by these different translations, provided that we are clear about the order between them. God's elective grace, undeserved and unwarranted by those God has chosen, always has priority and is the context in which God operates with his people. However, God's election does not rule out the possibility of God preparing the one elected by grace to be able to respond in faith to his call. Indeed, it requires it. Oberman keeps the correct order, and, therefore, the correct relationship between God's choice of Mary and Mary's readiness to receive and respond to God's choice of her in this way:

> The *Magnificat* [is] a poetic confession of justification '*sola gratia*' and '*sola fide*'. She believes the word of the angel and trusts God's promises: she knows that it is God's mercy which made him turn to her. The humility of Mary, then, is not seen as a disposition which provided the basis and reason for God's choice, but is regarded rather as the result of God's election and prevenient grace.[14]

God chooses us entirely out of mercy and grace, irrespective of our own qualities and strengths. But he prepares us to be able to respond faithfully when we hear his call.

Bodily assumed?

The notion of Mary as a prototype and model of our election in Christ is sometimes extended to other elements in Paul's cascade of the successive stages of God's salvation of his people:

> And those whom he foreknew he also predestined to be conformed to the image of his Son ... And those whom he predestined he also called; and those whom he called he also justified; and those whom he justified he also glorified. (Romans 8.29–30)

In itself this is entirely acceptable. What happens to Mary, through the elective grace of God and her Spirit-enabled faith and obedience, also happens to us through the same dynamic of God's action. But it is often used to defend belief in the bodily assumption of Mary to heaven – a belief that began to emerge after the fourth century and finds its clearest and most formal shape in the Roman dogma of 1950 which states that Mary 'was assumed body and soul into heavenly glory'.[15] Although, technically, the dogma does not equate Mary's assumption with her resurrection, one of the main drivers of belief in the assumption is that of Mary embodying (literally) the final eschatological destiny of all Christians to be bodily raised with Christ, and to participate fully in the new creation, the fulfilment of God's purposes.

The strength of the doctrine is its recognition that the redemption of the body belongs to the heart of our salvation and that any concept of the completion of our salvation which does not include the body misses the point of Jesus' resurrection and misunderstands the whole biblical story of creation, redemption and consummation. The weakness of the doctrine, however, and its fundamental flaw, is that it disrupts the eschatological pattern laid out in the New Testament and threatens the unique vocation of Christ as the incarnate God. Scripture does not teach that Mary was bodily assumed to heaven because it looks forward to the *future* coming of Christ to establish the new creation which his own death and resurrection has inaugurated. Through the gift of the Spirit, God has 'blessed us in Christ with every spiritual blessing in the heavenly places' (Ephesians 1.3). In this sense, we, with Mary, have been 'glorified'. We have been 'adopted as God's children' (Ephesians 1.5). We have redemption through Christ's blood, the forgiveness of sins (Ephesians 1.7). But this is by way of obtaining 'an inheritance' (Ephesians 1.11). Not everything is ours now because we are still waiting for 'the fullness of time', when 'God will gather up all things in him, things in heaven and things on earth' (Ephesians 1.10). Therefore, all Christ's followers, the faithful living and the faithful departed, remain 'in hope' (Romans 8.24), bound together with the fabric of God's creation as we wait for the coming of the new creation and the resurrection of our bodies that it will entail (Romans 8.24–25). Our confidence that God is committed to this plan and will complete it is based on the resurrection of Jesus Christ (1 Corinthians 15). It is because of his resurrection that we have received the Spirit as 'the pledge of our inheritance towards redemption' (Ephesians 1.14). Mary, in whose womb the new creation of Jesus Christ was formed, and who supported him in his ministry, stood by him at his death, saw him risen from the dead, witnessed the ascension and received the Spirit as the gift of the Spirit, this Mary, *model disciple Mary*, also waits with the rest of creation for the 'revealing of the children of God' (Romans 8.19). Her vocation is to bear Christ as his mother and to follow Christ as his disciple. The vocation of her son is to be the divine Saviour in whom all the promises of God are fulfilled and who remains the embodiment of her destiny, her hope of resurrection, as much as he is ours.

Mary: model of the faithful believer

We saw earlier that when Elizabeth declares in the Spirit that Mary is uniquely blessed by being chosen by God to be 'the mother of [our] Lord' (Luke 1.43), she goes on to say that

Mary is doubly blessed by God because she *believed* that God
would fulfil what was promised. Later in his Gospel, during the
cut-and-thrust of Jesus' ministry, Luke tells us about another
woman who recognized God's mercy and favour towards Mary
as the mother of Christ. Jesus had just cast out an evil spirit.
Although many in the crowd were amazed at God's messianic
power at work through Jesus, some used it as a chance to accuse
him of operating through satanic forces. Jesus grasped the
chance to teach about the coming of the kingdom through his
ministry. As he spoke, 'a woman in the crowd raised her voice
and said to him, "Blessed is the womb that bore you and the
breasts that nursed you!" But he said, "Blessed rather are those
who hear the word of God and obey it!"' (Luke 11.27–28).

Whereas Elizabeth, speaking in the Spirit, held together
Mary's calling to bear God's Son with her faith in God's word,
Jesus had to correct the woman in the crowd and make it clear
to her that the new eschatological family that God is gathering around the Messiah is constituted by faith and obedience.
Even his earthly family must meet this criterion – even his own
mother. Luke very much portrays Mary as a faithful believer,
and so the implication here is that Jesus recognizes that the
blessing under which his mother lives is rooted in her belief in
God's word and in her faithful following. This coheres with
Luke's account of the annunciation. Gabriel announces God's
favour towards Mary and she responds, 'Here am I, the servant of the Lord; let it be to me according to your word' (Luke
1.38). Of course there is a process Mary has to go through
before she arrives at this point. She is perplexed, disturbed and
confused. What would this mean for her, a young, unmarried
women? Gabriel addresses some of the questions that must
have been shooting through her mind, but there is no reason to
suppose that all her distress disappeared. But believe she does.
And in believing she commits herself to the consequences of her
faith. Luke here presents Mary to us as a model of faithful discipleship – the one who at the very beginning of Jesus' ministry
responds to God, offering herself in her weakness to be used by
the strength of God's grace.

Mary stood at a momentous moment in human history and God's purposes. Much has been made of the significance of her 'Yes' to God, and many have mused over what would have happened if she had said 'No'. But we too stand at critical moments in God's involvement and interaction with the world. We too are invited to welcome and to receive Christ (Luke 24; Revelation 2). We too have been called to be his servants, slaves, handmaids of the Lord (Acts 2.18). We are dignified with the title of co-workers (1 Corinthians 3.9) in God's kingdom. As we look to Mary we can see that the angel's promise that 'nothing will be impossible with God' (Luke 1.37), which runs as a continuous theme through Luke's Gospel, is indeed true and even extends, as Beverly Roberts Gaventa shows, to 'our consent to God's will'.[16] God chooses to place his treasure in precarious earthen vessels (2 Corinthians 4.7). But because 'nothing is impossible to God', he promises to achieve his promises in and through us. Mary's faithful, obedient response is a sign of God's covenant faithfulness to his world and is why, as well as blessing God for Mary, and acknowledging her as blessed by God, we also honour her as *bless-ed*. In responding to the *blessing of God* to bear the Messiah, she also bore the *beatitude of the faithful*, for 'blessed (*makarios*) is she who believed that there would be a fulfilment of what was spoken to her by the Lord' (Luke 1.42). This is first of several pronouncements of blessing in Luke's Gospel in which the attitudes that mark righteous life are identified. In presenting Mary as the first to show what it means to respond to the gospel, Luke has Elizabeth declare that the childlike trust of Mary, and her willingness to let God be God, is the primary sign that the messianic mission of Christ through the activity of the Spirit has impacted a person's life: '[she] received the word with joy inspired by the Holy Spirit, so that [she] became an example to all the believers' (1 Thessalonians 1.6–7).

Luke leaves us in no doubt that the Spirit was powerfully at work in Mary. He gives us multiple examples that the Holy Spirit had burst upon God's people with the sort of eschatological intensity that had been prophesied years before when the coming of the kingdom was foretold: angelic manifestations, divine action, human faithfulness, Mary's praise, Elizabeth's pregnancy, Joseph's dreams, shepherds' visions, Simeon's and Anna's waiting and rejoicing. Moreover, Mary demonstrates that discipleship involves welcoming the Spirit's activity in the world, receiving the Spirit's empowering in one's life, discerning the Spirit's work in others. She responds faithfully to God's word through the Spirit's strength. She is led by the Spirit to go 'with haste' to meet Elizabeth. She praises in the exuberant joy of the Spirit. She interprets Hannah's song in scripture and applies it to herself through the inspiration of the Spirit. She prophesies in the power of the Spirit. She hears God's word being spoken to her through the Spirit by a mysterious angel, a close relative and an elderly man and woman. She holds powerful experiences and events in her heart, waiting for the Spirit of truth to lead her into their true meaning. She prays to be 'clothed with power from on high' (Luke 24.49). She is enveloped in tongues of fire and, with all those who were gathered 'together in one place', she 'began to speak in other languages, as the Spirit gave [her] ability' (Acts 2.1–4). Mary's tenderness at the birth of her son, her concern for him during his childhood and ministry, her agonizing vigil at his cross, all display the greatest of the gifts of the Spirit – the love of the Son. If Mary can be seen as the first evangelical Christian, the first to believe and obey God's word about Christ, she can also be cited as the first charismatic Christian. She shows that believing in God's word cannot be separated from being filled with his Spirit. She shows that accepting the grace of the gospel includes expecting the Spirit's involvement in the physicality of the world. She shows that there is no theological space between confession of Christ and reception of the Spirit, and she challenges the practices of the church, pentecostal or sacramental, not to tear apart what God has joined together. Mary shows that gospel life is life in the Spirit and that *evangelical identity* is authentically *charismatic*.

Although Luke's infancy narratives give clear evidence that

Mary was justified by faith through her faith in God's grace, and that God's Spirit was at work in and through her, we should not imagine that she was instantaneously transformed into a perfect disciple. In terms of Paul's list of the saving stages of God's action, scripture allows us to say that she was predestined, called and justified (Romans 8.30) in the events surrounding Jesus' birth. But it leaves us in little doubt that she was not *immediately* 'conformed to the image of [God's] Son' (Romans 8.29). Even Luke implies that Mary's maternal protectiveness of her child obscured her full recognition of his messianic calling and his true place in his Father's house (Luke 2.48–51). Mark, whose briefer portrayal of Mary is generally less sympathetic than Luke's, implies that Mary was among the family members who went out 'to restrain Jesus' in the early stages of his ministry (Mark 3.21, 31–35). Indeed, later Mark has Jesus recount the saying that 'a prophet is not without honour, except in his own country, and among his own kin, and in his own house' (Mark 6.4). John records the curious exchange between Jesus and Mary at the wedding in Cana when Jesus seems both to distance himself from her (calling Mary 'woman' rather than 'mother') and to rebuke her for misconceiving the timing of his messianic work (John 2.3–4).[17]

In their different ways, each of the Gospel writers wants to make it clear that Mary's membership of Jesus' messianic community relies not on her motherhood as such but on her acceptance of the true identity of her son, and her faithful following of him in his eschatological mission. In fact, it seems quite likely that, despite the phenomenal events around his birth, full acceptance of the significance of Jesus may have been *more difficult* for the one who gave birth to him, nurtured him as a child and shared a house with him through many years of his adulthood. As a mother, her instincts would have been to protect her son from the dangers involved in his messianic mission. All the Gospel writers, however, show that Mary did reach that point in the end, that she became fully part of the messianic community on the basis of her faith in Christ and commitment to follow him. Luke does so in the scene of Mary praying with

other members of Jesus' family and with the 11 remaining apostles in the upper room after the ascension. For John, the choice
of scene is even more poignant. Mary, together with her sister
Mary and Mary Magdalene, is 'standing near the cross' (John
19.25) in defiant solidarity with Jesus. Jesus has only spoken
once before to his mother in John's Gospel. Now he speaks
for a second time. Again the address is the same – 'woman'
– but the content is more tender and the words full of allusive
possibility that are still being debated among Christians. 'Here
is your son', says the dying Jesus to his mother as he entrusts her
to the care of his 'beloved disciple', to whom he says, 'Here is
your mother' (John 19.26–27). Whether or not John intends us
to understand this in terms of Jesus reconstituting his messianic
community and establishing his embryonic church around two
representative figures who stand 'at the foot of the cross', it is
clear that Mary has proved that she belongs fully to his community of faithful, believing disciples.

Mary's slow, gradual movement towards maturity in faith,
her faltering steps towards full discipleship (which may have
included some backward ones), her apparently ambivalent
relationship to Jesus' community of disciples in the early stages
of his ministry, does not make her any less of a model of the
faithful follower of Christ. Rather, it authenticates her and
makes her a genuine pattern of Christian discipleship. Mary
may have made a decisive decision at the annunciation, but
following Christ involves successive decisions that shape us into
convinced and committed disciples. Making the right decision
at one point does not mean we will make the right decisions at
every point. And making the wrong decision at certain times
does not reverse God's call upon us. Peter and Thomas had to
discover the truth of this, as well as Mary. What counts is that
we keep going along 'the long road in the same direction', to
use Eugene Peterson's compelling phrase.[18] Mary shows that
through affection for Christ, openness to the Spirit working
through him and contact with his followers, we can grow into
the sort of disciples who play a full part in the life of his church
and in his messianic mission through it.

Through Mary's membership of the eschatological community, the new holy family of faith that Jesus was gathering around him, Mary shows that it is not the blood of family affinity that makes us Christians but the blood of Christ shed for us and in which we place our faith. She shows that obedience to Christ involves more than a personal, private love. It means joining his community and being with others who confess and follow him. She shows, as she did when she went to the house of Elizabeth and Zechariah but perhaps had to re-learn in the years that followed, that the Spirit's gifts belong to the community of faith and serve the mission of God's people. Just as she shows that Christian life is simultaneously word-believing and Spirit-receiving, she shows that it is at the same time a communal existence, participation in Christ's community. She shows that evangelical identity, as well as being authentically *charismatic*, is also fully *catholic* – for the life lived in the grace of the gospel, empowered by the Spirit, is shared in and with the community of faith.

Immaculately conceived?

Reflection on Mary's discipleship – particularly in relation to her obedient response to God's word through Gabriel – contributed to a tendency (at quite an early stage of the church's life), to seek to protect Mary's character from the influence of original sin and her behaviour from the actual practice of sin. The most formal and extreme expression of this trajectory in Marian theology is the doctrine of the Immaculate Conception. Mary's immaculate conception, first proposed by a Pelagian theologian in the fifth century, gained, after a somewhat turbulent process of refinement, general agreement in medieval theology and was finally promulgated in the Papal Bull of 1854 which teaches 'that the most blessed Virgin Mary was, from the first moment of her conception, by a singular grace and privilege of almighty God and view of the merits of Christ Jesus the Saviour of the human race, preserved from all stain of original sin'.[19]

The strength of the doctrine is that it underlines the choice of Mary before the 'foundation of the world' (Ephesians 1.4) and points to God's elective attention to the beginnings of her life (Jeremiah 1.5). If we allow that, having chosen Mary for his purposes from eternity, God prepared her for her actual call in earthly time, there is nothing to say this should not have begun from the moment she was conceived. Indeed, the same applies to us all. However, the weakness of the doctrine – quite apart from the fact that, like her bodily assumption, it has no clear basis in scripture – is that, by preserving Mary from the corrupting effects of inherited, endemic, original sin, Mary's solidarity with us as sinners in need of forgiveness through faith in the gospel and transformation through the continual work of the Spirit in the fellowship of the church is undermined. Of course, the doctrine does not actually teach that Mary was not a beneficiary of Christ's redemption. In fact, it claims, as Duns Scotus (one of its strongest medieval proponents) put it, 'Mary more than anyone else would have needed Christ as her Redeemer, since she should have contracted original sin . . . if the grace of the Mediator had not prevented this.'[20] Christ's atoning work was operative in her anticipatively. However, although scripture teaches that Christ's salvation was efficacious before his actual ministry (John 8.36; 1 Corinthians 10.4), at no point does it relieve any of God's people from the genetic predisposition towards disobedience which it sees as the burden of all humanity since the fall and which, according to some branches of Reformed theology, was assumed by Christ himself. It is Mary's situation *within* sinful humanity which makes her a genuine model of faithful discipleship. It is God's capacity to prepare her to hear his call and to enable her to respond faithfully, to renew her *through* her faith in Christ and to transform her into the image of his Son through the Spirit by one degree of glory to another, which gives us hope that he will do the same for those who follow her in the love of her child, Jesus.

Mary: model of the Christian community

As well as being a model of the faithful discipleship of the
believer, Mary can also be seen as a model of the community
of believers, the church. In many ways the same should apply
to any faithful believer. The characteristics of faithful discipleship are the characteristics of the life of the church. But Mary's
prototypical role as the first believer in the gospel – and her
distinctive relationship to the physical body of her son – make
her a particularly resonate symbol of the life of his body, the
church. This is a theme that can be found in the patristic period
and is particularly developed in the poetic writings of Ephraim
the Syrian in the fourth century. It has become a prominent
dimension in the Eastern Orthodox understanding of Mary.[21]

Mary *heard the word of God*. She heard God's word from
the angel, through the scriptures of her people, from the mouth
of her son and through the apostolic teaching. 'The holy word
of God' is the church's 'chief holy possession [which] purges,
sustains, nourishes, strengthens, and protects the church', said
Luther.[22] The word of God, 'sharper than any two-edged sword'
(Hebrews 4.12), forms and re-forms the church. Like Mary, the
church is called to hear the word and to obey it – to say 'let it be
to me according your word' (Luke 1.38), which for Mary, and
for the church, means *receiving and living in the Spirit*. Mary
opened herself to the Spirit at the annunciation, discerned the
work of the Spirit in Jesus' ministry and prayed for the coming
of the Spirit after his ascension. The church echoes that prayer
and pleads, not only on the 'Sunday after the Ascension', but
every day, every minute, 'leave us not comfortless; but send
to us thine Holy Ghost',[23] for 'The church is that community
that lives by the continual inspiration of the Holy Spirit.'[24] At
the centre of the Spirit's work in Mary was her calling to *bear
Christ* and to care for him: to have him formed in her and presented to the world. 'In the womb of Mary, you found a dwelling place on earth, O Christ: remain in our hearts for ever',[25]
the church sings on one of the days set aside to celebrate God's
work in her. 'My little children,' Paul writes to the Galatians,

'for whom I am again in the pain of childbirth until Christ is formed in you' (Galatians 4.19), and to the Thessalonians he says, 'We were gentle among you, like a nurse tenderly caring for her own children. So deeply do we care for you that we are determined to share with you not only the gospel of God but also our own selves, because you have become very dear to us' (1 Thessalonians 2.7–8). The church is called to be the body of Christ, and the divine commission of 'the saints [in] the work of ministry' is 'to build up the body of Christ . . . to the measure of the full stature of Christ' (Ephesians 4.12–13).

Mary *thought about Christ* and the extraordinary activity of the Spirit through him. She 'treasured all these words and pondered them in her heart' (Luke 2.19). The church is called to meditate on God's word, to keep our gaze fixed on Christ and to yield itself to the Spirit who 'interprets spiritual things to those who are spiritual' (1 Corinthians 2.13). *Mary waited*, sometimes alone, sometimes with others. The months of pregnancy, the 30 years of motherhood before Jesus' ministry, the testing years of ministry, the long hours 'near the cross', in the upper room. She was waiting for the hour. On one occasion it seems that her patience slipped, that her discernment failed (John 2.3–4). But at least she was looking for the hour, waiting for the revelation to come, for the Messiah to act, for the kingdom to break into the world. The church waits with all creation (Romans 8.19) for the revelation of the ultimate significance of Jesus Christ for the whole of space and time. Like Mary, there may be times when we glimpse the heavens open and the glory of the messianic kingdom touch the earth. There may even be moments when the church seems to be at the centre of the world's stage, when the nations turn to it in their search for light and beauty and peace. But for most of the time – at least in our time – the church waits, like Mary, on the edge – misunderstood, dismissed, even ridiculed: 'Is this not the carpenter, the son of Mary?' (Mark 6.3). What can the ultimate truth of everything that has ever existed anywhere have to do with the church, with its compromised past and ignominious present? In her waiting *Mary felt* the pain of waiting. 'Deeply troubled'[26] (Luke 1.29), desperately anxious (Luke 1.48), utterly confused (Mark 3.21), stricken with grief. Like Mary, the church waits, even the church at heaven waits and cries with us on earth and the whole of creation: 'How long?' (Revelation 6.10). This is the present eschatological existence of the church. But, like Mary, the church is to trust in God's promise and to give voice to the Spirit's song of praise and 'rejoice in God our Saviour' (Luke 1.46).

Mary suffered and rejoiced: 'Sad and rejoyc'd shee's seen at once, and seen / At almost fiftie, and at scarce fifteen . . .' writes John Donne in his poem, 'The Annunciation and Passion', which plays on the rare occasion when the Feast of the Annunciation on 25 March coincides with Good Friday.[27] Mary's commitment to Jesus took her to the cross, to the place of threat and danger where everything is risked for the gospel and trust in the promise of God is tested most. The church is called to stand for Christ against all the evil that is on the earth and 'under the earth'. The church is called to stand with Christ in the suffering places of the world, with him and in him, *as his body*, as he stands in solidarity with all who are oppressed by the prince and principalities of this world. And the church is called to stand in the place of praise – to rejoice that God 'has looked with favour on the lowliness of his servant' (Luke 1.48) and to proclaim that God 'has shown strength with his arm' (Luke 1.51) in the weakness of a child born to a poor girl. It is to 'break bread' with the exultant joy of the messianic banquet that awaits God's people when he shall have wiped away every tear from every eye (Revelation 21.4) and when swords shall no longer pierce the depths of their beings (Luke 2.35).

Mary worshipped. She worshipped the God of her ancestors in the words of the ancient song of Hannah, remixed by the Spirit for the eschatological praise of the fulfilment of the promise. At the birth of the 'Son of the Most High', she 'wrapped him in bands of cloth, and laid him in a manger' (Luke 1.32; 2.7), and surely, as Christina Rossetti imagines, she 'worshipped the beloved with a kiss'.[28] At his ascension her worship of Christ was corporate, public and jubilant (Luke

24.52). Mary *interceded*. 'They have no wine' (John 2.3), she said to Jesus, bringing in her own way, with her own limitations, the needs of those around her to Christ. Before Jesus' birth she *prophesied*, declaring to the people of God and the nations of the world that God's promise of old was being fulfilled. On the Feast of Pentecost, she *spoke in tongues*, filled with the Spirit of God's promised kingdom. The church is built to worship, and to worship in this sort of way: focused on the Christ who reconciles us to the Father, activated by the Spirit who brings to us the realities of the kingdom, equipping us with all his gifts and rooted in scripture, God's abiding word in written form.

Mary pointed to Christ and directed people to listen to him and to obey him. 'Do whatever he tells you' (John 2.5), she said to the stewards at the wedding, and (it seems reasonable to suppose) she proclaimed to the crowds at Pentecost. This is the church's greatest commission: to tell the world that 'all authority has been given' to Christ and to 'make disciples of all nations, baptising . . . and teaching them to obey everything that [he] has commanded' (Matthew 28.20). And, like Mary, we go as people who not only speak a message but are themselves caught up in the re-creative work of God, people who participate in God's kingdom and who belong to the reconstituted order of human and historical reality. We, Christ's people, are also highly favoured, greatly blessed, like his mother. We have been saved by Christ's blood and reconciled to his Father, baptized into Christ's life and grafted into his body, indwelt by Christ's Spirit and enlisted in his messianic service. Like Mary, we are called to respond to God's blessing upon us with humility and to demonstrate it with holiness.

Mother of the church?

The symmetry between Mary's spiritual virtues and the nature of the church, combined with her physical participation in the conception of Christ and the birth of the church, led at a fairly early stage to the mother of the Lord being seen also as the

mother of the church. On one level it was an innocent development of biblical imagery which simply recognized that being in
Christ means sharing in his relationships, for as Luther said,
'If he is ours, then we are in his place; where he is, there we
also are to be, and everything he has is ours, and therefore
his Mother is also our Mother.'[29] On another level, though, it
sets in motion a very unhelpful line of thought which soon not
only distances Mary from the main body of believers but also
distances Christ from his people and his world. Rather than
Mary being a member of the church who models to her fel-
low believers what it means to live for Christ, she becomes its
generator and guardian, the one who brings the church to birth
and watches over its life. In the worst excesses of Mariolatry
she becomes a dispenser of grace and a wielder of divine power
– the *redemptrix* who shares in the redemptive work of her
son. And rather than the faithful disciple who points others to
Christ, she stands in front of him, as if to protect people from
him and to prepare them for the ordeal of meeting him. In the
extreme she becomes the mother of mercy who hides the faithful under her skirt lest they are consumed by the judgement of
Christ – the *mediatrix* who arbitrates between Christ and the
world.

A softer and less controversial version of Mary's motherly
calling within the church is based on the notion of her continuing intercession, the belief that she is still laying the needs of the
world before her son as she did in Cana of Galilee. Views on
whether Mary is interceding for the world depend on all sorts
of other eschatological considerations about the nature of life in
Christ between death and resurrection. For my part, I am persuaded that scripture leads us to the picture of all the believers
who have gone before us – all the saints in Christ – sharing
in the light and life of Paradise (the heavenly existence of the
redeemed before the resurrection), in the presence of Christ.
Although parted from death from us, they remain bound to
us – in the fellowship of the Spirit – in a common hope for the
coming of the new creation and 'the redemption of the body'. I
see no reason why they should not be sharing in Christ's min-

istry of intercession as they did when they were alive on earth. In this sense, I think Philipp Melanchthon was right to say in his commentary on the Augsburg Confession that 'Mary prays for the Church'.[30] But she does so as a member of the church, in which no person or group is privileged over the other. She stands in solidarity with all Christ's people, living and departed. 'Truly our sister', as Pope Paul VI put it,[31] she shares in the prayer of the church made in and through the prayer of Christ which, in the words of Anglican–Roman Catholic International Commission, 'does not contest the unique mediatory work of Christ, but is rather a means by which, in and through the Spirit, its power may be displayed'.[32]

Mary: word, salvation and church

We noted at the beginning of the chapter how Mary has become a point of focus between catholic and evangelical positions in a number of key theological areas. Karl Barth was one who put this point most strongly, even so far as claiming that 'Marian dogma is neither more nor less the critical, central dogma of the Roman Catholic, the dogma from the standpoint of which all their important positions are to be regarded and by which they stand or fall.'[33] Barth's statement is a mirror image of the dismissive comment we met earlier by the Roman Catholic theological François-Xavier Durrwell and gives us little hope that there may be ways in which evangelical and catholic positions can mutually inform and reform each other. Nevertheless, it is true that a theological assessment of Mary's place in the purposes of God profoundly touches the three areas on which we have hitherto concentrated: the relationships between scripture and tradition, justifying and transformative grace, and Christ and his people. It is now time to gather the foregoing discussion of Mary into some concluding comments about what we can learn about these various relationships from a scripturally based and evangelically orientated understanding of Mary such as we have attempted in this chapter.

Mary and the relationship between scripture and tradition.

Although Mary only appears to receive one mention in the epistles, she figures prominently in the Gospels, significantly at the beginning of Acts and symbolically – though not all would agree – in the book of Revelation. For those of us who are not used to paying much attention to Jesus' mother, and perhaps, at the same time, are very wary of paying too much attention to her, the textured depth of some parts of scripture may remain hidden to us. If this is the case, then we need to be reminded that (as we said in Chapter 2) we are to sit under scripture, rather than stand above it, allowing scripture to speak its story to us, rather than us deciding in advance what it will be allowed to say. We are not to allow the *paradoseis* of our church life to eclipse anything that belongs inherently to the *paradosis* itself (a principle that is as true for catholic as for evangelical interpretations of scripture). Part of this process will involve us being, as the Methodist theologian Pauline Warner challengingly puts it, 'wary of our wariness'.[34]

I suggest that the sort of reading of scripture that will be the most profitable will be the approach advocated in Chapter 2. This involves reading scripture *evangelically* – in other words, *according to the gospel*. What does scripture teach us about Mary and the gospel of the one she bore and loved, served and proclaimed? To answer this question fully, scripture needs to be read *catholically*, that is, with others who have found and felt the reality of the gospel of Mary's son. By way of example, my own study of Mary in scripture has been most enriched by reading what scripture has to say with, on the one hand, Orthodox writers and, on the other, Roman Catholic feminist writers. The former are able to take us deeper into the patristic interpretation of Marian texts and thus behind what a distinguished Roman Catholic theologian has called 'the galloping Mariolatry'[35] of later centuries. The latter manage to cut through some of the traditional features of their church's theology and piety concerning Mary with a zeal that would make even the most ardent Protestant blush. But, with their affinity to Mary as a woman – and especially those who are able to empathize with her as a poor woman eking out an existence in a land run by corrupt (male) leaders and occupied by foreign (male) armies – catholic feminist theologians work with the sort of instinctive respect for Jesus' mother that is rare in evangelical exegesis. Reading scripture evangelically and catholically involves reading it *charismatically*, according to what the Spirit is saying today to the church about the gospel of God's salvation through Mary's son. What does scripture teach us today about the sort of faithful following and apostolic witness to the gospel that Mary embodied?

An evangelical, catholic and charismatic reading of the Bible leads us to affirm the necessity of the patristic interpretation insofar as it defined the doctrines of God to which scripture witnesses. The Christological disputes of the fourth and fifth centuries led to great debate over whether Mary should be seen as *Christotokos* (bearer of Christ, as argued by Nestorius and the Antiochine school) or as *Theotokos* (bearer of God, as argued by Cyril and the Alexandrian theologians). In 431 the Council of Ephesus decided in favour of the Alexandrian position on the grounds that this best protected the full implications of Nicea's earlier affirmation of the full divinity of Jesus Christ – that the birth, life, death and resurrection of Jesus were the actual experiences of the divine Son of God, the second person of the Trinity. By calling Mary *Theotokos* it allowed no escape from the radical Christian conviction that in Jesus Christ the eternal God has been through human birth in all its physicality, human life in its joys and pains, human death in its suffering, and resurrection in its new and permanent future for humanity. In Jesus Christ, truly human and truly divine, God was born, God lived and God died. This is why John of Damascus, several centuries later, said, 'It is proper and true that we call the holy Mary the *Theotokos*, for this name expresses the entire mystery of the economy.'[36] Mary's dignity as *Theotokos* – bearer or mother of God – arises from the gospel. It is an evangelical statement. It is a bold affirmation of the immediate logic of the gospel of the grace that 'in Christ God was reconciling the world to himself' (2 Corinthians 5.19). It is an authentic, Spirit-led interpretation of scripture and a proper outworking, in the spirituality and theology of the patristic period, of the inner workings of the *paradosis*. In this sense, it is the *paradosis* of the church explicating the originating *paradosis* of the faith that is enshrined in holy scripture.

Hence, the place of Mary in the life of the church affirms the necessity of the gospel tradition held within scripture, and the theological tradition developed within the church to interpret scripture according to the genetic structure of its originating tradition. At the same time it also warns against a degenerating development which, though it has a connecting logic to the originating tradition, is so distanced from its fundamental data that it becomes a distortion of it. Ironically, we need look no further than Ephesus in 431 for evidence of this danger. Immediately after the bishops declared that Mary was truly *Theotokos* the excited crowds, who had been demonstrating for exactly that affirmation, burst into exuberant acclamations of 'Praised be *Theotokos*' and held a torchlight procession through the city. There were scenes uncomfortably reminiscent of the near riot in Ephesus four centuries earlier when people took to the streets proclaiming, 'Great is Artemis – or Diana – of the Ephesians' (Acts 19.28, 34) in an attempt to suppress Paul's preaching of the greatness of Jesus Christ and his call to abandon the idols of any other religion. Indeed, the Collyridian sect went so far as to worship Mary as divine just as Diana had been honoured in the Roman cult, causing Epiphanius, the Bishop of Ephesus, to protest in gospel fashion, 'The body of Mary is holy but she is not God . . . Let no one adore Mary.'[37]

In her study of Mary from a Roman Catholic feminist perspective, Elizabeth Johnson divides the history of Marian thought and practice into two millennia and two models. She shows that while the first millennium generally kept to Epiphanius' teaching and treated Mary as an inspiring companion in the faith and evidence of the gospel's veracity, the second millennium increasingly viewed her as a matter of theological and spiritual interest in her own right, promoting her as a patron of the faith – someone who could be turned to for religious purposes in ways that deflected from the sole mediation of Christ and was therefore *contrary to the gospel*. Elizabeth Johnson's account of how these two forces clashed at the Second Vatican Council, with the former overcoming the latter at the points that mattered, is a fascinating one that unfortunately cannot detain us here. The critical matter for our purposes is that the story of Mary in the theology and devotion of the church underlines the case made in Chapter 2 for an understanding of tradition as the *inner centre of scripture*, the fundamental faith in Jesus Christ passed on faithfully and explained fully in the church's teaching. This faith is, on the one hand, supremely simple and can be stated in the few statements Paul uses in 1 Corinthians 15.3–5. On the other hand, it is extraordinarily deep – as deep as the depths of God – and requires an ongoing theological and spiritual tradition to search it out under the Spirit's guidance in a way that is according to the scriptures and so promotes the one in whom 'all things hold together', and through whom 'God was pleased to reconcile all things'. In this person – Jesus of Nazareth – 'the fullness of God was pleased to dwell' and to be born of Mary, one of the poor of the earth. Only where the gospel of Christ (the originating tradition) and its apostolic witness in scripture is the criterion of the church's ongoing tradition will it support rather than distort the gospel, remaining its servant and not becoming its master.

Mary and the relationship between justifying and transformative grace.

In the earlier discussion we found that it was truer to the text of scripture and to the whole thrust of the gospel to interpret the angelic greeting to Mary as the 'favoured one' (*kecharitōmenē*) in terms of God's choice of her purely on the basis of his grace and not on the basis of her own goodness. Mary's response was an act of faith, trusting entirely in God's mercy and not in her own moral or spiritual strength. 'Hence,' says Luther, 'she does not glory in her worthiness or unworthiness, but solely in the divine regard, which is so exceedingly good and gracious that he deigned to look upon such a lowly maiden, and to look at her in so glorious and honourable a fashion.'[38] We also acknowledged, though, that God prepares people to respond in faith and that Mary's election included the prevenient work of the Spirit leading her to the point at which she could say her 'Yes' freely and fully to God.

The freedom and the fullness of Mary's response to God help to uncover the layering of authentic, saving faith in a way that shows the complementarity of the classic Protestant and catholic positions on justification recognized, as we saw in Chapter 3, in the twentieth-century dialogue between Roman Catholics and Lutherans. Feminist perspectives underline how important it is for Mary's response to be free and not forced, to be an act of her own will rather than as a result of being overwhelmed by the will of God. This is a young, vulnerable woman who has been chosen to conceive a child out of wedlock, a fate that would normally consign a person to a life of ignominy and poverty or, if the law was strictly applied, death by stoning. It was critical that she should freely consent to this call, that God's gracious but demanding choice of her should be reciprocated by her willing faith in the good and gracious purposes of God. We are saved, Paul tells us, by grace through faith. Both are necessary, and yet both, he insists, are 'not our own doing' but 'the gift of God' (Ephesians 2.8). Mary's faith-filled response to God was a Spirit-inspired response, a result of the work of the Spirit leading her to the point at which she could respond to God in freedom and fullness.

The fullness of Mary's response is shown in her embrace of what Dietrich Bonhoeffer was to call 'costly discipleship': 'Here I am, the servant of the Lord; let it be with me according to your word' (Luke 1.38). This was no attempt to cash in on any sort of offer of 'cheap grace'. It was an acceptance of all the consequences of faith in the God of grace who is committed to the costly coming of his kingdom. And Mary was to pay a high price indeed – the death of the son she carried and bore and nurtured. Bonhoeffer also said, 'Only the believers obey, and only the obedient believe.'[39] Mary's 'Yes' to God shows that justifying faith, faith that depends entirely on the gracious, undeserved, unwarranted mercy of God's call, cannot be separated from obedience to the will of the merciful God. Indeed, 'the disobedient cannot believe; only the obedient believe'.[40] Faith not only fulfils itself in discipleship, it *finds* itself in discipleship. It was as Mary stepped out into what Bonhoeffer calls 'the fresh air of decision' that she found that God had not only elected her to be the mother of his Son but had equipped her with the faith to believe his word and to follow his way.[41] Mary shows that although God justifies purely on the basis of his grace to us and not on the basis of our love for God, the faith that responds to God's grace will 'work through love' (Galatians 5.6).

Mary and the relationship between Christ and the church.

In Chapter 4 we described the relationship between Christ and the church as organic *and* asymmetrical. On the one hand, Jesus Christ is intimately connected to his people, so much so that a primary biblical image is of the church as his body. In later chapters, when we move on to consider the ministry of the church (its actions and practices), we will see that this understanding of the church as the bodily presence of Jesus underlies any claim about the presence and work of Christ through the church. On the other hand, Christ is distinguishable from the church. He is not subsumed into it or contained by it. The church does not possess Christ: it receives him as the gift of the Spirit. Jesus is the head of the body, and the body remains entirely dependent on him and on his will and energy. More formally, the church is the recipient of his salvation and is permanently in need of his saving effect. Jesus Christ is the Lord of the church and Saviour of his people. Our exploration of Marian thought and devotion has shown that it is important to maintain the proper order and dynamic of this relationship when considering the place of Jesus' mother in the life of the church. All the while that Mary is seen, in Pope Paul VI's words, as 'truly our sister', our *compañera* in the faith, as a Latin American hymn puts it, she serves the gospel of her son by pointing us to a free and full following of Christ and the kingdom she bore him to bring. When Mary is raised to a place where, in some way, she gives the benefits and blessing of his kingdom, then, contrary to her decision to be a servant of the Lord, she is put into a place that is properly occupied by her son. This is not to deny that Mary has a special place in the life of the church. Her 'unique vocation' as *Theotokos*, her calling to be the mother of the church's Lord, ensures that she has a particular dignity within the body of Christ and that we have a particular relation to her. Elizabeth was right to say – and we are right to say with her – that she is blessed among all the women of the world. But Elizabeth said in the same voice, 'and blessed is the fruit of your womb' (Luke 1.42) and it is this confession that Mary, along with all the saints and servants of the Lord, desires to hear from the lips of every person. In this sense, Mary is – as her own Magnificat anticipated – a very 'bless-ed' model of the church because she praises the God of her salvation and proclaims to the world the fulfilment of 'the promise made to her ancestors' that 'the mercy of God is for those who fear him from generation to generation' (Luke 1.46–55). As Luther tells us in his great commentary on the Magnificat:

> Mary does not say, 'My soul magnifies itself' or 'exalts me'. She does not desire herself to be esteemed; she magnifies God alone and gives all glory to him. She leaves herself out and ascribes everything to God alone, from whom she received it. For though she experienced such an exceeding great work of God within herself, yet she was ever minded not to exalt herself above the humblest mortal being.[42]

The church has a high calling, a *Marian calling* to see Christ formed in the world. Like her we are to see ourselves as the handmaid of the Lord, the servant of the kingdom, drawing others to him and his work and not to ourselves and our efforts.

Conclusion: Mary and the gospel

We have seen in a number of ways that Mary does, indeed, belong to the gospel. First, we cannot have Jesus without Mary. This is true on a physical, historical level. In Mary, Jesus was conceived and delivered into this world. It is true on a theological level. Mary's obedient response to God's word through the angel was a critical and necessary stage in the history of our salvation. It is true on a relational level. By being related to Jesus we are related to everyone to whom he is related. Mary of Nazareth is our sister in the faith because she is a member of Jesus' messianic community. She is *in Christ* as other followers of him are in Christ. Jesus' relationship with each member of his body is unique, Mary included. She remains his mother and he remains her son. Jesus' dealings with his disciples after his resurrection demonstrate the continuity of his relationships with his followers during his earthly ministry. The same is true for his relationship with his mother. He remains bound to her in filial love. Whatever we may say about the changed character of our relationships in heaven, the eternal character of love requires that they are nothing less than what they were on earth. They are fulfilled rather than forsaken. Jesus' continuing relationship with Mary as mother arises from the permanence of his humanity. He does not discard what it means to be human at his ascension: he exalts it. Hence, through Jesus we relate to Mary our sister in the particular place she occupies in the community of Christ, the place of his mother. In loving Jesus we are to enter into his love for all his people, including his love for his mother.

Second, Mary belongs to the gospel as an example of the grace of the gospel in action. God's regard for Mary in her 'low estate', God's choice of this poor peasant girl to bear his beloved Son reveals the way the God of the gospel works in our world to put it right. And so Mary, Elizabeth Johnson writes,

. . . sings pregnant with hope, bearing the Messiah, embodying the historical reversal she proclaims. Who shall mother the Messiah? Not a well-protected queen, not someone blessed with a bounteous table and a peaceful life, not a well-regarded woman of influence. Indeed, there is nothing wrong with these things; peace and abundant nourishment are among the blessings hoped for in the messianic age. But the world is distorted by sin. People accumulate power and wealth at the expense of others. Suffering is rampant. And the pattern persists through the generations. Into this unjust situation comes the choice of God, Creator and Redeemer of the world. Hearing the cries of the oppressed, seeing their misery, knowing well what they are suffering, coming down to redeem, the Holy One aims to turn the unjust order of things upside down and make the world right again, being faithful to the covenant promise. In the deepest revelatory insights of Jewish and Christian traditions, there is no other God.[43]

The action of God to and in Mary embodies the dynamic of the gospel not only in the sense of the extraordinary strength of God's grace but also in the faith-filled and faithful response to the grace of the gospel that God engenders in her. She shows what can happen when we believe and obey God's word in Christ. Protestant thought has been rightly protective of the saving role of Jesus' vicarious humanity. Emphasizing that it is Jesus' obedience to God's call to him to be the Messiah that saves us, Protestant thought has been rightly suspicious of anything in Marian thought and piety that might obscure the saving effect of Jesus' vicarious humanity. For example, ideas in catholic theology of Mary fulfilling the vocation of Israel in her 'Yes' to God sound deficient to evangelical theological ears, which, rightly in my view, define Jesus as the representative Israelite who is faithful where the people fail and even goes to the cross to bear God's judgement on them as one of the people. However, there is something that Mary does that Jesus cannot do. She shows us how to follow Christ, to become a disciple of Christ through 'her pilgrimage of faith',[44] and to be filled with the Spirit because of Christ. To be sure, she is not unique in this regard. Indeed, she is one of many in the 'great cloud of witnesses' (Hebrews 12.1), and part of her role in the life of faith is to remind us of this extensity of the church through the communion of all the saints. But the intensity of the love she has for her son is the love that we are called to share.

Perhaps Martin Luther, reformer of the church but respecter of Mary, should have the last word in this chapter's attempt to regard Mary from the perspective of the gospel:

> Thus regarding her, you will be moved to love and praise God for his grace, and drawn to look for all good things to him, who does not reject but graciously regards poor and despised and lowly mortals. Thus your heart will be strengthened in faith and love and hope.[45]

6

Worshipping God[1]

Christian worship is the most momentous, the most urgent, the
most glorious action that can take place in human life.
Karl Barth

Introduction

So far we have considered three doctrinal areas – word, justification and church – where evangelical and catholic thought have
been in significant disagreement. We have also looked at Mary,
partly because her different status in evangelical and catholic
spirituality is so noticeable and partly because she has been a
focus of debate in each of these areas of Christian theology. I
hope to have shown that by a careful process of listening to the
other, and, where possible, by responsible recasting of some
of the issues in the kiln of the Spirit, the complementarity of
evangelical and catholic perspectives can be seen and a way
found to hold them together in the 'boundless riches of Christ'
(Ephesians 3.8). The next three chapters apply this method to
the worshipping life of the church. This chapter explores three
of the marks of worship that derive from evangelical principles
about the gospel, catholic instincts about the church, and charismatic concerns about the vitality of the Spirit. It then goes on
to identify three practical implications for evangelical worship
that arise from this analysis. The chapter's lens is fairly wide. It
deals with panorama rather than particulars, broad proposals
for worship rather than detailed theological reasoning. That
comes in later, in Chapters 7 and 8, where the lens is changed
to give a closer angle on liturgy, baptism and Eucharist. We
begin this set of three chapters with some general comments on
the nature of evangelical worship.

Evangelical worship is worship of the God of the gospel. It is worship according to the gospel of Jesus the Messiah, the one whom God sends to the world to fulfil the divine mission. As a result, because the gospel comes to us by the Spirit for life in the messianic community of Christ, worship of the God of the gospel is necessarily catholic and charismatic. Worship according to the gospel pertains to and participates in the life of the whole church, the whole Christ, head and body, in and by the Spirit. It is orientated simultaneously to the God who sends the Messiah, to the people who follow the Messiah and to the world to whom the Spirit, through the messianic community, seeks to make the Christ known.

Essentially, evangelical worship is living *before* the God of grace, living *for* others in the God of grace, and living *towards* the world for the God of grace. It involves the whole of life, especially life that serves and seeks the coming of the kingdom of God, but it includes all that Christians do 'when they come together'.[2] Hence, although an evangelical understanding of worship extends to the expansive experience of living a gospel life before the presence of God, it certainly includes all that happens when Christians gather for intensive expressions of their life of love before God.[3] Likewise, evangelical worship refuses to reduce these intensive moments of worship to the modes of exaltation and adoration – *the sacrifice of praise*, for short – still less to particular feelings of worship experienced by the emotions or the spirit in the giving of thanks and praise. Evangelical worship, worship according to the gospel, embraces all the ministries of the Spirit in which the word of the gospel is heard and seen,[4] celebrated and received, expressed, embodied and enacted: the reading and preaching of scripture; the gathering, praying, singing and dismissal of the people; initiation, reconciliation, healing, ordaining, marrying, burying and so on.

Within its circle of commitment to the gospel, the church and the Spirit, this form of worship will aim to hold together that which the flawed history of Christian worship and spirituality has forced apart: word and sacrament, prophetic and mystical, personal and communal, simple and ceremonial, ordered and spontaneous, exaltation and edification. As in every other aspect of its life, evangelical worship is to take Jesus Christ, the one in whom 'all things hold together', as its pattern, conforming itself to his image. He is the word and sacrament of God, the prophet and the mystic, the one who could pray alone and with others. He broke bread simply with his friends and rode ceremonially into Jerusalem. He learnt the prayers of home and synagogue and spoke to God with radical freedom. On the same occasion he could switch from ecstatic exaltation of God to sustained edification of his disciples. His integration is our inspiration.

Gracious, cross-centred worship

The first mark of worship I want to consider is *grace*. Christian worship is *gracious*, full of grace, the 'grace of our Lord Jesus Christ'. The grace of the gospel is proclaimed, received, expressed, manifested in evangelical worship worthy of the name. Evangelically speaking, although the grace of God stretches across the whole action of God from creation to consummation, its defining centre is – as we have seen in other chapters – the cross of Christ. Jesus says to the Samaritan woman, 'the hour is coming, and is now here, when the true worshippers will worship the Father in spirit and truth, for the Father seeks such as those to worship him' (John 4.23). The one whose life was a life of worship, and who would enable others to offer worship in spirit and truth, stood before the Samaritan woman. In this sense, the 'hour' had come. But John is clear that the time, the 'hour', culminates on the cross. This would be the 'hour' of the Son's glorification through his perfect worship of the Father (John 17.1) and, therefore, the gateway to the gift of the Spirit (John 16.5–15; 19.30). It is as we believe in him 'lifted up' and receive the Spirit from his wounded side that we share in his eternal life of worship (John 3.14–15; 12.32; 20.20–22). That is saving faith.

The cross, the saving death of Jesus Christ, therefore stands at the core of evangelical worship. God in Christ addresses the incapacity of Jewish, Samaritan, Greek and Roman worship – the inadequacy of the worship of all the nations and cultures – to deal with the enslavement of the human heart to evil, to acknowledge the depths of human rebellion against God, and to perceive the true nature of God. Through the cross, evil is faced and faced down, sin is acknowledged and judged, human nature is reconstituted by radical obedience, and divine nature is revealed as holy, triune love. All the sacrificial instincts of human worship are fulfilled in the sacrifice of the Son of God. All the mediatorial attempts of humankind are subsumed in the priesthood of Christ. Jesus the perfect sacrifice and Jesus the righteous priest, who offered himself to the Father 'by the eternal Spirit' (Hebrews 9.14), is the one through whom we can approach the throne of grace. The Roman Catholic Catechism puts it well: 'From the first community of Jerusalem until the Parousia, it is the same Paschal mystery that the Churches of God, faithful to the apostolic faith, celebrate in every place.'[5] This is a profound definition of worship. The churches of God, inspired by the Spirit from Pentecost to Parousia, celebrate the cross of Christ. In so doing, of course, our celebration will extend across all the mighty acts of God – remembering and rejoicing in the grace of God displayed in the ministry of Jesus, proved in the resurrection of Jesus, made known in the history of Israel, and confirmed in the life of the early and continuing church. But at the still centre of it all stands the wondrous cross on which the Prince of Glory died, the cross that demands our soul, our life, our all. Essentially, therefore, *worship according to the gospel* is the celebration of the presence of this crucified Lord coming to us by the power of the Spirit to take us deeper into his risen life and further into his messianic mission.

Communal worship

The second mark of worship we are considering is its *communal* character. The 'grace of our Lord Jesus Christ' is brought to us by the 'fellowship of the Holy Spirit'. The Spirit, as Calvin (following Augustine) liked to say, is the 'bond of union' uniting us with Christ and with his people.[6] The Spirit connects us with the 'historical church', the continuous embodiment of God's covenant with humanity, stretching across the centuries of Jewish and Christian tradition. The Spirit connects us with the 'geographical church', the present manifestation of God's work in Christ across all the continents and among all the traditions, including those with whom we gather in our bit of history and geography through the 'local church'. The Spirit connects us with the 'heavenly church', those who have gone before us in the faith and who wait in the nearer presence of Christ for the coming of the kingdom's fullness. The Spirit connects us with the 'eschatological church', the community of the redeemed that includes not only the saints on earth and in heaven but also those whom the Spirit will draw into the people of God through the ongoing messianic mission of Christ. This is the catholic and apostolic breadth of the Spirit's work in our worship: to connect us with all those to whom Christ is connected, to bring us into fellowship with, as Luther liked to say, 'Christ and *all* his saints'.[7] Hence, as Vielhauer says in his important study of worship, 'The goal of divine purpose is not pious individuals but one holy catholic apostolic church in the profoundly and radically eschatological meaning of the New Testament.'[8]

This sort of fellowship is formational. Indeed, it is transformational. To be connected with Jesus Christ and to be connected with his people and his mission is to be changed. 'Blind worshippers remain every day the same', said Luther.[9] Christ re-formed human nature from self-centredness and transformed it into other-centredness. Jesus' capacity to live *before* the God of grace and to live *for* others in the God of grace and *towards* the world for the God of grace – his obedient life of messianic worship – is formed in us through our relationship with him in the Spirit. The worship of the church provides a sustained system for intensive encounter with Christ so that his 'worshipping self' can be formed in us.[10] Christopher Irvine calls the church's worship 'God's studio' in which God fashions and shapes us into the likeness of his Son in whom he has (quoting Athanasius), 'renewe[d] his image in humankind' by allowing it to be 're-drawn on the same material' through the mercy and mystery of the incarnation.[11] This transformative process happens on at least two interconnected levels – *relational* and *educational*.

The opportunities for *relating* to Jesus Christ in worship are myriad. Jesus meets us in the other worshippers, ministers to us through the various members of his body, speaks to us through the scriptures, confronts us through preaching, reveals himself in the breaking of the bread, gives us words to pray to his Father, baptizes us with the Spirit of God, invites us to call him Lord and sing his praise, anoints us with gifts of the Spirit, ministers healing, brings us mercy, forgiveness and love, and sends us out with his blessing for his work. The heart of worship is the presence of Christ calling us into deeper communion with him so that we may be changed, and so that he may change the world through us.

Relationships involve *education*. As we grow in understanding others, so our fellowship with them deepens. The disciples' fellowship with the risen Christ on the way to Emmaus grew in intensity as they learnt more about the necessity of his death through his words, and discerned, in his familiar actions at a meal, the reality of his resurrection. Worship provides this sort of Emmaus education. It is a structured context for the proclamation and enactment of the gospel that in turn allows our lives to be structured by the pattern of the gospel and gives us the energy to tell others that 'The Lord has risen indeed, and he has appeared to Simon' – to us! (Luke 24.34).

The creeds of the church explicate the historical and theological basis of the gospel. They evolved as words for worship defining the identity and describing the activity of the God whom the church worships. Worship according to the gospel will habituate the followers of Christ into the doctrines of creation, redemption and consummation articulated in the creeds. This involves far more (though not less) than reciting the words of the creeds. It requires a systematic programme of proclamation and enactment through kerygmatic word and liturgical action. In faithful preaching and teaching, the graciousness of God is expounded and explained. Through symbol, sacrament, sound and silence the activity of God is seen, touched and felt. In the rhythm of the liturgical year and the discipline of structured reading of scripture the mighty acts of God are rehearsed and retold.

This process of liturgical education in the credal teaching of the church involves certain essentials of the gospel in order to maintain scripturally faithful worship. For example, it will at least incorporate the following. First, a proper expression of the relationship between God and creation which respects the ontological difference between the Creator and the created but which rejoices in God's blessing of and involvement in that which God creates by grace. This is the basis of the doctrine of worship. Second, a presentation of the true dynamics of salvation which preserves the priority of God's grace and the giftedness of any response which humanity, helpless of itself, makes to God. This is the order of sacramental theology. Third, an understanding of the kingdom which honours the anticipation of its presence in heaven and on earth but looks and works for the fullness of its coming in the new heaven and new earth of God's future. This is the motivation for mission. It is not for nothing that orthodoxy means 'right praise'. The law of prayer is the law of belief. Evangelical theology, gospel truth, is nurtured through the repeated celebration of the gospel in worship.[12] The educational dimension of worship leads to a personal encounter with the risen Christ because it does not just speak about the gospel, it *performs* the gospel. It provides access to the reality of the gospel – to the gracious presence of the risen Christ through the persons, words and actions of his people in the power of his Spirit. The gospel is proclaimed.

Truth is told. Forgiveness is offered. Peace is shared. The kingdom is manifested: we are welcomed to God's table, we are lifted to heaven, we sing 'Alleluia!' and we cry 'Maranatha!'.

The liturgical experience of the gospel is a communal experience. It happens with others, through others. It educates us into the corporate reality of our salvation – that 'there is no gospel without the church'; that we are not only bound to other members of Christ in the gospel – *we rely on them for the gospel*. Evangelical theology is rightly sensitive to any suspicion of instrumentalism in the life of faith. History has proved the ease with which the freeness and directness of the gospel is tethered or tamed by ecclesiastical device, even within evangelical practice. However, scripture shows that the communication of the gospel involves God's use of human and material instruments or means of grace – 'for how are they to hear without someone to proclaim him?' (Romans 10.14). 1 Corinthians 12—14 spells out how we are dependent not only on the preacher but on each member of Christ's body for the ministry of the Spirit of God. The danger comes when we are tempted to turn the economy of God's grace into an economy of our power, when we take the instruments of divine choosing and make them instruments of human control, when the servants of God's gift become managers of God's favour. The line between a gospel-serving instrumentality and a gospel-denying instrumentalism is a thin one, but fear of the latter should not deter us from recognizing and rejoicing in the former. As Miroslav Volf says, 'the transmission of the faith occurs through interpersonal ecclesial interaction'.[13]

Spiritual worship

The third mark of worship I want to consider is that it is *spiritual* – it is of and in the Spirit. Through the 'fellowship of the Holy Spirit' we know 'the grace of our Lord Jesus Christ', by which we experience the 'love of God' (2 Corinthians 13.13). Because worship is a celebration of the presence of Christ and a performance of his gospel among his people, it is an experience of the loving of God with and through others as a *witness* to the world and eschatological *sign* of the kingdom. Worship is a personal and communal experience of being loved *by* God and expressing love *to* God. Worship does not just refer to the reality of God's love in Christ, it is a realization of the love of God for the world in the present experience of his people. This is what it means to 'worship in the Spirit': we worship in the one by whom the love of God 'has been poured into our hearts' (Romans 5.5).

The dependence of the church's worship upon the activity of the Spirit is acknowledged in the *epiclēsis*. The *epiclēsis* is the invocation of the Holy Spirit traditionally located in the eucharistic prayer. But it is much more than a liturgical formula. It is a recognition of the church's need for what William Law and John Wesley in the eighteenth century called the 'perpetual inspiration of the Spirit'.[14] It is a confession of our inability to approach God in worship by our own power and goodness. It is an acknowledgement that, in the words of Albertus Magnus in the thirteenth century, the Holy Spirit 'makes the church holy' and that 'the Spirit communicates that holiness' in all manner of ministries, including 'the sacraments, the virtues and the gifts that he distributes in order to bring holiness about and finally in the miracles and the graces of a charismatic type such as wisdom, knowledge, faith, the discernment of spirits, healing, prophecy and everything that the Spirit gives in order to make the holiness of the Church manifest'.[15] The *epiclēsis* is the acceptance that the Spirit is the leader of our liturgy.

The Spirit's ministry in our worship is to lead us to the presence of Christ and to the kingdom that Christ brings, so that we may participate in the eschatological love of God for the world demonstrated on the cross. In this way worship is a *prolepsis* – a foretelling of the kingdom of God, an anticipation of the fulfilment of God's purposes for the whole of creation. The Spirit, the *arrabōn* (pledge), the *aparchē* (first–fruit), yearns within us for the renewal of creation. The Spirit manifests the coming reign of God's love among us now as we do that for which we were created and redeemed, and that which we shall enjoy for ever. Of course, worship in this age remains only a *prolepsis* of the *eschaton*, not the *eschaton* itself. It is always marked by lament for what is not yet here and by desire for the completion of God's purposes and the fullness of Christ's presence. But it is a real 'taste', as the letter to the Hebrews puts it, of the 'powers of the age to come' (Hebrews 6.5), and it is a taste that makes us want to have more and compels us to say to others – 'Taste and see that the Lord is good' (Psalm 34.8).

Although our experience of God in worship is a real experience of the reality of God (it is brought to us by the Word *of God* and the Spirit *of God*) it is nonetheless mediated through the material means that God chooses to use. As John Colwell, the evangelical Baptist theologian, says, 'God mediates [his] mercy and grace, by his Spirit, through human and created instrumentality.'[16] *Mediated immediacy* (to use the Scottish Presbyterian Donald Baillie's term) has always been acknowledged by evangelical theology in relation to the word. God comes to us in the humanity of Christ, and speaks to us through the 'prophetic writing' (Romans 16.26) of scripture and through the anointed preachers of its truth. But it goes further than this. The Spirit's work throughout all of our worship has a sacramental character. The Holy Spirit inspires our adoration of God in worship by affecting our spirits and by providing ways for us to express our adoration. Both movements of the Spirit – inspiration and exhalation – are mediated through the material. Even the intensification of Spirit-inspired praise through glossolalia involves the physicality of the human body. The Spirit of truth enables the edification of the worshipping community by 'renewing the mind' (Romans 12.2) through a series of embodied ministries by which we are built up in the truth (Ephesians 4.15; 2 Timothy 2.15; Romans 15.14). Even the dramatic in-breaking of God's word through a prophetic word in worship is mediated through the prophet's voice. The Spirit of hope empowers us through our worship to take our part in the missionary work of Christ by equipping us with all manner of spiritual gifts communicated in very material ways.

Even the overwhelming power of God that may be experienced in prayer ministry involves the prayers – and often hands – of those who are ministering the love of God. In each dimension of our worship, God's own Spirit is the means of our worship. God, through the Spirit, gifts the members of Christ's body to minister the grace of Christ. God, through the Spirit, takes the ordinary things of human life to communicate the extraordinary life of Christ. God, through the Spirit, plays what the Desert Fathers and Mothers called 'the five-stringed harp' of our senses to awaken us to the mercy of Christ.

Practical implications

In his study of worship in the New Testament churches, Ralph Martin identifies three types of worship in the embryonic Christian communities of the first century: didactic, charismatic and eucharistic. Interestingly, these relate quite closely to the three marks that we have been considering in this chapter as they emerge from fundamental principles of the gospel, the church and the Spirit. They each have something to say to the practice of evangelical worship today.

Recovering catechesis through scripture in worship.

Worship that is gracious will have a *didactic* character. It will tell of the grace of the gospel. It will be *catechetic*, communicating the events of our salvation to us and teaching about their significance. Without careful scriptural teaching through the systematic reading of scripture, expository preaching of scripture, and scripturally based liturgy and hymnody, our memories will become disconnected from the corporate memory of the church and either hit a blockage and then boredom, or wander into fantasy and then apostasy. One would expect careful attention to the reading and preaching of scripture to be a given in evangelical worship. Sadly, in my experience this is not always the case. Personally, I have become tired of readings – often only one in a service – read badly, to a congregation that appears to have little expectation of being addressed by God's word, followed by a sermon that pays little more than lip-service to the passage as it launches into a talk on a theme. The Reformers were passionate about the place of scripture in worship. They were committed to the restoration of systematic attention to scripture in liturgically coherent ways to the worship of the church. In my own church, Thomas Cranmer's programme for 'the public reading of scripture' (1 Timothy 4.13) was just as important to the reform of the church as his revision of the eucharistic liturgy. His work has been continued and creatively applied by contemporary evangelical liturgists who argued for systems for the reading of scripture that are both *catholic* and *congregational*. They secured the adoption of 'open and closed lectionary seasons' in the liturgical revisions of the Church of England.[17] These unite the church around common readings during the incarnational and paschal cycles of the Christian year, and allow congregations to use alternative lectionary material at other times during the year to serve their particular pastoral or missionary needs. They provide evangelicals, in one church at least, with a systematic structure for the catechetical reading and preaching of scripture, both in terms of the provision of patterns of readings and in the freedom to depart from them in responsible ways.[18] The challenge is to use what has been offered. Unless we hear the gospel through the whole of scripture, read and expounded to us, our worship will not be centred on the gospel, and our capacity to connect with the great events of our salvation, and to live the new life in the Spirit that they make possible, will be seriously thwarted (2 Timothy 3.16–17).

Re-enlivening the liturgical tradition.

Worship that is communal will be *charismatic* because the agent of Christian community is the Spirit of fellowship (2 Corinthians 13.13). The Spirit brings us into communion with Christ so that together, as one people, we can share in the communion of the life of God. We worship the God of the gospel in the truth of God's grace and in the Spirit of God's life (John 4.23). In much of contemporary evangelical practice, liturgy has been condemned as the enemy of the Spirit. In the UK this began during the charismatic renewal of the 1960s and 1970s when there was a very definite reaction against structured forms of worship. It gathered pace in the 1980s and 1990s (despite the significant – and generally charismatic-friendly – revision of the liturgy) under the pervasive influence of Vineyard forms of worship. In the early years of the twenty-first century this widespread suspicion, or even wholesale rejection, of liturgy has hardened into a missionary strategy. Only very recently I was speaking to a vicar of a very vibrant, pioneering church in central London who said that his team of cutting-edge, mission-focused leaders is convinced that liturgy will play no part in forms of worship accessible to postmodern urban people.

So strong is this antipathy between the charismatic and the liturgical in many evangelical circles that it needs some sustained attention, which is why some of the next chapter will be devoted to uncovering its deeper causes and to reaccommodating the liturgical into today's evangelical culture. Suffice it to say at that point that along with James Smith's and Graham Hughes' shrewd analyses of evangelical worship, I do not think that contemporary evangelicalism's rejection of the deep wisdom of the liturgical tradition is sustainable. Neither do I think it is true to the originating worship of the earliest churches, which, as Ralph Martin has shown, combined 'coherence' (recognizable patterns across the churches) and 'contingency' (immediate responses to the dynamics of each church).[19] I propose a confident, grateful, Spirit-led use of the church's liturgy. I long to see planners and presiders of worship so understanding the structures of worship that they can move freely within them. I look for songwriters to put the classic texts of worship, which the Spirit of truth has given to the church – many of them in the Bible itself – to a contemporary musical idiom so that, once again, they can rest in the hearts and minds of evangelicals and rise to their lips in worship. I yearn for sustained periods of sung worship, glossolalia, prophecy, healing, woven into the movement of liturgical worship by Spirit-led leaders. I hunger for the biblical symbols of the grace of the gospel – bread, wine, water, oil, light – to be received with prayer and thanksgiving and used faithfully and joyfully. I desire all the good things that God has given to the church – the wisdom of the liturgical inheritance, the enlivenment of the Spirit, the powerful teaching of scripture – all serving the grace of the gospel and helping us to celebrate the presence of the risen Christ with his people.[20]

Reclaiming the sacraments.

We worship the God of the gospel in the truth of God's grace and in the Spirit of God's life in the materiality of this world as bodily beings. This is why Jesus' ministry began with his baptism and why the ministry of the church began with tongues of fire 'appearing among' Jesus' followers and 'resting on them' (Acts 2.3). It is why John C. Lambert's statement in 1903 has stood the test of scholarly time: 'there is nothing in early Christianity more primitive than the sacraments'.[21] It is why new disciples in our day, young and old – who may have never even heard of 'sacramental theology' – instinctively want to ritualize and symbolize their conversion to Christ in dramatic actions of the church and with a profusion of water. It is why evangelical worship needs to recover a vibrant sense of the gospel realities of the sacraments.

Martin Stringer, a contemporary liturgical theologian and anthropologist, identifies 'the meal' and 'spirit-filled worship' as two discernible givens of early Christian worship. He concludes his study of the sociological history of Christian worship by saying 'that if these two could ever be successfully reunited then Christian worship would be launched again in a round of renewal'.[22] Here is a mandate for an ecclesially rich and Spirit-open form of evangelical worship if ever there was one. It is a theological and spiritual travesty that the Eucharist is sidelined in evangelical and charismatic spirituality. We are commanded by Jesus Christ to do it, and evangelicals in every century testify to the *encounter* with the presence of the risen Christ that lies at the core of the Eucharist. Here, as Handley Moule loved to say, we have 'a personal interview with the Lord'.[23] The breaking of bread is a *performance* of the gospel in the church by the Spirit. The self-sending, self-sacrificing, self-sharing[24] God of the gospel gives his beloved Son to us as we remember his death and receive his life. The communion of the body and blood of Christ is an *experience* of the loving of God in which we taste the future that God has for the world – a kingdom of reconciled humanity and transfigured creation.

The Spirit of God has used the Eucharist throughout evangelical history to celebrate the presence of Christ, perform the gospel and convey the love of God. Listen to Martin Luther, John Calvin, Thomas Cranmer, John Owen, Richard Baxter, John and Charles Wesley, George Whitefield, John Newton, Charles Simeon, Daniel Wilson, Edward Bickersteth and Handley Moule, to name only a few of the faithful witnesses.[25] They – and many others with them – would agree with Thomas Haweis, one of the leading figures of the eighteenth-century Revival, that those who avoid the Lord's Supper 'confirm that they have no friendship for Christ'.[26] As Philip Seddon has argued, it is time to reclaim a holistic evangelical spirituality by reuniting the sacramental word of grace with the preached word.[27] For too long evangelicals have been *apophatic* in their sacramental theology – saying what baptism or the Eucharist is not, in order to say (eventually) what they might be. And for too long charismatics have been *anarchic* in their worship – welcoming the power of the Spirit in 'extraordinary' mediations but forgetful of the pledged presence through the 'ordinary' gifts of water, bread and wine. Of course there are exceptions, for the Spirit does not tire of causing people to desire baptism (Acts 8.36) and of making Christ 'known in the breaking of the bread' (Luke 24.35). But there remain serious tendencies towards reductionism in evangelical and charismatic sacramental practice – a way of doing the sacraments that implies that the real locus of God's activity is to be found elsewhere. Let us do what the Lord commands and the Spirit speaks through scripture. Let us proclaim the cross in speech and actions through all the ministries of the Spirit, including the baptism into Christ's death (Romans 6.4) and the feast of his victorious life (Revelation 19.7–8).

7

Touching grace

It touches the body and cleanses the heart.
Augustine

The next two chapters take forward some of the ideas on worship proposed in the previous chapter, particularly in relation to the role of the liturgy and the sacraments in evangelical life and worship. This chapter concentrates on liturgy and baptism, the next on the Eucharist. Fundamental to the discussion that follows is the concept of *mediated immediacy* (that the reality of God's presence is mediated to us through human and created forms), which was implicit in almost everything that was said in the previous chapter, and especially in relation to the Spirit's work in worship.

Evangelicalism and the liturgy of the church

One of the rooms in my house has a picture rail running around the walls about half a metre from the ceiling. Curiously, though, I do not make any use of it. That is not to say that I do not have any pictures on the walls: quite the opposite in fact. The walls are strewn with paintings, drawings and prints. I have the pictures but I do not use the picture rail. I simply nail in a hook at whatever point on the wall I would like to hang the picture. In other rooms the picture rail has been taken down – dismantled during an exercise of modernization and despatched as a relic of the past. I often think that those two ways of treating picture rails are similar to the way much of contemporary evangelicalism treats the liturgy, particularly in Anglican evangelicalism, which lives within a liturgical church but often fights against it. For some evangelicals – especially Anglicans, often of the older sort – liturgy is an honourable feature of the church's life that should be respected. It is kept on in the service – more so in situations where a certain dignity and formality seems to be more appropriate, such as the Lord's Supper or funerals – but it is not used for the *worship*. The words, and a minimum of the action, are retained perhaps out of deference to the past or because of obedience to present authorities, or perhaps out of a nebulous sense that they might do us some good at some point. But the worship itself – the personal and corporate engagement with God – is positioned to happen on another level. The introductions and connections made by whoever may be steering the service, the songs of worship and the prompts of the 'worship leader', the words of the intercessor (or, in more charismatic worship, the prophesier), shape and stimulate the worship rather than the movement and words of the liturgy itself. Other evangelicals – including some Anglicans, especially charismatics – have decided to abandon the liturgy pretty much altogether, creating 'liturgy-free zones' where worship can be freed from the fetters of an outdated tradition, often even reducing the thanksgiving prayer of the Eucharist to a reading of the institution narrative in 1 Corinthians 11.

Evangelical attitudes to liturgy have been forged from theological instincts, historical influence and cultural pressure. We now discuss each of these in turn.

Theological instinct.

Evangelicals – particularly those affected by charismatic renewal – instinctively place great emphasis on the freedom of Christian worship, a liberty that flows from the accessibility of God in Christ. Our relationship with God is personal, and our worship of God, whether we are by ourselves or with others, is to be personal: in words that belong to the moment rather than inherited from the past or imposed by others. It is to be *free*, dictated by the dynamics of relationship rather than the conventions of religion. It is to be a *genuine response* to the gospel activated by the Spirit, not a ritual determined by the church. However, this bi-polarity between the freedom of engagement with the accessible God, and the shapes, forms and words of the liturgical tradition, does not actually correspond to the depth and breadth of biblical faith. God's *immediacy* is *mediated*.

The shape and the words of the liturgy have the capacity to be used by God to bring about encounter and engagement with his real presence. Indeed, the mediation of God's activity through human history requires that the story of God's work is told faithfully and responded to appropriately. It is this telling and re-telling of the story of salvation in theologically accurate ways so as to gather hearers of the story *into* the story, making them active participants in God's redemption of the world, that makes liturgical shape and liturgical words necessary to Christian worship. Furthermore, it would seem that God's creation of the human brain with its predilection for patterns in order to find meaning, and repetition in order to sustain memory, makes liturgy an effective tool for the Spirit's work of calling to mind the mighty works of God and enabling us to live within their truth (John 16.12–15).[1]

There is plenty of evidence for this among the Spirit-filled people of God. The Israelites constructed an elaborate liturgy for the dedication of the temple, and God's presence was manifested in ways which exceed all expectations (2 Chronicles 5—7). The Spirit inspired a great prayer of praise in Hannah, reworked it on the lips of Mary and then established it in the life of the church (1 Samuel 3.2–10; Luke 1.46–55). Jesus told his disciples not to 'heap up empty phrases' in their prayers 'as the Gentiles do' and then went on to teach them a prayer which became a permanent part of the prayer life of the church (Matthew 6.7–13). Jesus' command to 'do this in remembrance of me' was situated within a people formed by the liturgy of temple, synagogue and home. This command to recall him through words and actions ensured that those who followed him would take their place in this tradition of prayer that saw no dichotomy between frameworks and forms on the one side, and freedom and authenticity on the other.

John Wesley's Journal records a notable example of this combination of spontaneous response to the present movement of the Spirit with the use of the Spirit's gift of words from the past:

> Mr Hall, Hinching, Ingam, Whitefield, Hutching, and my brother Charles were present at our love feast at Fetter Lane with about sixty of our brethren. About three in the morning as we were continuing instant in prayer the power of God came mightily upon us, insomuch that many cried out for exulting joy and many fell to the ground. As soon as we recovered a little from the awe and amazement at the presence of His majesty, we broke out with one voice, 'We praise Thee, O God, we acknowledge Thee to be Lord'.[2]

It is a wonderful example of the blending of evangelical piety, the presence of the Spirit and the richness of the church's liturgical tradition. The Moravians who met in Fetter Lane had led Wesley to the gospel realities of evangelical faith. He and other future leaders of the evangelical Revival were praying well into the night, no doubt extempore, and most probably for the conversion of many others. The Spirit came with the sort of physical effect of which we read in 2 Chronicles 7 when Solomon's temple was dedicated, and the words which these evangelical leaders used to voice their praise was the ancient song of the church, first inspired in the hearts and minds of fourth-century creators of worship and soon commonplace in the liturgy of the church, East and West, and so a staple feature of Wesley's prayer life: *Te Deum laudamus*, 'We praise thee, O God . . .'.

Historical influences.

The origin of contemporary evangelical attitudes to liturgy can, in fact, be traced back to the ferment of church life in seventeenth-century England out of which modern evangelicalism was to sprout in the eighteenth century.[3] Three approaches to liturgy emerged. Quakers and other charismatic groups jettisoned any pre-arranged forms and words of worship, trusting instead that the Spirit would lead and guide each occasion of worship and each moment within it in new and different ways. Puritans proposed the *Westminster Directory* with its guidelines and examples to help ministers construct and lead worship appropriate to the situation and to the Spirit's work among their people at that time. Anglicans, with their Book of Common Prayer, required set texts to be used within an invariable order and a carefully prescribed practice. But the Quakers generally stopped quaking in the Spirit and silenced the dynamism of Christian worship. Presbyterian Puritans ignored the sensible advice of the *Directory* and often slipped into Unitarianism. Anglicans redefined liturgy as mandatory words on a page and oppressed worshippers with a level of regulation made possible by the printing press but actually alien to the character of Christian worship and to the intention of the liturgical tradition.

Nevertheless, these three liturgical preferences have left their mark on the consciousness and culture of evangelicalism. In reaction to straitjacket definitions of liturgy as *these words on this page at all times and places*, some evangelicals have become, or yearn to become, 'Quakers', even if they are officially bound to liturgical norms. They have taken down the picture rail. Others, often simply out of obedience, retain the liturgy but in a wooden sort of way, simply ploughing through the texts because they are there, rather than using them spiritually to shape the worship. They have kept the picture rail but hang their worship elsewhere. The Puritan *Directory*-type approach resonates with the best of evangelical instincts both for the contextualization of worship and respect for the wisdom of the church's liturgical tradition. However, history teaches us that without the 'Anglican' insistence on the use of certain Spirit-proved texts and on the necessity – not just advisability – of patterns and structures made credible by common use, worship will all too easily slide into the syrup of the surrounding culture, mirroring contemporary assumptions and attitudes, rather than facing people with the transcendent and transforming themes of the historic liturgical tradition. Similarly, the lesson of history is that the 'Quaker' openness to the Spirit belongs with the wise use of the liturgy. From the *Didache*'s invitation to 'the prophets to give thanks as much as they wish' in the second century, to contemporary – if rare – examples of the blending of the charismatic and the liturgical in the twenty-first century, the church's liturgical tradition at its most dynamic and wholesome teaches us that liturgy is to be used 'in the Spirit'. The liturgy of the church and liberty of the Spirit are not opposites that have to be chosen between, but gifts that need to be woven together in the rich ecology of the gospel.

Cultural pressure.

Evangelicalism combines a robust commitment to the truth of the gospel with a capacity for cultural adaptability. On the one hand, the gospel's counter-cultural claims are fully acknowledged and every attempt is made to ensure that they are not diluted. On the other hand, the culture of the church is systematically critiqued in order to dismantle any barriers which may have arisen between the gospel and its missionary context. This is most evident in contemporary evangelical worship with its espousal of an unchanging gospel and its adoption of styles of worship that resonate with contemporary culture.

Liturgy has generally fared badly as a result. The theological anxieties and negative historical legacies already present in evangelicalism have been reinforced by the felt need to adapt its worship to contemporary culture's apparent preference for informality and intimacy on the one hand, and its suspicion of whatever is not new and of the moment on the other. Planners and leaders of worship in evangelical churches often fear that scripted liturgy will introduce an element of artificiality and distance in worship which will be off-putting to contemporary worshippers and alien to those outside the church. Similarly, it can be felt that liturgy plays into the cultural relegation of the church to a past, remote era, with people repeating in a mindless, uncritical fashion words bequeathed from the past, not forged out of the present experience of God. Christians, it is argued, must challenge this parody head-on and show that the faith is relevant and contemporary and modern. The worship of the church should be keeping up with a fast-changing world, not relying on the ways of the past and the inheritance of history.

The task of distinguishing the core characteristics and values of the gospel from the church's own cultural packaging is a critical function not just of missionary theology but of liturgical theology itself. However, it is a complex and difficult one. It is not just a case of trying to remove the kernel of the gospel from the husk of the church. The church, as we maintained in Chapter 4, belongs to the gospel, and some of its practices are necessary for the health of the gospel. Furthermore, the attempt to present the gospel and to embody the gospel in ways that cohere with the culture in which we find ourselves is fraught with danger. How do we prevent the culture seducing the church into a shape and style that tames, even distorts, the gospel? How do we avoid so close an association with the cultural characteristics of this age that we find it even harder to relate to the next? I am not trying to pour cold water on the adaptation and creativity that has been such a mark of evangelical worship over recent decades. I am simply suggesting that liturgy may not be the enemy of missionary engagement with the culture than it is often assumed to be.

Anthropology, for example, indicates that the underlying characteristics of liturgy are integral to human life. The neurons of the brain search for patterns and connections, the ear listens for beauty, the heart is moved by poetry. Children learn by repetition and lovers communicate their feelings in a small repertoire of signs and words. Meals with friends and family have an order and set of conventions. When we get up in the morning we like to do things in a certain way and get irritated if we cannot. Reality television programmes follow a basic and very predicable ritual. Communities cry out to be organized for corporate expressions of grief in times of crisis. Liturgy is not alien to human life. Life is liturgy.

Cultural analysis also warns us against jettisoning liturgy. One of the interesting features of contemporary culture, and evidence of its *post*modernity, is a renewed respect for the old and an appreciation of its wisdom. The cultural fascination with the culturally different which fuels the tourist industry may make the ancient texts and patterns of the liturgy, and their capacity to convey the past into the present, deeply attractive just at the point when evangelicals risk forgetting them.

Finally, the church's preservation and promotion of the orthodoxy of the gospel demonstrates the necessity of liturgy to the mission of the church. The Apostles' Creed was forged in missionary strategy as the baptismal confession of new converts to Christ. The Nicene Creed was hammered out in the struggle with movements within the church that undermined the logic and implications of the gospel: God's creation of the world, Christ's lordship over all things and the Spirit's activity in and through the church. The eucharistic prayers of the church are careful compositions designed to tell the story of salvation, to celebrate the presence of Christ with his people and to anticipate the coming kingdom of God. The prayers of confession, forgiveness and blessing mark out the ways of living that bring joy and wholeness, and which God honours with his presence. The formative function of Christian worship has long been acknowledged. It is expressed in the ancient principle *lex orandi, lex credendi*, which can be fairly paraphrased as 'the way we pray is the way we believe'. Little wonder, then, that Charles Simeon commended those who:

> delight to draw nigh to God, and to pour out their hearts before him: and *this*, not only when some fluent person is exhibiting his gifts, but when the prayers of our Liturgy (better than which were never composed by mortal man) are offered up in the presence of the congregation . . . Whilst they 'draw nigh to God, God will also draw nigh to them', and will 'manifest his acceptance' of them by some special tokens of his love. In former times he often testified his acceptance of the sacrifices by sending fire from heaven, to consume

them upon the altar: now he will do the same, as it were, in a more secret way: he will send his Spirit into the soul as a Spirit of adoption, he will 'shed abroad his love there', and will fill it with an abundance of grace and peace.[4]

A definition of liturgy

Having said a good deal about liturgy, it is time to be more precise about what I actually mean by the word. The Greek word *leitourgia* is derived from *laos* (people) and *ergon* (work). Originally in the classical Greek world it referred to state projects or public works – essentially public acts of service or activities that were for the good of all. Later, when Greek was used to translate the Hebrew Bible, it was applied to the religious activity of worship. It is one of several words that the New Testament uses to describe worship, such as in Acts 13.2 where the Christians in Antioch 'make liturgy (*leitourgounton*) to the Lord'. What is clear is that *leitourgia* did not refer primarily to words, even less prescribed words on a page. We need, therefore, a multi-layered definition of liturgy. This recovery of meaning may help to reaccommodate the concept of liturgy into evangelical life.

Expansively *leitourgia* covers the whole of the church's obedient response to the mercy of God – all of its *communal service* to the God of grace. (In this sense, everything we do in faithful response as members of the body of Christ is liturgy.) Intensively it refers to all that Christ's people do when they come together in that concentrated form of response that we know as worship. (In this sense, every congregation is a liturgical community, gathered to worship, to 'make liturgy before the Lord'.) Technically, it defines how on those occasions we structure and articulate our response to God through actions and words. (In this sense, all acts of worship are liturgical – they are all a *service* – and can be analysed liturgically. A Pentecostal meeting will have its ways of structuring and articulating worship just as surely as will a Coptic Mass.) Narrowly, it refers to words that have become *set* in the practice of the church and are enshrined in a written text that has some form of recognition or authorization. (In this sense most churches will have an element of liturgy – the Lord's Prayer and the Grace, perhaps – but some will have more than others.)

There is another layer to the meaning of liturgy which is somewhat more theological. Drawing on the etymology of the word, much play in liturgical writing is often made of liturgy – in the intensive and in the technical senses – being *the work of the people*. In many ways this has been very healthy and has served basic Reformation principles, rescuing worship from the domain of the clergy and emphasizing the way we are all called to participate fully in worship and to exercise the ministry God has given us within the worshipping community. However, if used too loosely and liberally it can undermine the deeper principles of the Reformation – that *all* we have, including our obedient response to God, is God's gift to us. In fact, the Second Vatican Council, which did so much to reform the liturgy in the Roman Catholic Church, and to influence the revision of the liturgy in other liturgical churches in the West, protects these fundamental principles when it describes liturgy as 'an action of Christ the Priest and of his Body which is the Church'. It is:

> the public worship which our Redeemer as head of the Church renders to the Father, as well as the worship which the community of the faithful renders to its Founder, and through him to the heavenly Father. In short, it is the worship rendered by the Mystical Body of Christ in the entirety of its head and members.[5]

All Christ's people are called to worship, to 'make liturgy', to give obedient, communal service to God, and so it is *the work of the people*. But it is only this because it is first a *gift of the triune God*. By the power of the Spirit through whom Christ offered himself to the Father and by whom Christ was raised from the dead, we are brought into relationship with the ascended Christ, the *leitourgos* (Hebrews 8.2), and we participate in his praise of the Father. The Spirit brings us into communion with Christ who not only 'prays for us as our priest' but 'prays in us as our head', as Augustine said.[6] Through his priestly *leitourgia*, his full and complete service to God on behalf of his people on the cross, we are entitled to serve, 'made worthy to stand in God's presence', permitted to 'offer a sacrifice of praise to God' (Hebrews 13.15). Because he took *our place* and offered for us the service of obedience which was counted as the sufficient sacrifice for sin, we can enter into *his place*, his 'spiritual territory',[7] singing his songs (Hebrews 2.12) and praying his words:

> Our Father in heaven,
> hallowed be your name.
> Your kingdom come . . . (Matthew 6.9)

In this theological sense, liturgy is the ordering of our participation in the trinitarian life of God and of his kingdom. Baptism, therefore, is the primary liturgical event. We are baptized in the name of the Father and of the Son and of the Holy Spirit. By the Spirit we are incorporated into the messianic life and community of Christ and anointed to take part in his messianic work. Through the Spirit we join with Christ in crying '*Abba! Father!*' (Romans 8.15–17) and praying 'your kingdom come' (Matthew 6.10). Baptized 'in the name of the Father and of the Son and of the Holy Spirit' we take our part in that movement to the nations which calls all people to become disciples of the Christ who is with his people 'always, to the end of the age' (Matthew 28.18–20).

By way of example, we can see that baptism clearly involves what I have called the *expansive* and *intensive* meanings of liturgy, but it also includes the *technical* and *narrow* senses of the word. Obedience to Jesus' command to baptize involves *people* (followers of Christ and those who want to join them as followers), *actions* (primarily the use of water) and *words* (some form of confession of Jesus as Lord and use of the trinitarian formulae). Hence, because of Jesus and apostolic practice, baptism is the appointed way of structuring and articulating our response to God through actions and words (my technical meaning of liturgy) by using certain words which have been set in the practice of the church from the earliest time and have the highest authorization (my narrow sense of the word).

There is no reason in principle, therefore, why evangelicals, including charismatics, should shudder at the idea of being liturgical (properly understood). Quite the contrary in fact. We should be ready to receive this gift that the Spirit gives to us through the church, and consider how it can be best used to order and structure our participation in God's life and in God's purposes for the world. As one example of this, the following section explores how the liturgical tradition can help to structure our experience of time and history so that it is ordered towards God's life and purpose.

The structuring of time

The story that the liturgy tells and enacts is the story of God's dealings with the world from creation to consummation.[8] As we saw in the previous chapter, it is a story with a direction, a movement. It is leading somewhere. It has an end, a fulfilment, a *telos*. It is orientated towards the kingdom of God. We find our place within the story when we see that we too are heading towards God's kingdom. As the story's dramatist, the liturgy orientates Christ's people to the coming of God's kingdom on various levels and in many ways.

The liturgy anticipates the kingdom by reordering an assembled group of people and their corporate activity into 'a faithful representation of the kingdom of God'.[9] Sins are forgiven. Wounds are healed. God's word is heard. Human beings of different gender and tribe, social status and age are at peace with each other. All God's people join with angels and archangels to sing 'Holy, Holy, Holy'. We are placed at God's table and eat the bread of heaven (John 6.25–71) and the new wine of the kingdom (Luke 22.18). The gap between heaven and earth is closed. The God of heaven dwells with the people of the earth, and the people of the earth are lifted into the heavenly realm. In this way the liturgy of God's people does not just *speak* of the kingdom, it *shows* the kingdom. It demonstrates what the kingdom will be like. We glimpse the new heaven and the new earth. But of course it is only a glimpse. We taste the new wine of the kingdom but it is only a taste, only a sign. The Spirit is still groaning and sighing in us and in the whole of creation for the coming of the new creation. Christ is still praying within us for the kingdom to come. There is praise but there is also lament: tears as well as joy, absence as well as presence, war in the world – and in the church – as well as peace in the heart. However, the tension and dynamic between the two is itself an impetus to the messianic work of the kingdom. By *showing* us the kingdom through the liturgy, the Spirit sends us out to announce the time of the Lord's favour, to say that '*now* is the day of salvation' (2 Corinthians 6.2), to establish footholds for the coming kingdom in the world and to teach the world to live in the expectation of the coming of the judge of all the earth.

Underlying the liturgical reordering of time in events of worship is the yearly rehearsal of the story of salvation in the liturgical year. God's history is impressed on the months and seasons of the year, reminding us that the repeating cycles of the earth's year are, in fact, one more turn of a wheel in the direction of God's kingdom. Ahead of the world, the church's liturgy begins the year with Advent, setting its sights on the end of the story, confidently asserting its belief that the Saviour will come to judge the earth, banish the evil one and to establish the Lordship of God where 'God himself will be with [his peoples] . . . and death will be no more' (Revelation 21.3–4). The long road that has led to this promise of victory is retold in the Advent readings and then spread before the church in the months ahead. The momentous events of the incarnation when divinity inhabits humanity are re-told at Christmas and we are emboldened to pray that 'we may share in the life of [Christ's] divinity'.[10] Epiphany follows Christmas as the Spirit reveals the extraordinary patience of the God who waits until the time is right to announce the coming of the kingdom, *and* the overwhelming compassion of the God who associates with 'the rejected, the helpless, the despised and the excluded', healing them and allowing them 'to re-enter the worshipping community of Israel'.[11] As Epiphany begins with the child Jesus honoured by the mysterious Magi from strange lands, so it ends with the child Jesus in the arms of the old saint Simeon who prophesies that, before this child becomes 'a light for revelation to the Gentiles', a sword will pierce his mother's heart (Luke 2.28–35). If we are to share in Jesus' glory, like Mary we have to share in his sufferings (Romans 8.17). The kingdom comes with a price, and the full cost is counted over the days of Lent with its tumultuous final and holy week.

Lent is a long journey. It is a route-march over six weeks that begins slowly and gathers pace towards its last two weeks, as the spectre of the cross looms larger. Six weeks to learn and re-learn that discipleship involves discipline, and that feasting in the kingdom begins with fasting in the desert, battling with the forces of evil and the temptations of the flesh. The last week of Lent is the last before Jesus' death. From the fourth century the church's liturgy has re-lived those unrepeatable events, forcing us to see representations of thorns, nails and the terrifying cross so that we may 'survey the Wondrous Cross on which the Prince of Glory died'. All this is so that 'with the eyes of our heart enlightened' we may:

> know what is the hope to which [God] has called [us], what are the riches of his glorious inheritance among the saints, and what is the immeasurable greatness of his power for us who believe, according to the working of his great power. God put this power to work in Christ when he raised him from the dead and seated him in the heavenly places, far above all rule and authority and power and dominion, and above every name that is named, not only in this age but also in the age to come. (Ephesians 1.18–21)

This is the resurrection faith which the liturgy proclaims in the darkness of the early hours of Easter morning, through the weeks of the Easter season to the celebration of Christ's ascension and the week's wait for the renewal of the Spirit on the feast of Pentecost.

In the Anglican tradition, the remainder of the year is bracketed on the one side by Trinity Sunday and on the other by the feast of Christ the King. Trinity Sunday is the theological conclusion to the cycle of the incarnation (which took us from Advent to the Presentation of Christ) and the cycle of redemption (which ran from Lent to Pentecost). The story of God's descent to the earth and the story of humanity's ascent to heaven is the story of the triune God who structures us into his life and orders us for his service. The feast of Christ the King, a relatively recent addition to the calendar, is an *affirmation* at the end of the year that we are called to live under the reign of Christ even in this 'in-between time', and a preparation for the greater feast of Advent when we celebrate the coming of the Son with all the fullness of God's kingdom which 'will have no end'.

The liturgical year is an exercise in *stretched-structuring* of our participation in the life of God and his mission. It reorders our sense of time and reorientates us to the realities that lie behind the course of the world's history. By overprinting the world's time with the story of God's time it imprints upon us the fundamental features of Christian faith and takes us deeper into the life of the Saviour of the world. Running alongside the stretched-structuring of the year is the *concentrated-structuring* of each Sunday celebration. Although every Sunday is a Sunday in the liturgical year and will be flavoured by the stage of the year, each Sunday stands on its own as a concentrated opportunity to encounter the incarnate Christ, to look at his cross, to rejoice in the resurrection, to receive the power of the Spirit and to be sent to proclaim the kingdom. Congregations are not forced to be solemn in Lent or required to rejoice at Easter. There may be a work that God wants to do that overrides the focus of the season. God is not bound by the liturgical year.

But the wisdom into which the Spirit has led the church is that good use of the liturgical calendar enables Christians to be shaped by all the historical realities upon which the gospel is based and helps to form us into a Christ-centred, cross-based, Spirit-filled people.

Sacramental dialogue partners

I have chosen two partners to help us to explore God's use of the material in his saving purposes. One, representing the catholic tradition, is Thomas Aquinas. The other, representing the evangelical tradition, is Martin Luther. In many ways they seem quite extreme choices, and, so it might be thought, unlikely to share much in common or to yield much fruit in dialogue. Certainly, Aquinas is not a usual source for evangelical theology. Architect of the doctrine of transubstantiation, bedfellow of Aristotle and Greek philosophy, constructor of so much of the medieval theology that the Reformation sought to deconstruct, it is little wonder that the 'Angelic Doctor', as he is fondly known in catholic circles, is viewed with suspicion, even antipathy in the evangelical world. Luther, on the other hand, of course, is a hero.[12] His study and teaching of scripture, leading to a paradigmatic conversion experience and an unflinching commitment to the reform of the church, exemplify evangelical confidence in the power of the gospel over the ways of the church. Traditionally, in the catholic tradition Luther has been viewed with just as much suspicion and antipathy as has Aquinas among evangelicals: a destroyer of the unity of the church rather than its reformer; a neglecter of generations of biblical interpretation layering wisdom upon wisdom, rather than a biblical exegete; a single-issue protagonist unwilling to submit to the authority of others and to allow diversity of opinion, rather than an uncompromising contender for the gospel. Stereotypes are seldom accurate, as Roman Catholic theology, to its great credit, has shown with its reassessment of Luther and its increasing appreciation of much of his theology, some evidence of which we saw in Chapter 3. What follows is an attempt to see how far the *catholic* sacramental theology of Thomas Aquinas (especially his baptismal theology), and the *evangelical* theology of Martin Luther support and complement each other. We will then go on to consider how, as suggested in the previous chapter, distinctively *Spirit-orientated* perspectives can help us to hold together the gospel-serving insights of both traditions.

Catholic commitments: securing gift

Although Aquinas' sacramental language has a technical, almost legal feel to it, which makes it sound somewhat impersonal, perhaps off-putting, it is in fact full of the gospel. For example, even though much of his sacramental theology works within a framework of cause and effect, Aquinas is abundantly clear that the cause of the sacraments is *grace* and that the effect of the sacraments is *grace*. God is the 'principal cause of grace' and the grace of God is the 'sufficient cause' of the salvation of the world.[13] More specifically, salvation is caused by the passion of Christ. It is because of the grace of God manifested in Christ and through his death that human sins are forgiven, relationship with God renewed and the new creation established. In this sense, Aquinas' theology stands for the fundamental convictions of *sola gratia* and *sola Christi* that would drive the Reformation 400 years later. At the same time, Aquinas is clear that sacraments are necessary for salvation.[14] This is because 'they produce their effects in virtue of the Passion of Christ which is, in a certain manner, applied . . . through the sacraments'.[15] Here, Aquinas relies on an understanding of instrumentality that differentiates between a 'conjoined instrument', such as the hand of a person ('the principal agent'), and a 'separated instrument' which the principal agent uses by his 'conjoined instrument', such as a tool in the hand. 'Thus it is right', Aquinas argues, 'that the power to bestow salvation should flow from the divinity of Christ through his humanity into the actual sacraments.'[16] Furthermore, this divine instrumentality involves both the material element ('the sign only') of the sacrament, such as water in the case of baptism, and the minister of the sacrament, the person whom God uses to confer the sacrament.[17]

The effect of the sacraments is twofold. First, we receive the grace of God's forgiveness, and second (and consequently), we are in some way qualified and equipped to live lives of worship of God, including the concentration of our relationship with God in the liturgical life of the church. Being fitted for worship involves conferment of a certain character, for in order to be able to live before (and to give praise) to the trinitarian God of holiness, we need to be not only forgiven but also configured into the character of Christ: 'it is manifest that sacramental character is specifically the character of Christ, seeing that a configuration to his priesthood is imparted to the faithful through sacramental characters which are nothing else than a certain kind of participations in the priesthood of Christ deriving from Christ himself'.[18] This character, in fact, is only actually communicated by three of the seven signs which Aquinas, in line with medieval theology, defined as sacraments: baptism, confirmation and orders. Baptism and confirmation provide the incorporation into Christ and the strengthening of the Spirit that are then lived out and lived into through the other sacraments. Orders simply provide the mechanism for the 'handing on' of the sacraments.[19]

The whole structure of Aquinas' thought is rooted in an incarnational understanding of God which accepts that God deals with the world through its own created realities. It accepts that because God assumes the humanity of Christ into his divine life, God also uses the things of this world (for example, water and people) as tools in the hand of the risen Christ, just as surely as Jesus used the fish and bread of the child and the actions of the disciples to reveal his glory and to feed those who came to him. It is a structure of thought designed to ensure that Christian existence is securely set within the reliable activity of God: it identifies what instruments God uses and how God uses them so that it can be confident of the result. It is a structure of thought that looks back to the objective action of God in the past, accepts the objective action of God in the present and looks ahead to the objective fulfilment of all God's promises in the future: the sacraments are 'at once commemorative of that which has gone before, namely the Passion of Christ, and demonstrative of that which is brought about in us through the Passion of Christ, namely grace, and prognostic, that is, a foretaste of future glory'.[20]

This is not all that Aquinas says. Indeed, it is somewhat misleading to isolate Aquinas' teaching on the objectivity of God's action through the sacraments from his equally strong insistence on the word and faith, but I do so in order to identify the fundamental instinct of the catholic tradition before and after Aquinas: that God has made himself available and accessible through Christ in the life and action of the church.

Evangelical commitments: securing response

'What is the good, then, of writing so much about baptism and yet not teaching . . . faith in the promise?', wrote Martin Luther in 1520 in his *Babylonian Captivity of the Church*.[21] As we shall see later, this was not a charge that can be fairly levelled at Aquinas himself, but it was certainly how Luther viewed the church's sacramental theology and practice as he had received it. Aquinas' proper stress on the objectivity of God's action in the sacraments (an emphasis which, as we shall see later, Luther also wanted to affirm), had become reduced – as far as Luther and the other Reformers were concerned – to a mechanical system and an arithmetical equation which appeared to require only that the sacraments were properly performed and that certain minimal conditions were met.[22] 'Sacraments do what they do not by their own power, but the power of faith, without which they do nothing at all',[23] Luther argued. Although he accepted that everything that God gives to us is mediated in some way, and that God uses 'vicarious instruments', Luther wanted to secure the personal realities of the gospel and to demonstrate that the sacraments find their meaning in the God who speaks words of gracious promise and invites human beings to hear them and to believe them.[24] 'On no account ever consider the word and the water apart, or separate them', he said.[25] The sacraments are expressions of the word. They are situations in which the word is spoken. They are presentations of the divine promise and they require response. 'Where there is a divine promise, there everyone must stand on his own feet; his own personal faith is demanded.'[26] Luther's guiding biblical text for the interpretation of baptism is Mark 16.16: 'The one who believes and is baptized will be saved; but the one who does not believe will be condemned.'[27] It is only as we respond to the word spoken to us in baptism – the word of grace, of forgiveness, of reconciliation with God – that we receive what baptism signifies: 'everything depends on faith'.[28]

Catholic and evangelical commitments combined

Although Aquinas does not speak of faith with Luther's passion and energy, he is in no doubt as to the necessity of faith to the full appropriation of baptism. This is evident in at least five places in his teaching on the sacraments and on baptism in his *Summa Theologiae*.

The first place is in Aquinas' affirmation of Augustine's fundamental principle of sacramental theology – that it is the adding of the word to the sign that makes it a sacrament; hence 'baptism is consecrated by the words of the gospel'.[29] For Aquinas (as it was for Augustine) this is not simply a liturgical requirement to ensure a sacrament's validity (that is, the form of words that needs to be applied to the matter and action of the sacrament), though it is certainly that. Rather, it is a theological conviction that the effectuality of any action of the church derives from the proclamation of God's word. Much follows from this principle, as the following will show.

Aquinas' second, and closely related discussion about the role of faith is when he examines the faithful figures of Israel's history. Aquinas is clear that their salvation lay in the *future* passion of Christ, which, inasmuch as our Old Testament forebears placed their faith in the gracious, saving purposes of God, was the cause of their salvation. Hence, he can say that 'the Fathers of old were justified by faith in the Passion of Christ as we ourselves are'.[30] Although, unlike Luther, Aquinas is prepared to locate a devolved, mediated power to the sacraments, he is equally insistent that it is faith that receives all that God gives through them: 'Thus the power designed to remove sins inherent in the sacraments works chiefly through faith in Christ's passion.'[31] Hence, he would have been quite happy to say with Luther that 'my faith does not make the baptism, but receives baptism'.[32]

The third place where Aquinas makes critical space for faith is in his discussion of 'the water, the blood and the Spirit'. Here Aquinas, making use of Cyprian, the fourth-century bishop, argues that the effects of baptism can be realized in a person independently of water baptism. A person can be incorporated into Christ and conformed to his character by martyrdom (the baptism of blood) or by 'the power of the Holy Spirit . . . when the heart is moved by the Holy Spirit to believe in and love God to repent of one's sins' (the baptism of the Spirit, or more literally, the baptism of the 'blowing').[33] Baptism remains necessary for Aquinas, but baptism is not defined simply by the pouring of water but by its *spiritual effect*, which may be present through active faith, even when the sacramental sign is absent.

The fourth place where Aquinas' estimation of the role of faith in the sacramental process can be found is in his discussion of the possibility of salvation without baptism. For those who have not been baptized and who have no desire to be baptized, their fate is sealed. They are not saved because they are 'not incorporated into Christ through whom alone salvation is possible'.[34] However, those who *desire* baptism with an active faith have been 'reborn in the heart' and inwardly sanctified, even though they have not been through the water of baptism itself.[35] Here, and in the discussion about the baptism of blood and of the Spirit, Aquinas is merely applying a general principle of medieval sacramental theology that God's 'power is not restricted to visible sacraments'.[36]

Finally, the distinction alluded to above between sacramental validity and effectuality allows Aquinas to underline the necessity of faith to the sacramental process. He describes situations in which a person has been properly baptized but where the effects of baptism have not been received because of sin or the intention to sin. He is clear that baptism 'cannot confer salvation' in such a case and will only do so when the person truly repents. In other words, a sacrament may be *valid* but not *efficacious*.

Aquinas is glad to call baptism 'the sacrament of faith'[37] and would agree with Luther that it calls for the continual exercise of faith in Christ so that its gift of forgiveness – through the putting to death of our sins on the cross and the gift of new, redeemed life through the resurrection of Christ – can be personally and fully appropriated. 'Thus,' said Luther, 'you have been once baptized in the sacrament, but you need continually to be baptized by faith, continually to die and continually to live.'[38] Aquinas would have said 'Amen.'

Not long after Luther had unleashed the zeal for reform long latent in the life of the church, the Reformation began to take a turn that caused him great concern. It is a tendency to which evangelical faith and life has remained prone. It arises from the logic of faith. When talking about the Eucharist, Luther himself had proclaimed, 'Therefore I can hold mass every day, indeed, every hour, for I can set the words of Christ before me and with them feed and strengthen my faith as often as I choose. This is truly spiritual eating and drinking.'[39] Herein lies the evangelical dilemma. If we are saved, justified, sanctified by faith in the word of the gospel (that Christ's body was given for us on the cross), why do we need such outward forms as baptism and the Lord's Supper? Surely the word is sufficient? What is the need of the sacraments? Only recently, an ordinand – a deeply committed and spiritual person – came to see me to ask exactly that question. 'I just don't get it,' he said, 'why do we make such a big thing of the Communion?'[40]

Actually, as we have seen, it was not a problem of Luther's making. It was implicit in Aquinas' theology which allowed for the effects of a sacrament to be received by faith without a drop of water touching the body. After looking at how Luther addressed the problem, we will see what help Aquinas is able to add. In the next chapter we will see how John Wesley responded to exactly the same issue in his dealings with the Moravians.

Luther appealed to the freedom of God's choice. In his treatise, On the Councils and the Church, completed in 1539, Luther identified seven 'holy possessions' which God has given to the church and by which we can recognize the presence of 'the holy Christian people'. 'The holy word of God', the gospel preached (Luther calls it 'the external word') is the first of these, and the one on which everything else depends. Baptism is the second, and 'whenever [we] see this sign [we] may know that the church, of the holy Christian people, must surely be present'.[41] Earlier we quoted Luther chiding the more radical Reformers, saying,

> if God were to bid you to pick up a straw or to pluck out a feather with the command, order, and promise that thereby you would have forgiveness of all sin, grace, and eternal life, should you not accept this joyfully and gratefully, and cherish, praise, prize, and esteem that straw and that feather as a higher and holier possession than heaven and earth? . . . [whereas] you do not regard the water of baptism, the bread and wine, . . . the spoken word, and the laying on of man's hands for the forgiveness of sin as such holy possessions [when] God himself wishes to be effective and wants them to be his water, word, hand, bread, and wine, by means of which he wishes to sanctify and save you in Christ.[42]

Essentially, Luther's argument is that God has chosen to accompany his word of promise with certain signs which, by virtue of God's free choice, become the place in which God's word can be found, given and received. Luther's *Larger Catechism*, published ten years earlier, made an impassioned defence of water baptism (including infant baptism) and was extremely critical of 'our wiseacres, with their modern ideas, who make out that faith alone will save us'.[43] He entirely affirmed that 'nothing works in us but faith'.[44] But faith, he argued, 'must have something to believe, that is, to which it can cling, on which it can stand and rest'.[45] Baptism, he contended, provides this because it 'embodies God's word and command' and has 'God's name attached to it'.[46] God has chosen to fix his word of forgiveness and adoption to baptism. Therefore, Luther commended others to do as he did – 'to cling to the water', to write on the dust of the table when the devil is tempting one to despair 'I am baptized'[47] and, 'to know that baptism is in force all through life, even until death, yes . . . even to the Last Day'.[48]

Aquinas would very much have agreed with Luther that water baptism is an ordained sign, given by Christ himself, and that therefore it is a non-negotiable reality in the ministry of the church. Furthermore, although the priority of the word and the receptivity of faith must be acknowledged, baptism is God's ordinary means of initiating people into Christ. Therefore, although we may say that God is not bound by the sacraments, we are. *We* cannot choose to bypass the ordinary means of God's activity, even if *God* does so from time to time. Beyond this, Aquinas would appeal to three other theological realities to explain why and how God uses baptism for his saving purposes.

The first is to do with human nature, especially fallen human nature. We are embodied beings who, by definition, live and breathe in the created order. Therefore all of our knowing is reached 'deductively through [our] experience of physical and sensible realities'.[49] We make sense of things through things, and God helps us to perceive and receive his salvation through the visible and tangible realities of life. Although he recognizes that our sin has given us an 'an affection for physical things' (which has the potential for damage) and intensified our proneness 'to involve [ourselves] with physical things' (again in a way that could be unhelpful), Aquinas' fundamental point is that God relates to us 'in a manner appropriate to [our] own nature'.[50]

Aquinas' second – and main – rationale for God's use of the sacramental lies in the incarnational decision of God. As we saw earlier, God chooses to assume humanity in order to reach humanity. God's redemptive identification with the created order extends to the point at which God 'conjoins' humanity to the divine nature of the eternal Son so that God can truly and fully reach, touch and transform humanity. Jesus Christ, the incarnate Son, becomes the primordial sacrament, as twentieth-century theology was later to affirm. Jesus is the one 'in whom all things hold together', the fundamental *symbol* where divinity and humanity meet and from whom flow all the actions of the church which bring human beings face to face with the grace of God.[51]

Third, again as we saw earlier, God's reach through the incarnation involves the use of instruments by which the divine humanity – the ultimate instrumentality of God – acts. Baptism is one of these instruments in the hands of the risen Christ enacted through the ministry of the church, like a saw to a carpenter. In this way baptism does not just illustrate the washing away of sins, it *effects what it figuratively expresses*.[52] It is an effectual sign of grace. Luther was somewhat suspicious of such language and preferred to avoid anything that could imply an autonomous power to a sacrament independent of the word on which it relies and the faith which it demands. Anglican sacramental theology, however, has been quite comfortable with describing baptism and Eucharist as *effectual signs*, which effect what they signify.[53] It does so, in line with Aquinas, within an understanding of the need for the sacraments to be 'rightly received' in order for us to share in the blessing that they are designed to give. It is simply a way of following through Luther's basic principle that 'my faith does not make the baptism, but receives baptism'.[54] The gospel is to be received through faith in the word of grace which is embodied in and applied through the sign of grace. Liturgically,

Anglicanism, in common with other traditions, expresses the divine instrumentality at work in the sacraments by the notion of consecration. The water of baptism and the bread and wine of the Eucharist are set apart and 'sanctified by God's word and prayer' (1 Timothy 4.5) in the belief that God chooses to use these appointed signs as means – at this moment in his economy of grace – to *effect* his purposes regardless of the immediate *affect* they may have on the faith of the participants. When we turn to the Eucharist in the next chapter, we shall see that the concept of consecration is necessary in order to secure the appointed role of the sacrament in the encounter with the risen Christ.

Catholic and evangelical secured in the Spirit

We have seen how, in their different ways, Aquinas and Luther were theologically committed both to the reality of God's gift in the sacraments and to the necessity of our faithful response to the gift of God. Aquinas' teaching about the application of grace through the sacraments, and Luther's language about God's promise being attached to the sacraments, were different ways of preserving the objectivity of God's action in the sacramental life of the church. Similarly, Aquinas' assumption that the grace freely given is to be freely received, and Luther's insistence that the promise divinely uttered is to be believed in human hearts, are complementary ways of promoting the inter-personal realities of God's work which require a subjective response from those with whom God acts.

However, the careful balance of their theology has not always been maintained by the traditions which have been inspired by them. I can remember many baptism services in evangelical churches where the point has been made, and then underlined, and then made again, that it is faith that saves, not water. So careful has the minister been to avoid any hint that mere participation in the physical act of water baptism is sufficient in itself, that the gift and promise of God's presence and action *by means of this sacrament* have been thoroughly undermined. To be fair, though, this sacramental caution has often been fuelled by experiences of forms of church life that appear to downplay the call to repent and believe. At their most suspicious, evangelicals fear that the catholic tradition has constructed a complex sacerdotal and sacramental machinery that overrides the relational and covenantal basis of God's dealings with humankind. Times have moved on since evangelical Anglicans took catholic Anglicans to court over these matters as they did in the nineteenth century, but many of the instincts remain, to the detriment of both traditions.

One reason why the balance of gift and response, so carefully weighted in the best of medieval and Reformation theology, was so easily disturbed, may be because of a relative neglect of the role of the Spirit in the sacramental process. Aquinas and Luther both rooted their sacramental theology in the doctrine of the incarnation, making little use of the doctrine of the Holy Spirit. This is not to suggest that they, or those who followed them, denied the involvement of the Spirit in sacramental activity. It is simply to register that the nature of the Spirit's involvement was assumed rather than expounded. For example, although Luther says that God will work through the sacraments 'with the Holy Spirit',[55] he does not explore the way in which the Spirit works. The following section is a brief attempt, with the help of some biblical images of the Spirit, to show how an emphasis on the Holy Spirit in sacramental theology enables one to affirm both the activity of God and the receptivity of humanity in and through materiality.

Sweeping wind and breath of life.

The Spirit is the wild wind (*ruach*, in Hebrew) sweeping over the 'void and darkness' bringing the creation into being as gift of the triune God, the breath (*ruach* again) of the word that God speaks (Genesis 1.1–4). God breathes this divine breath of life into human beings and they have the capacity to receive life, to inhabit the creation, find their place within it, and to interpret the world as God's gift, discerning how God would have them flourish in this home he has made for them (Genesis 2.7). As God's breath, penetrating the cosmos with divine life and energy, the Spirit sustains all things in life and keeps them from returning to dust, to the nothingness from which they came (Psalm 104.29–30).

Cloud of presence and gift of speech.

God's presence through the Spirit to all things is identified and intensified in his presence to his chosen people. The divine presence in the Spirit becomes visible as God delivers his people from the forces of violence and destruction (Exodus 14.19), as God leads them to the land of his promise (Exodus 16.10), as God reveals his law of life to them (Exodus 19.20) and as God dwells with his people, speaking to his servant Moses and guiding Israel through the vicissitudes of the wilderness and the opportunities of the new land. This is the cloud of God's presence. Through the Spirit by whom God spoke the world into being, God makes his presence known in the cloud, which both reveals and veils. Under the sign of the cloud, Moses speaks with God face to face, and as the greatest of the prophets (Deuteronomy 34.10–12) demonstrates the intimacy of the prophet's relationship with God and the availability of God's word. The prophet can be close enough to God to feel his breath and hear his word. The God who is so utterly other that his presence consumes those who are not qualified to be near him, and whose thoughts are so far beyond the intellectual capacities of created beings to be wholly out of reach, speaks through his Spirit to his appointed servants and gives to his people the ears to hear and the mind to understand the word of the Lord.

Anointing gift and power of truth.

The identification of God's presence through the Spirit and its intensification among the people of Israel comes to a point of ultimate concentration in the brooding of the Spirit over the young woman Mary and in the incarnation of the Son in and through her. The Spirit who brings Jesus to birth anoints him for ministry, speaks, heals and delivers through him, leads him to the cross and is the power by which he is raised from the dead. There is a double aspect to this anointing. Not only does the divine Spirit act *through* the humanity of Jesus, the Spirit acts *on* the humanity of Jesus, opening it up to the full potential of human life, shaping, teaching, fashioning it into the full stature of God's intention to humanity, equipping it for the moral and spiritual struggle with the legacy of the fall and the forces of evil – a battle that reaches its fulfilment and victory in his Spirit-enabled obedience on the cross. The Spirit at work in and through Jesus is present and active around Jesus, opening people up to the eschatological life of the kingdom that Jesus is bringing. Mary says 'Yes' to God. John follows the Messiah. Nicodemus wonders at the new life of the Spirit. The materially poor and the poor in spirit are actually the most receptive, the most ready to rely on the power of God's Spirit, knowing the poverty of their own resources. The anointed Jesus promises this Spirit to his disciples and assures them that he will lead them into truth of all that he is and all that God will do through him.

Tongues of fire and rushing wind.

The promised Spirit comes, and the anointing of Jesus to speak God's word and heal with God's power rests on all his followers in the upper room. Jewish pilgrims and traders from across the nations hear the word of God *in their own tongue* through the interplay between the Spirit of God and the physicality of human voices and ears. The very ordinary followers of Jesus say and do extraordinary things as the Spirit of God transforms them into a body of people empowered to act as the body of the anointed Christ. Peter the betrayer becomes Peter the preacher. He interprets the story of Christ, people are 'cut to the heart' and call out 'What should we do?' (Acts 2.37).

And what is the answer? 'Repent, and be baptized every one of you . . . *so that* your sins may be forgiven; and you will receive the gift of the Holy Spirit' (Acts 2.38). The Spirit's ecology of gift and response is the culture in which we have lived since the first days of our faith.

Three principles for sacramental theology emerge from this short exploration of the work of the Spirit in creation, Israel, Jesus and the church. The first is double-sided. Because of the way we have been created by the word of God through his Spirit we cannot, and are not meant to, reach beyond our human, embodied, material existence. Our relationality, intellectuality and spirituality are bound to our physicality.[56] Hence, God's dealings with humanity through his Spirit are always mediated by the material of creation. Nevertheless, because God has bound himself to the creation through his Word and Spirit, we deal *directly* with God in and through the created means that God uses to relate to us. This is what is meant by *mediated immediacy*. It is the real and personal presence of God that we meet in and through created, material reality. The world is the arena of God's gift.

The second principle is that the Spirit who brings the presence of God to the creation works with what has been created in order that it may *receive* what has been given to it. However, the creative action of God through the Spirit involves giving to the creation space to be the creation. Or to put it another way, God allows creation to occupy the space that is not God. It is given a genuine freedom to be itself. We know that this freedom is abused and that there is a persistent spoiling of creation through sin and evil infecting the smallest cells to the most sophisticated structures of society, with the result that some materiality fails to receive all the life that is offered. Cain spills Abel's blood. Sodom, Nineveh, Babylon become cities of shame. Job's skin is covered in sores. One criminal repents, the other jeers. Although the Spirit of God enables us to confess that Jesus is Lord, and our faith is itself a gift of the grace of God, sinning against the Holy Spirit remains a possibility. The gift can be rejected, the promise ignored, the Lover shunned, the Saviour mocked and the waiting Father made to wait for ever.

The third principle is that because we are made by the Spirit to inhabit a material world, the world is our field of meaning about God and an environment of encounter with God. Our knowledge and experience of God cannot bypass the structures of our physicality and materiality, even though they transcend them. 'The world is', as Oliver Davies puts it, 'a divine text, made up of signifying matter, and we are the creatures who are hosted at its core, as interpreters animated by the Spirit, and as agents whose own body life has been taken up and shaped by divine creativity.'[57] Within the world's 'signifying matter' are particular signs that God uses to reach and to relate to his people. Among the many signs hallowed by God's use, from ancient Jewish past to contemporary Christian practice, are the signs raised by Jesus' command into the realm of the Spirit's redemptive work, bringing the life of the new creation into the presence of the old – water, bread and wine. Here, in the dominical sacraments, God's gracious gift of life in Christ is *really given* by the Spirit to be *really received* through the Spirit.

It is a powerful thing when sacramental practice is enlivened with the realities of the gospel through the dynamic of the Spirit. Michael Heras, the senior priest of a large Roman Catholic parish in the United States, describes the difference that the Alpha course – with its evangelical emphasis on what one parishioner called the *reachability* of Christ, and its charismatic stress on the *activity* of the Spirit – made to his parish:

> Our church has changed completely. It's God, God, God, grace, infusion, life. Our people have fallen in love. They're in love with the person of Jesus and his Holy Spirit as the gift of the Father. Beforehand, some of the people were in love with the idea of being in love with Jesus – a big difference. That's the problem with sacramentalism sometimes. People get caught up with lighting the candles, making a sign of the cross, kneeling, standing, genuflecting, doing this and that

and then getting caught up with this whole drama instead of thinking, 'Why are we doing that?' Now it has so much meaning and people are openly weeping at the Stations of the Cross and just get lost in adoration and weeping at Mass.[58]

Here, participation in the sacramental life of the church has become infused with the experience of the gospel through the *gift-giving* and *response-enabling* work of the Spirit. This is the sort of combination of catholic and evangelical commitments which, as I have argued, can be held together by the unifying work of the Spirit. It is the spiritual fullness that John Valton experienced during the evangelical Revival when he received Holy Communion and described in a letter to John Wesley that he had a 'gracious season . . . for the Lord was in the means'.[59]

8

Breaking Bread

Happy is the Christian who can say, 'I scarcely need that
memorial'. But I am not such an one; and I fear, my brethren,
that the most of us need to be reminded by that bread and wine,
that Jesus died; and need to be reminded by the eating and the
drinking of the same, that he died for us.
Charles Spurgeon

Introduction

This chapter differs in form from most of the others. Rather
than comparing evangelical and catholic emphases, and then
seeing how far they can be united in a Spirit-focused approach,
it sets out how the thought and practice of two theological
figures achieved a remarkable level of integration, and remain
an inspiration for the shape of evangelical life being proposed
by this book. One of them – John Wesley – will come as no
surprise. He has already made an appearance at several points
so far. The other is Charles, his brother. They shared much in
common: a similar upbringing in a large clergy family; membership of the Holy Club while at Oxford, with its commitment to
disciplined discipleship; ordination in the Church of England;
disappointment in a mission to Georgia; evangelical conversion
within days of each other in May 1738, one through reading
Luther on Galatians and the other through hearing Luther's
commentary on Romans being read; then an extraordinary
ministry of preaching, writing, hymnwriting and leadership in
the Revival which swept the nation in the eighteenth century. It
is true that John preached more than Charles and that Charles
wrote more hymns than John. It is also true that John, though
the younger of the two, became the senior theological partner

in the fraternal ministry and was not afraid of criticizing some of Charles' hymns, occasionally distancing himself from them. But, for the reasons I shall explain in a moment, when it comes to the heart of their eucharistic theology, they wrote and sang with one voice.

My method in this chapter will be even more specific. I am going to concentrate on two texts – the *Hymns of the Lord's Supper* and the theological Preface published with the Hymns in the first edition of 1745 and then in the eight editions that followed.[1] The Preface is an unusual document: 'The Christian Sacrament and Sacrifice, Extracted from Dr. Brevint'. Daniel Brevint was an Anglican exile during the period of the Commonwealth in the mid-seventeenth century. While living in France and working as a tutor among the French nobility, he wrote an essay for his pupils designed to take them beyond the eucharistic controversies of the time and into the heart of sacramental faith and experience. The result, according to the Methodist scholar Ernst Rattenbury, was 'a beautiful devotional booklet, positive in its sacramental and evangelical teaching'.[2] Although not very well known at the time, it was spotted by Daniel Waterland (who wrote what became the eighteenth century's standard Anglican study of the Eucharist). Waterland was keen for Brevint's tract to be 'reprinted for the honour of God and the benefit of the Church'.[3] It was the Wesleys who took up the challenge.

They did more than reprint it, though. John carefully edited it, reducing it by two-thirds and reworking some of Brevint's wording when he thought it was wanting. Charles used it to structure and to inspire the hymnbook. He followed the main structure of Brevint's text, albeit contracting his original eight sections into six, and turned many of Brevint's images, expressions and words – especially from the prayers with which he concludes each of the sections – into poetry and song. It is quite likely that John wrote a small number of the Hymns and probable that a few of them came from other sources. But most of them were Charles's remixing of Brevint's text into a powerful collection of hymns, rich in theology and passionate in emotion. They were published in the name of John and Charles

Wesley, so it is clear that the Hymns as well as the Preface had been through John's theological sieve and that they represented his views on the sacrament as much as Charles'.

I have chosen to base this chapter on close readings of the *Hymns of the Lord's Supper* and of the Wesley–Brevint Preface for a number of reasons. First, the texts are an archetypal example of the Wesleys' methodology. They were not theological revolutionaries. Just as in their evangelistic ministries they sought to revive the life of the Spirit in the church, so in their theology they aimed to revive the great spiritual tradition of the church. Essentially they would have understood tradition in the way we defined it in Chapter 2 – as the biblical heart of the faith which had been passed on by the patristic church. But they were happy to interact with all of those whom they believed were engaging responsibly with the biblical tradition, whether medieval writers, magisterial Reformers, English dissenters, contemporary continental Roman Catholics or High-Church Anglicans. They were willing to *receive* this theological tradition and then *rework* it according to the spiritual dynamics which were themselves being revived in their time – the power of the gospel to convict and convert, the work of the Spirit to change individuals and reform society, and the calling of the church to minister the gospel and to be the authentic community of the gospel.

My second reason for choosing the texts is because they show the fruitful results of this sort of method. They give us an example of what can happen when instincts about the reality of Christ's presence and activity in the life of the church that lie at the core of catholic faith, are brought together with convictions about the cross and of faith that form the centre of evangelical experience, and with insights about the work of the Spirit that are at the root of pentecostal life. In this way they demonstrate a distinctively evangelical and authentically charismatic form of eucharistic spirituality. Through some generous peppering with other quotations from notable evangelical sources, I hope to show that although their texts have been neglected in evangelical circles, and the vitality of their gospel-serving and Spirit-filled eucharistic devotion has been lost in evangelical culture, the Wesleys' experience of Christ in the Lord's Supper is by no means unique in evangelical history.

The third reason I have chosen to focus on the Wesleys' eucharistic theology, and on these texts in particular, is because they anticipate many of the considerable agreements in the eucharistic theology arrived at in the last third of the twentieth century. Their insistence on the reality of Christ's presence in the Eucharist (while stressing the role of faith in any encounter with Christ), the place they give to the Spirit in communicating Christ's presence through bread and wine (while avoiding static or mechanical categories of sacramental transaction), and their willingness to explore and to restore the sacrificial dimension of the sacrament (while celebrating the uniquely saving character of Christ's death) gave their theology an empathy and energy that was ahead of their time.

All of this is not to say that the Preface and the Hymns are beyond criticism. From an evangelical perspective there are some points where they sail very close to the wind, especially in a few of the Hymns. But it is to recognize that the Wesleys achieved a remarkable co-inherence of the fundamental themes of gospel, church and Spirit in their eucharistic theology and practice. As in other areas of their ministry, they demonstrated not only the theological dynamic of an ecclesially orientated and Spirit-enlivened form of evangelicalism, but also its spiritual vitality in lives revived by the power of the gospel in the life of the church through the work of the Spirit.

The Christian Sacrament and Sacrifice and the Hymns of the Lord's Supper

'The Importance of Well Understanding the Nature of this Sacrament.'

John shortens Brevint's opening section considerably. The concise result is worth quoting in full because it sets out some of the main themes that are developed in the rest of the work.

The Sacrament ordained by Christ the night before He suffered, which St *Paul* calls The Lord's Supper, is without doubt one of the greatest mysteries of godliness, and the most solemn feast of the Christian religion. At the holy Table the people meet to worship God, and God is present to meet and bless the people. Here we are in a special manner invited to offer up to God our souls, our bodies, and whatever we can *give*: and God offers to us the Body and Blood of the Son, and all the other blessings which we have need to *receive*. So that the holy Sacrament, like the ancient Passover, is a great mystery, consisting both of *Sacrament*, and *Sacrifice*; that is, of the religious *service* which the people owe to God, and of the full *salvation* which God hath promised to the people.

How careful then should all Christians be to understand what so nearly concerns both their happiness and their duty! It was on this account that the devil, from the very beginning, has been so busy about this Sacrament, driving people either to make it a *false God*, or an empty ceremony. So much the more, let all who have either piety towards God, or any care of their own souls, so manage their devotions as to avoid superstition on the one hand, and profaneness on the other.[4]

From the outset we can see how John both affirms evangelical principles and extends them to include catholic emphases. First, he defines the Lord's Supper as one of the 'greatest of mysteries of godliness' and as 'the most solemn feast of the Christian religion' in which there is a 'special manner' of spiritual activity. Second, he describes the Eucharist as a sacrament in which we receive 'the Body and Blood of the Son, and all the other benefits [of] which we have need', and as a sacrifice in which we 'offer up to God our souls, our bodies and whatever we can *give*': both a testimony to our salvation from God and a service we render to God. Third, he exhorts his readers to treat the Eucharist as neither 'a *false God*' nor 'an empty ceremony'. Thus, John introduces some of the perennial questions of eucharistic theology, questions that for evangelical theology have a particular sharpness. Does the Eucharist involve a unique communication with God in an unequalled level of intensity? What is the manner of this communication, and what level of mutuality between God and the Church does it involve? How should we approach the Eucharist, what should be our level of expectation and what implications does this have for the way it is celebrated? The Wesleys' answers to these critical sacramental questions will unfold as we work through the text.

'Concerning the Sacrament, as it is a memorial of the Sufferings and Death of Christ.'

In a way reminiscent of Aquinas,[5] Wesley begins his analysis of the sacramental character of the Eucharist by referring to its simultaneous orientation to the past, present and future, aligning a verb and a noun to each. The sacrament represents the past sufferings of Christ, of which it is a memorial. It conveys the 'present graces' of Christ's sufferings, of which it is a means. It assures us of future glory, of which it is a pledge. This section of the Preface explores the first of these dimensions – the sacramental representation, or 'memorial' of Christ's passion. Three of the Hymns will help us to see how the Wesleys developed this theme. We begin with 'Come, to the supper come'.

> Come, to the supper come,
> Sinners, there is still room;
> Every soul may be His guest,
> Jesus gives the general word;
> Share the monumental feast,
> Eat the supper of your Lord.

> In this authentic sign
> Behold the stamp Divine:
> Christ revives His sufferings here,
> Still exposes them to view;
> See the Crucified appear,
> Now believe He died for you.   (8)[6]

This short hymn has a strangely familiar ring to evangelical ears. It is familiar because it challenges sinners to believe that Christ died for them. It is strange because it casts familiar evangelistic language into a more unfamiliar sacramental shape. Paul's contention that 'as often as you eat this bread and drink this cup, you proclaim the Lord's death until he comes' (1 Corinthians 11.26) is taken with the utmost seriousness. The Lord's Supper is the 'authentic sign' of Christ's saving death. It has 'the stamp Divine' of God's purpose imprinted upon it, so that participants may 'see the Crucified appear' and 'now believe he died for [them]'. The hymn sings what the Preface says: the sacrament bears the 'Divine appointment, and the express design that God has to revive hereby, and to expose to our senses, Christ's sufferings as if they were present *now*'.[7] The Preface makes several parallels with the Passover commemorations to underline both the abiding character of past, historical acts of redemption, and the representational function of liturgical symbolism. In the spiritual dynamic of sacramental remembrance, Christ 'invite(s) us to His sacrifice', not of course to repeat what cannot (by definition as an historical event) be repeated, but to encounter and appropriate the eternal effects of the saving action of the triune God in human history.[8]

Although the Wesleys' vivid use of the representative character of the Eucharist may seem somewhat alien to contemporary evangelical spirituality, it is by no means out of line with the classic tradition of evangelical practice. A century before, the Puritan leader John Preston (drawing on Augustine's foundation), succinctly said, 'The Gospel [meaning the preached word] is that of an offer of Christ to all that will take him for remission of sins. In the sacrament there is an offer of Christ to us. The Gospel presents it to us under audible words, and the sacrament presents it to us under visible figures.'[9] This was very much the experience of John Bunyan, the Puritan preacher and the writer of *Pilgrim's Progress*, who testified, 'I discerned the Lord's body as broken for my sins, and that his precious blood hath been shed for my transgressions.'[10] Later, Isaac Watts wrote one of the few hymns that remain in the evangelical consciousness, 'When I survey the Wondrous Cross'. One can see why this remarkable hymn, originally composed for Communion, caused Charles Wesley to say that he would have gladly given up all his other hymns to have written it.

> See from His head, His hands, His feet,
> Sorrow and love flow mingled down!
> Did e'er such love and sorrow meet,
> Or thorns compose so rich a crown?

> His dying crimson, like a robe,
> Spreads o'er His body on the tree;
> Then I am dead to all the globe,
> And all the globe is dead to me.

Here we see the same ease with a dynamic liturgical symbolism which the Wesleys showed. In common with Isaac Watts, Matthew Henry and later evangelical writers such as John Newton, the Lord's Supper is 'expressive'.[11] It displays the suffering and death of Christ, drawing participants close to them (placing us 'near th'accursed wood'), giving us sight of the cross (so that we may 'see him bound and bruis'd and slain'), inviting us to respond to the saving reality of the passion, calling us – whether believers or not – to put our faith in Christ's suffering and death (to 'believe He died for [us]').[12] So powerful has been the dramatic effect of the sacrament that tears have not been uncommon in evangelical celebrations of it. Charles exhorted worshippers to 'Weep . . . with tears of humble love'.[13] John Newton sang:

> Let me dwell on Golgotha,
> Weep and love my life away!
> While I see him on the tree
> Weep, and bleed, and die for me![14]

And Charles Spurgeon regularly wept when he administered the sacrament.

The Wesleys' conviction that the sacrament could be a 'converting ordinance' was born out of their experience of conversions taking place as the Lord's Supper was celebrated.[15] Although not a traditional part of evangelical evangelistic practice, there is no doubt that the sacrament has played a critical part in the journey of many people to an evangelical faith. Particularly noteworthy are the leading evangelical figures of Charles Simeon and Daniel Wilson, both of whom found Christ breaking through to them at the breaking of the bread and themselves reaching out to him in saving faith. 'At the Lord's table I had the sweetest access to God through my blessed Saviour',[16] wrote Charles Simeon after his first Communion; and Daniel Wilson said in similar vein of his own experience, 'On last Sunday morning, I took that solemn and important step, and the Lord was with me. Never did I enjoy so much the presence of my dear Redeemer, as I have since that time.'[17]

'Come, to the Supper come' has allowed us to examine the *affective aspect* of the Lord's Supper – its capacity to stimulate the senses, inspire the imagination and move the faith of the worshippers. The next hymn I have chosen from this section changes the angle and focuses on God the Father, moving the attention to the influence of the Eucharist on God himself.

Father, hear the blood of Jesus
Speaking in Thine ears above;
From Thy wrath and curse release us,
Manifest Thy pardoning love;
O receive us to Thy favour,
For His only sake receive,
Give us to our bleeding Saviour,
Let us by Thy dying live.

'To Thy pardoning grace receive them',
Once He prayed upon the tree;
Still His blood cries out, 'Forgive them,
All their sins were purged by Me.'
Still our Advocate in heaven

Prays the prayer on earth begun,
'Father, show their sins forgiven,
Father, glorify Thy Son!'   (14)

Again the language is familiar to evangelical spirituality but
the sacramental context is surprising. The hymn is clear, as is
the Wesleys' theology generally, that humankind is the deserv-
ing subject of the wrath of God and that the only way to the
'pardoning love' and 'favour' of God is through the event of the
cross in the past ('All their sins were purged by Me') and the
application of the benefits of the cross in the present ('Father,
show their sins forgiven'). All this belongs to the heart of evangelical teaching, and the Wesleys were as good at writing about
it, preaching it and singing it as anyone. What is interesting,
though, in this hymn and in others in the collection, is the space
that the Wesleys give for the ministry of the church or, more
correctly, the continuing ministry of Christ through the church.
The event of the cross is eternally efficacious, but its application involves the continuing prayer of Christ ('Still His blood
cries out, "Forgive them"') *and* of the church in such a way
that the two coincide in what we may call an *effective ecclesial
echo* ('Father, hear the blood of Jesus speaking in Thine ears
above').

We will see more evidence of this, and greater clarity on how
it relates to the action of the Eucharist, in later sections of the
Preface and Hymns. But before leaving this hymn with its focus
on the atonement, it is worth noting how the Wesleys plumb
the trinitarian depths of the cross. They are totally committed
to a juridical understanding of the cross, believing that it is an
exercise in 'Divine justice', judging sin, condemning evil, and
propitiating the wrath of God. At the same time, they show
how the one whose 'body mangled, rent' in 'last tremendous
agony' *is* 'My God, that suffers there', for 'the great Jehovah
. . . the 'God of angels dies'.[18] 'Let us fall amazed', says the
Preface, 'at that stroke of Divine justice, that could not be satisfied but by the death of God.'[19] The cross is the demonstration
of 'unexampled grace' because there God chose to be 'crush'd

beneath our load'.[20] This burden is the load of human self-destruction and the load of evil's desire to wreak hell upon us on the one hand. On the other, it is God's determination to deal with the disobedience that destroys us by the obedience that remakes us, and to defeat the powers that kill us with the higher power that brings us back to life. The 'death of God' brings the 'death of sin' because it is: 'The death by which our foes are kill'd, the death by which our souls are heal'd (24.2).

The angle shifts again in the third hymn I have chosen from this section, this time to the Holy Spirit.

> Come, Thou everlasting Spirit,
> bring to every thankful mind
> All the Saviour's dying merit,
> All His sufferings for mankind;
> True Recorder of His passion,
> Now the living faith impart,
> Now reveal His great salvation,
> Preach His gospel to our heart.
>
> Come, Thou witness of His dying,
> Come, Remembrancer Divine,
> Let us feel Thy power applying
> Christ to every soul and mine;
> Let us groan Thine inward groaning,
> Look on Him we pierced and grieve,
> All receive the grace atoning,
> All the sprinkled blood receive.   (16)

It is generally accepted that, compared with the Eastern tradition, Western theology and liturgy has understated the role of the Spirit in the Eucharist. I say *understated* because although pretty much every Christian theologian and liturgist would acknowledge that the Eucharist depends upon the activity of the Holy Spirit, the presence and power of the Spirit in the sacrament have often been implicitly assumed rather than explicitly explained in the Western theological and liturgical tradition. The result has been a practical neglect of the Spirit's capacity to mediate between contrasting positions and to hold together that which we so easily, but unnecessarily, tear apart. John Calvin, perhaps because of his liking for the Eastern Fathers, was much better than most. The Wesleys, perhaps because of their respect for Calvin's eucharistic theology and their similar attraction to the Eastern tradition, gave considerable attention to the Spirit's work in the Eucharist.

'Come, Thou everlasting Spirit' is a very interesting example of how an emphasis on the Spirit might help to avoid damaging dichotomies in a critical area of eucharistic theology – the meaning of *anamnēsis*. *Anamnēsis*, a word drawn from the lips of Jesus in the accounts of the Last Supper, became a much-debated liturgical term in twentieth-century eucharistic theology, especially in the area of ecumenical dialogue. Evangelicals have been suspicious sometimes, and with just cause, of catholic approaches to *anamnēsis* which talk in terms of making past events present through some form of ritual process. Evangelical instincts about the historicity – the once-for-all-ness – of the saving events, are correct. On the other hand, catholic instincts about the corporate liturgical character of Christian remembering and of the need to connect with the past in the present, are also rightly placed. Both emphases are held together in this hymn by Charles' evocative descriptions of the Spirit.

We cannot remember the events of salvation by ourselves. It is impossible. We were not there. But the Spirit of God recalls the words and works of Christ in the life of the church and allows us to share in the continuing corporate memory of the church that reaches back to the event itself. Through the reading, hearing and preaching of scripture, and through the performance of the scriptural story in liturgical action, the Spirit who, as 'Witness of His dying' was 'the True Recorder of [Christ's] passion', animates the 'death-recording rite' of the Eucharist as the 'Remembrancer Divine'. Reconnecting us with the events of Christ's life, death and resurrection, the Spirit declares their meaning to us (John 16.14) and applies 'Christ to every soul and mine'. Notice also how this pneumatological approach to *anamnēsis* takes us through and beyond another of the polarities that appear to separate catholic from evangelical understandings of the Eucharist. Evangelicals and catholics have disagreed sharply over whether the focus of the Eucharist is the humiliated body of Christ, his past and crucified body (generally the evangelical view), or Christ's glorified body, his present and risen body (generally the catholic view). However, viewed pneumatologically, such a divide is unnecessary. The Spirit, using the scriptural story, takes us to the death of Christ but does not leave us there. In remembering the historical Christ we are carried to the present and eternal Lord, and, through the Spirit – and by means of all that the Spirit uses for this purpose – our fellowship with the risen Christ is renewed and deepened.

'Concerning the Sacrament as it is a Sign of Present Graces.'

Fellowship with the risen Christ through the commemoration of his death is very much the theme of the next section and the one that follows. This section looks at the sacrament in terms of sign ('a *figure* whereby God *represents* present graces') and the following one considers it as a means ('an *instrument* whereby God *conveys* them').[21] In fact, 'sign' and 'means' are difficult to distinguish in sacramental theology, the one implying the other. It is even more difficult to put liturgical and experiential space between them, which may explain why Charles chose to conflate these two sections in the Hymns. Nevertheless, the two main points that the Preface seeks to make are worth noting. First, like Aquinas and Calvin, the Wesleys show that throughout the history of salvation, God's 'ordinary way' is to 'confirm the *word* and the *gift* with the addition of some sign'.[22] The burning bush, the fiery cloud and now bread and wine are simply ways by which God assures us of his presence and blessing.

Second, the signs that God chooses resonate with the grace that God communicates. Water, for example, illustrates the cleansing that God gives through baptism. It is consistent with the reality it represents and therefore provides rich seams of symbolic connection. Similarly, in Daniel Brevint's own words, bread and wine 'bear the character of a sacrament'.[23] They are able to be meaningful signs of Christ's salvation because of their representative capacities. For example, before bread and wine are able to nourish and gladden us they have to be 'cut down, ground, and baked with fire' or 'pressed and trodden under foot'.[24] In this way, in their own character, they illustrate the sufferings that Christ had to endure in order to be able to save and sustain us. Furthermore, by their nature as food-stuffs, bread and wine are apt signifiers of our *continual* need for spiritual nourishment and strength. Just as our physical bodies cannot survive without regular food and drink, so our life in God requires regular sustenance through all the means that God has given. The capacity of the eucharistic elements to represent both the one sacrifice of Christ and the ongoing need for spiritual sustenance through the blessings of the sacrament was exploited in a number of places in the Hymns, such as here in verse 1 of 'Worthy the Lamb', which celebrates God's justifying work in the 'pardoning' and his sanctifying activity in the 'hallowing grace'.

> Worthy the Lamb of endless praise,
> Whose double life we here shall prove,
> The pardoning and the hallowing grace,
> The dawning and the perfect love.   (38.1)

The representative character of the elements plays an impor-tant part in an area of Anglican sacramental apologetics that lies behind the Preface and finds voice in the Hymns. Article 28 of the Church of England's Articles of Religion argues that 'transubstantiation overthroweth the nature of a sacrament'. As well as not wanting to require belief in anything that cannot be demonstrated by scripture, and a hesitancy to explain the inner workings of the sacrament, Anglican theology has been suspi-cious of the doctrine of transubstantiation on the grounds that it involves the overriding of the essential reality of bread and wine by the presence of Christ's body and blood. Anglicans, even those of quite catholic persuasions, have argued that this displacement of the natural by the supernatural undermines the sacramental character of the elements and their designation as representative signs. The first two verses of hymn 57, especially the last two lines of verse 2, put these reservations into song:

> O the depth of love Divine,
> Th'unfathomable grace!
> Who shall say how bread and wine God into man conveys!
> *How* the bread His flesh imparts,
> *How* the wine transmits His blood,
> Fills His faithful people's hearts
> With all the life of God!
>
> Let the wisest mortal show
> How we the grace receive
> Feeble elements bestow
> A power not theirs to give.
> Who explains the wondrous way,
> How through these the virtue came?
> These the virtue did convey,
> Yet still remain the same.   (57)

'Concerning the Sacrament, as it is a Means of Grace.'

In the previous section the Preface concentrated on the *affective* function of the sacrament, its ability to influence and to stimulate the human spirit by its symbolic power. This is an important base for eucharistic doctrine but it is insufficient in itself to secure the purposes of God in the sacrament. For this, the Wesleys knew that it was necessary to define the *effective* role of the sacrament, and specifically of the sacramental bread and wine. Bread and wine are not simply signs that point us towards something, in the way a signpost tells us where to find a certain place. They are *effectual signs* that *take us* to where they direct us. They convey what they communicate. They provide what they promise.

Draw near, ye blood-besprinkled race,
And take what God vouchsafes to give;
The outward sign of inward grace,
Ordain'd by Christ Himself, receive:
The sign transmits the signified,
The grace is by the means applied.

Sure pledges of His dying love,
Receive the sacramental meat,
And feel the virtue from above,
The mystic flesh of Jesus eat,
Drink with the wine His healing blood,
And feast on th'Incarnate God.

Gross misconceit be far away!
Through faith we on His body feed;
Faith only doth the Spirit convey,
And fills our souls with living bread,
Th'effects of Jesu's death imparts,
And pours His blood into our hearts.   (71)

Notice here how Charles is insistent on the instrumental function of the sacrament – it really does do something, and really
does give something – while at the same time emphasizing the
role of both faith and the Spirit. Here we begin to touch on
the genius of the Wesleys' work and its abiding value. We will
look at their understanding of the dynamics of the Spirit before
going on to look at the dynamics of faith; though, of course,
the two are closely bound together, as the hymn makes clear.

Although the sacrament is 'a sure communicating sign' and
'an instrument ordain'd to feed',[25] it is not a mechanical device
or some sort of automated spiritual transaction which ignores
the personal and relational character of God's dealings with
his people. On the one hand Christ promises his presence. On
the other hand we implore him for his presence. God gives, but
the church asks. The way that God gives is by the power of the
Holy Spirit, and this is exactly what the church asks for in its
prayer and worship.

Come, Holy Ghost, Thine influence shed,
And realize the sign;
Thy life infuse into the bread,
Thy power into the wine.

Effectual let the tokens prove,
And made, by heavenly art,
Fit channels to convey Thy love
To every faithful heart.   (72)

Notice again how the objectivity of the Spirit's divine gift is held in tension with the need for faithful human subjectivity. Another hymn shows that far from being in irreconcilable tension, they are, in fact, interfacing aspects of the work of the triune God who saves us by grace *through* faith (Ephesians 2.8).

Jesu, my Lord and God, bestow
All which Thy sacrament doth show,
And make the real sign
A sure effectual means of grace,
Then sanctify my heart, and bless,
And make it all like Thine.

Great is Thy faithfulness and love,
Thine ordinance can never prove
Of none effect, and vain;
Only do Thou my heart prepare
To find Thy real presence there,
And all Thy fulness gain.   (66)

The Wesleys are clear that the divine gift of the Eucharist is nothing less than the 'true and real presence' of Christ and that the elements play a critical part as 'effectual means of grace' in communicating Christ to the participants in the Lord's Supper.[26] However, they are equally clear that the gift of Christ can only be received by faith and that the location of the presence of Christ is to be found in the relational encounter between the believer and Christ. Their interest in what God does *in* and *with* the bread and wine lies only in what God does *through* them. Hence they pray, 'Thy power into the means infuse, and give them now their sacred use', so that 'Receiving the bread, on Jesus we feed'.[27] The dialectic the Wesleys maintain between the gift of God through the liturgical commemoration on the one hand, and the receiving faith of the participants (both of which are enabled by the Spirit), takes us to the heart of biblical teaching about the Eucharist: 'The cup of blessing that we bless, is it not a sharing (*koinōnia*) in the blood of Christ? The bread that we break, is it not a sharing (*koinōnia*) in the body of Christ?' (1 Corinthians 10.16). Paul – as the Preface notes – was in no doubt that something real, powerful and dynamic was happening as Christ's people gathered to celebrate the Lord's Supper. Why else were some getting 'weak and ill' and some 'nearly dying' (1 Corinthians 11.30) in their 'unworthy' gatherings? But the focus in scripture, whether here in Paul, or in the Synoptic accounts of Jesus' table fellowship during his ministry, or the Johannine teaching on Jesus as the bread of life, or Hebrews' eucharistic allusions, or the glimpses of the 'marriage feast of the Lamb' in the book of Revelation (19.7), is on the *encounter with Christ and participation in his life*. This is why evangelical attention, at its best, has been on the reality of the gift of the Lord's Supper; for in the words of the seventeenth-century Puritan Thomas Goodwin:

> We have to do with Christ himself, his person. We are to put upon him, let into him immediately and directly, and are to converse with him, as a spouse with her husband, in the nearest intimacies.[28]

This is why the catholic concern to secure the *givenness* of the gift and not allow it to be subject to the vagaries and vulnerability of human response is also correct, and thoroughly scriptural. The Wesleys, as we shall see, achieved this by their faithfulness to the promises of God in scripture (which promise Christ's presence in the Eucharist), their overarching theology of grace (in which the 'Love Divine' always takes the lead), and their strong doctrine of the Spirit (who responds to the prayer of the church and is active in the actions of the church).

I used to work regularly with an Orthodox theologian when team-teaching theological students. On one occasion he was involved in a passionate exchange with an ordinand from the Reformed tradition about the bread and wine of the Eucharist. My Orthodox colleague said that for him the presence of the Lord's body and blood in the eucharistic elements was non-negotiable – without the presence of Christ in bread and wine the Eucharist makes no sense. I remember joining the discussion along these lines: 'If you would be happy to say that the *gift* of Christ's body and blood through the eucharistic elements is non-negotiable, then I could fully agree with you.' My friend's response, generously, was to accept that 'gift' is the right category because it preserves the promised, gracious activity of God in the Eucharist and the proper response of Christ's people in welcoming the Christ who comes to us in the sacrament.[29] Perhaps our ready agreement had something to do with my friend once being a Methodist because this conviction that Christ is really given by the Spirit through bread and wine to be really received by Spirit-endowed faith through bread and wine is exactly the balance the Wesleys achieved in their theology of the presence of Christ in the Eucharist. It is essentially the position at which the Anglican and Roman Catholic International Commission arrived in its Agreed Statement on the Eucharist:

> The sacramental body and blood of the Saviour are present as an offering to the believer awaiting his welcome. When this offering is met by faith, a lifegiving encounter results. Through faith Christ's presence – which does not depend on the individual's faith in order to be the Lord's real gift of himself to his Church – becomes no longer just a presence *for* the believer, but also a presence *with* him. Thus, in considering the mystery of the Eucharistic presence, we must recognize both the sacramental sign of Christ's presence and the

personal relationship between Christ and the faithful which arises from that presence.[30]

The Wesleys' instincts about the necessity of the means of grace from their High-Church Anglican background put them in good stead when dealing with the 'stillness teaching' of Peter Molther that was taking hold of the Moravian Fetter Lane Society in the 1740s, and was threatening the early days of the Revival. In many ways Molther's teaching was a working out of the evangelical dilemma we mentioned in the previous chapter. 'Why do we need the sacrament if Christ is received by faith?' Molther was taking the evangelical emphasis on faith and the charismatic experience of the immediacy of God's presence to an extreme conclusion. All that we need to do before God is to be still and to await his presence and work. The outward forms of prayer and fasting, and even scripture and preaching, are ultimately unnecessary to the spiritual life. We should seek the direct experience of God that comes from waiting for God to manifest himself and impact the soul. The Wesleys' response in terms of human obedience and God's promise was much more than a dutiful appeal to scriptural command or to the teaching of the church. It was an impassioned plea to engage with the spiritual possibilities of a divine appointment, and it trumped the stillness teaching with a combined affirmation of the *effective* purpose of God and the *affections* of the worshipper. We met some of the lines of the hymn in Chapter 3. It is now worth looking at it in full.

> It seemed to my Redeemer good
> That faith should *here* His coming wait,
> Should here receive immortal food,
> Grow up in Him Divinely great,
> And, fill'd with holy violence, seize
> The glorious crown of righteousness.
>
> Saviour, Thou didst the mystery give,
> That I Thy nature might partake;

Thou bidd'st me outward signs receive,
One with Thyself my soul to make;
My body, soul, and spirit to join
Inseparably one with Thine.

The prayer, the fast, the word conveys,
When mix'd with faith, Thy life to me;
In all the channels of Thy grace
I still have fellowship with thee:
But chiefly here my soul is fed
With fullness of immortal bread.

Communion closer far I feel,
And deeper drink th'atoning blood;
The joy is more unspeakable,
And yields me larger draughts of God,
Till nature faints beneath the power,
And faith fill'd up can hold no more.   (54)

The hymn does not deny the place of faith, it simply affirms that Christ deemed 'That faith should *here* His coming wait'. The Moravian principles are not wrong in themselves. Life in Christ and the Spirit involves waiting to be encountered by Christ in the Spirit. But in Christ's gracious provision he has designated certain places where he can be found and particular means to communicate his life. The sacrament is one, 'the prayer, the fast, the word' are others. They do not override faith. They invite faith.

It is interesting that in the Wesleys' defence of the sacrament as one of the appointed means of grace, Charles writes that 'chiefly here my soul is fed with fullness of immortal bread'. A 'closer communion' is felt: a 'deeper drink' of 'th'atoning blood' is taken and with holy inebriation 'joy is more unspeakable', with the 'larger draughts of God' until, saturated with grace and overcome in the Spirit, 'nature faints beneath the power, and faith fill'd up can hold no more'. In other hymns, and in the more measured language of the Preface, the Wesleys make no excuse for believing that the Eucharist is the 'grand channel' of God's grace and that, 'well used, it exceeds in blessing as it exceeds in danger of a curse' other means of grace.[31] Similar testimonies can be found among other evangelical leaders across the centuries.

> It is a universal unimpeachable persuasion among all Christians that there is a near intimate communion and participation of him in the supper of the Lord. He is no Christian who is otherwise minded.[32] (John Owen, seventeenth-century Puritan)

> I believe that our Saviour does seal the most sacred ordinance with a peculiar blessing.[33] (Charles Simeon, late eighteenth century)

> The nearest approach to God of which our present state admits . . . [is involved in the] partaking of the consecrated emblems of the body and blood of Christ.[34] (Daniel Wilson, early nineteenth century)

> There is a blessed manifestation of the Divine Presence to the soul to be here expected.[35] (Edward Bickersteth, mid-nineteenth century)

> [The Supper has] a special and peculiar blessing attached to it. That blessing, I believe, consists in a special and peculiar presence of Christ, vouchsafed to the heart of every believing communicant . . . and a special revelation of Christ's sacrifice of his own body and blood to his soul.[36] (John Charles Ryle, nineteenth century)

These significant figures of evangelical life and ministry – and other voices could be added to them – show that the Wesleys were not alone in regarding the Eucharist as a unique and unrivalled form of God's ministry to us, bringing a 'special presence of Christ'. Elsewhere I have contended that the Eucharist is unique in terms of its *functional intensity* rather than its *ontological density*.[37] That is a shorthand way of saying that I do not think it necessary to claim that Christ's presence to us in the Eucharist is different in kind from his presence in other appointed ways. Indeed, I cannot make sense of different forms of the presence of any person. It is the same Christ who encounters us in the Eucharist as speaks to us in the word, meets us in the fellowship, lifts us in our worship, hears us in our prayers, and so on. Neither do I think it necessary to associate Christ's presence in a more intrinsic way with the bread and wine of the Eucharist than with the other sacramental means God uses to relate to us, as if the point of the Eucharist is Christ inhabiting them rather than using them to inhabit us.

I do believe, though, that it is entirely scriptural to regard the Eucharist as an intensive encounter with Christ, offering an intensive participation in his life. This can be argued from three scriptural perspectives. The first is the cumulative effect of the Eucharist that Luke describes in the Emmaus story. Jesus meets the disciples on the road, they speak to him and he to them. He unfolds the scriptures to him and then 'they recognize[d] him . . . in the breaking of the bread' (Luke 24.31, 35). This is the *sealing of the word* that Calvin and the other Reformers held dear. The sacrament reinforces what the word says, allowing it to penetrate. It connects our receptivity to the ministries of the Spirit already operative as the people of God worship together. Celebrations of the Eucharist contain the main ways in which God reaches us – fellowship, teaching, prayers and sacrament. So it is not surprising that they are especially wholesome and fulfilling.

The second plank in the argument for the intensity of the Eucharist is the concentration on the cross and the constitution of the Christian community that dominates Paul's teaching about the Lord's Supper in 1 Corinthians 10—11. Whereas other means of grace will quite properly range widely, the Eucharist will always focus on the cross. Whatever the current liturgy of the church or the fashion of theology, Jesus has ensured that we cannot dissociate the sacrament from his death.

Talk of 'body and blood' will not allow it. And however high or low the ritual of the church, and however individualistic the culture, the Eucharist requires some sort of corporate celebration. It binds us together with each other as 'we partake of the one bread' and share in the one 'body of Christ' (1 Corinthians 10.16–17). The cross is at the centre of Christian existence and the church is the community of the cross. The Eucharist takes us to the place where Mary stood, at the foot of the cross by the 'bleeding love' of the Saviour, where we find those who are bound to Christ and where Christ commands us to be bound to them (John 19.26–27).[38]

The third plank in the argument is the coterminous moment of belief in the Christ whom 'God has sent' to give his life 'for the life of the world' (John 6.29, 51) and the eating of the sacramental bread that John tells us about in his sixth chapter. Here we find the dynamics of faith coinciding with the celebration of the Supper. The sacrifice by which we are saved is so presented to us that our faith – by which we accept the sacrifice as ours and receive the Saviour who made it – is summoned. The bread of the Eucharist and the bread of life are so connected in the saving and sacramental purposes of God that, as Saravia, a Lutheran Reformer said, 'whoever has the bread certainly and really has the body, and whoever has the wine has the blood'.[39] All of this is not, as Robert Bruce, the sixteenth-century Scottish Presbyterian said, that we 'may get any new thing [in the sacrament]', but rather 'that [we] may get the same thing better than [we] had in the Word . . . that we may get a better hold of him than we got in the simple Word . . . and that we may possess Him more fully, it is a better thing'.[40]

I recognize that my own failing attempts to explore the gift of Christ's presence in the Eucharist will not satisfy everyone, even with the guidance of the Wesleys. Some will think that I – and perhaps John and Charles before me – have gone too far. Others will wonder what stopped us going further. It is fitting, therefore, that before I conclude this section with a Wesleyan hymn that accepts the mystery of the Eucharist while celebrating its reality at the same time, I include a quotation from Calvin to the same effect towards the end of his magisterial study of the eucharistic presence in his *Institutes*.

> Now, if anyone should ask me how this presence of Christ in the Eucharist takes place, I shall not be ashamed to confess that it is a secret too lofty for either my mind to comprehend or my words to declare. And to speak more plainly, I rather experience than understand it. Therefore, I here embrace without controversy the truth of God in which I may safely rest.[41]

God incomprehensible
Shall man presume to know;
Fully search Him out, or tell
His wondrous ways below?
Him in all His ways we find;
How the means transmit the power –
Here he leaves our thoughts behind,
And faith inquires no more.

How He did these creatures raise,
And make this bread and wine
Organs to convey His grace
To this poor soul of mine,
I cannot the way descry,
Need not know the mystery;
Only this I know – that I
Was blind, but now I see.

Now mine eyes are open'd wide,
To see His pardoning love,
Here I view the God that died
My ruin to remove;
Clay upon mine eyes He laid,
(I at once my sight received),
Bless'd and bid me eat the bread,
And lo! My soul believed.   (59)

'Concerning the Sacrament as it is a Pledge of Heaven.'

So far, with the Wesleys, we have explored the Eucharist in
its past reference as a memorial or commemoration, and in
its present dimension as a gift of Christ's presence with all his
blessings. We now move on to consider the future aspect of the
sacrament. All three tenses are celebrated in hymn 94.

> O what a soul-transporting feast
> Doth this communion yield!
> Remembering here Thy passion past,
> We with Thy love are fill'd.
>
> Sure instrument of present grace
> Thy sacrament we find,
> Yet higher blessings it displays,
> And raptures still behind.
>
> It bears us now on eagle's wings,
> If Thou the power impart,
> And Thee our glorious earnest brings
> Into our faithful heart.
>
> O let us still the earnest feel,
> Th'unutterable peace,
> This loving Spirit be the seal
> Of our eternal bliss!   (94)

The Eucharist is a 'soul-transporting feast' in which we are con-
fronted by the realities of Christ's past passion, transformed
by encountering his presence now and carried into our future
inheritance so that we 'feel th'unutterable peace' of our eschatological salvation. All this is brought to us by the Holy Spirit,
who 'seals' in our present the 'bliss' that lies in the future with
the 'earnest', or 'sacramental pledge'.[42] The lengthy hymn 93,
from which I quote in part below, explores this future and its
connection with our present in a fuller way.

Come, let us join with one accord
Who share the supper of the Lord,
Our Lord and Master's praise to sing;
Nourish'd on earth with living bread,
We now are at His table fed,
But wait to see our heavenly King;
To see the great Invisible
Without a sacramental veil,
With all His robes of glory on,
In rapturous joy and love and praise
Him to behold with open face,
High on His everlasting throne!

Then let us still in hope rejoice,
And listen for th'archangel's voice
Loud echoing to the trump of God,
Haste to the dreadful joyful day,
When heaven and earth shall flee away,
By all-devouring flames destroy'd:
While we from out the burnings fly,
With eagle's wings mount up on high,
Where Jesus is on *Sion* seen.

By faith and hope already there,
Even now the marriage-feast we share,
Even now we by the Lamb are fed;
Our Lord's celestial joy we prove,
Led by the Spirit of His love,
To springs of living comfort led.   (93)

This is a rich hymn, packed with biblical imagery. There are three themes that I would like to single out. First, in line with Aquinas, Calvin and the sacramental tradition generally, Charles shows how sacraments belong to this age and will be eclipsed in the age to come by the realities they represent. Nevertheless, they have a direct connection to these eschatological realities. The Lord whom we will one day meet face to face invites us to his supper *now*. The praise we will offer *then* is one with the praise we offer *now*. The 'marriage-feast' of the future uses the same table at which 'we now are . . . fed'. The connection between the present celebration of the sacrament and the future consummation of the kingdom is carefully made by the use Charles makes of *waiting*. Just as we are to wait here in the sacrament for Christ to come to us and feed us with this life-giving presence now, so we also 'wait to see our heavenly King' who will descend 'to take His bride in triumph home' at the end of the age. Second, Charles is faithful to the linear eschatology of the Bible in seeing the kingdom as a future reality which will involve 'heaven and earth flee[ing] away' and the new Sion, the new Jerusalem – the new creation where Christ reigns – emerging from the ashes of the old order. Third, this future reality is anticipated by 'faith and hope' as the Spirit leads us into the eternal realm of love, manifesting the conditions of the kingdom of the reign of God in the kingdom of this world, penetrating the present with the one reality in whom the new creation is already found, and the kingdom has already come – the Saviour who promised that he would not eat the bread and drink the cup 'until the kingdom of God comes' (Luke 22.16, 18), and whose 'celestial joy we prove' as he feeds us with the bread of heaven and the cup of salvation.

Although Charles quite rightly sees the kingdom as a future reality for which we wait, he also, quite properly, has a concept of the present heavenly realm where Christ is interceding, the angels and saints worshipping and in which we share through the celebration of the sacrament.

> How glorious is the life above,
> Which in this ordinance we *taste*;
> That fullness of celestial love,
> That joy which shall for ever last!   (101.1)

The present activity of Christ is an important theme in the Wesleys' understanding of the sacrificial dimension of the Eucharist, to which we now turn.

'Concerning the Sacrament, as it is a Sacrifice. And First, of the Commemorative Sacrifice.'

Thou Lamb that sufferedst on the tree,
And in this dreadful mystery
Still offer'st up Thyself to God,
We cast us on Thy sacrifice,
Wrapp'd in the sacred smoke arise,
And cover'd with th'atoning blood.

Thy death presented in our stead
Enters us now among the dead,
Parts of Thy mystic body here,
By Thy Divine oblation raised,
And on our *Aaron's* ephod placed
We now with Thee in heaven appear.

Thy death exalts Thy ransom'd ones,
And sets 'midst the precious stones,
Closest Thy dear, Thy loving breast;
Israel as on Thy shoulders stands,
Our names are graven on the hands,
The heart of our Eternal Priest.

For us He ever intercedes,
His heaven-deserving passion pleads,
Presenting us before the throne;
We want no sacrifice beside,
By that great Offering sanctified,
One with our Head, for ever one.   (117)

Here we see what the Wesleys envisaged the ascended Christ to be doing in heaven. He is *praying* for the world, *pleading* his passion and *presenting* his people to the Father. The Wesleys are in no doubt that Jesus Christ 'did fully once for all atone' and that his sacrifice is 'all sufficient'.[43] Their biblical schooling in the Reformation tradition, their evangelical experience of salvation, and their liturgical formation through Cranmer's layering of phrase upon phrase about the completed atonement of the cross, would not allow them to forget for a moment the fullness, perfection and sufficiency of Christ's sacrifice.[44] At the same time, their reading of scripture, especially of Hebrews and Revelation, their evangelical experience of the *presence and purpose* of the ascended Christ, and their spiritual formation in a tradition which took seriously the *practice* of the church, meant that they gave full expression to the heavenly ministry of Christ and to the liturgical ministry of the church. We can see the former in this hymn and the latter in the hymn that follows it in the collection and which we will look at in a moment.

As we have said, Christ's ongoing ministry involves prayer, pleading and presentation. But before considering each of them we must begin with the *person*. Jesus is the beloved Son of God who has become our *priest*. As our priest he carries us on his heart into the holiest presence of God in the way that Aaron, the priest of old, with the names of the tribes of Israel written on his breastplate, could only prefigure. As the priest who made an offering of himself 'once for all', 'a single sacrifice for sins' (Hebrews 10.10, 12), his sacrifice is 'eternal' (126.3). Because Christ's past and complete sacrifice was made *in his person*, its effect remains *present in him,* waiting to be applied through his *priestly activity*, his advocacy. He prays for us on the basis of his passion, the only ground of our acceptance, forgiveness and reconciliation. It is in this sense that the Wesleys conceive of Christ pleading his passion. It is not a case of the plaintive priest imploring a reluctant God for the sacrifice to be accepted: that is already fully achieved. His presence in heaven is the proof that he 'appeared once for all at the end of the age to remove sin by the sacrifice of himself' (Hebrews 9.26). And it is most certainly not a case of an earnest Son begging a disappointed Father to accept that what he has done is good enough. The Wesleys leave us in no doubt that not only was the cross an intra-trinitarian event in which the eternal God suffers human death in the person of the Son, but also that the ascension is an act of the triune God in which the Son sits down 'at the right hand of the Father' (Hebrews 10.12) 'to appear in the presence of God on our behalf' (Hebrews 9.24). As our brother and priest in the presence of God, Christ presents us to the Father in himself, in his person, in his redeemed humanity. By his presence and through his prayer he pleads for the blessings of his sacrifice to be *applied to our receiving faith* as 'we cast us on [His] sacrifice'.

Hymn 118 explains what casting ourselves on his sacrifice involves, and how it relates to the Eucharist:

> Live, our eternal Priest,
> By men and angels blest!
> Jesus Christ the Crucified,
> He who did for us atone,
> From the cross where once He died,
> Now He up to heaven is gone.
>
> He ever lives, and prays
> For all the faithful race;
> In the holiest place above
> Sinners' Advocate He stands,
> Pleads for us His dying love,
> Shows for us His bleeding hands.
>
> His body torn and rent
> He doth to God present,
> In that dear memorial shows
> *Israel's* chosen tribes imprest;
> All our names the Father knows,
> Reads them on our *Aaron's* breast.
>
> He reads, while we beneath
> Present our Saviour's death,
> Do as Jesus bids us do,
> Signify His flesh and blood,
> Him in a memorial show,
> Offer up the Lamb to God.

From this thrice hallow'd shade
Which Jesus' cross hath made,
Image of His sacrifice,
Never, never will we move,
Till with all His saints we rise,
Rise, and take our place above.   (118)

Here again we see the three themes of prayer, pleading and presentation that Christ performs *passively*, in his presence before
the Father, and also *actively*, in his ministry as priest of his
people. At the same time, we see the ministry of the church coinciding with his ministry. The presentation 'above' is mirrored
in the presentation 'below'. As the crucified Christ appears in
God's presence for us, we 'Do as Jesus bids us do . . . Him in
memorial show'. The last thing the Wesleys want to do is to
undermine the completeness of the cross. Hymn 124 affirms
this with absolute clarity. Christ's sacrificial death on Calvary
'did fully once for all atone'. His sacrifice is 'all-sufficient' and
'all complete'. But they do want to explain how we 'reach this
everlasting sacrifice', how we appropriate the atonement.[45]
That is why they remained committed to the *commemoration
of the cross* in the Eucharist, singing in the same hymn:

Yet may we celebrate below,
And daily thus Thine offering show
Exposed before Thy Father's eyes.   (124.1)

There is no doubt that this 'Yet' strikes a surprising chord in
evangelical ears and so we must ask whether the sound the
Wesleys want to make for the church's action is dissonant
with the gospel or actually the outworking of the gospel's own
music. It is probable that their use of the word 'show' here
and elsewhere (e.g. 122.1) can be traced to their exegesis of 1
Corinthians 11.26 where, in the King James' Version, which of
course would have been the translation they were using, Paul
says, 'As often as ye eat this bread, and drink this cup, ye do
show [*katangellete*] the Lord's death till he comes'. In John

Wesley's *Explanatory Notes upon the New Testament* he interprets the showing of Christ's death in this way: 'Ye proclaim, as it were, and openly avow it, to God and to all the world, till he come, in glory.'[46] But is John right? Can the 'setting solemnly forth before the eyes of God' of Christ's sacrifice in the Eucharist (as the Preface puts it) be justified evangelically?[47] I think that it can, provided we do so carefully.

It is important to remember John's little clause, 'as it were'. We are in the realm of the sacramental and the spiritual, not the historical and the literal. Historically, Christ's sacrifice was shown to the Father at a particular point in time. This was the only literal showing, the only actual offering. But its spiritual significance remains, and the spiritual processes by which we encounter and appropriate it continue. It is these that are sacramentally enacted in the Eucharist, not the historical event itself. With this in mind, we can see that the great works of God in human history are proclaimed before God in acknowledgement and thanksgiving, as well as to the church and the world in communication and challenge. This is what is going on in 1 Peter 2 where the boundaries between the worshipping life of the church and its missionary calling seem to blur. The proclamation of 'the mighty acts of God' is as much an affirmation and celebration of the church's identity as 'the chosen race, a royal priesthood, a holy nation, God's own people' (1 Peter 2.9), as it is a statement to the world. The connection between proclamation, praise and appropriation is a very close one. We proclaim all that God has done for us because we want to praise God for what he has done and to appropriate his saving action more fully. This is why elsewhere I have called the Eucharist 'a sacrifice of proclamation',[48] because in the sacrament we proclaim that, in the words of the Preface, 'the meritorious sufferings of our Lord [are] the only sure ground whereon God may give, and we obtain, the blessings we pray for'.[49] In this sense, the Eucharist is an act and exercise of faith, of *evangelical faith*.

It is here that 'faith presents the crucified'.[50] It is here that faith bows before God's mercy. It is here that faith puts its hope only in the one sacrifice by which sin is condemned in the Son who takes our place. It is here that faith falls before the thrice-holy God who bears the weight of his wrath against the world's evil in his own self. And it is here that *receiving faith* holds out empty hands to *giving grace* and waits for them to be filled with the body of Christ, broken for us, and lifts up the lips of a parched soul to taste the cup of the new covenant in Christ's blood. In this evangelical sense, the Wesleys were not alone in their daring invitation to 'offer up the Lamb to God'. Calvin had got there before them:

> It is necessary that each of us should *offer Christ to the Father*. For, although He only, and that but once, has offered Himself, still a daily offering of Him which is effected by faith and prayers, is enjoined to us.[51]

Similar sentiments were expressed by other Reformers in the sixteenth century and by leading Puritans in the seventeenth. Where the Wesleys went beyond them was in claiming, with Brevint, that the sacrament is *the most* 'blessed . . . instrument' to set forth Christ's one sacrifice 'before the eyes of God'.[52] To be sure, this cannot be proved by scripture but neither is it denied by scripture provided we see the Eucharist in the terms used earlier, as an opportunity for *intensive encounter* with Christ and his work rather than as something unique in effect and exclusive in power. As the appointed commemoration of the cross, we should be expecting the Eucharist to exercise our faith and renew our recognition that Christ is 'the pioneer and perfecter of our salvation' (Hebrews 12.2), and that we enter 'the sanctuary by his blood' and in his body (Hebrews 10.19). After all, if, as Tom Wright is fond of saying, Jesus did not give us a theory of the atonement, 'he gave us a *meal*',[53] why should Christ's Supper not be the most intensive encounter with the complete sufficiency of his sacrifice and the place where we pray most confidently – 'Then through Him the sinner see, Then in Jesus look on me' (119.4)?

'Concerning the Sacrifice of Ourselves and of our Goods.'

The last two sections of the Preface can be dealt with together because they deal with the same theme: how we receive and respond to the one sacrifice of Christ. Hymn 128, the first in the penultimate section of the hymnbook, summarizes the main theological principles with which John works in the Preface and with which Charles works in the rest of the hymns in the collection.

> All hail, Thou mighty to atone!
> To expiate sin is Thine alone,
> Thou hast alone the wine-press trod,
> Thou only hast for sinners died,
> By one oblation satisfied
> Th'inexorably righteous God.
>
> Should the whole church in flames arise,
> Offer'd as one burnt sacrifice,
> The sinner's smallest debt to pay,
> They could not, Lord, Thine honour share,
> With Thee the Father's justice bear,
> Or bear one single sin away.
>
> Thyself our utmost price hast paid;
> Thou hast for all atonement made,
> For all the sins of all mankind:
> God doth in Thee redemption give:
> But how shall we the grace receive?
> But how shall we the blessing find?
>
> We only can *accept* the grace,
> And humbly our Redeemer praise,
> Who bought the glorious liberty;
> The life Thou didst for all procure
> We make, by our believing, sure
> To us who live and die to Thee.

While faith th'atoning blood applies,
Ourselves a living sacrifice
We freely offer up to God;
And none but those His glory share,
Who crucified with Jesus are,
And follow where their Saviour trod.

Saviour, to Thee our lives we give,
Our meanest sacrifice receive,
And to Thine own oblation join,
Our suffering and triumphant Head,
Through all Thy states Thy members lead,
And seat us on the throne Divine.   (128)

In verses 1–3 we see the by now familiar Wesleyan affirmation of the completeness of the atonement and the incapacity of
human effort to contribute to our salvation. Verse 3 ends with
the question about how we receive what Christ has done for us,
how 'we the blessing find'. The answer begins as we would
expect it to in the world of Reformation theology and evangelical piety – 'We only can *accept* the grace'. We do so by faith,
and in so doing, the 'atoning blood' of Christ's past, once-for-
all sacrifice is applied to us today. But then the thought moves
in a more unexpected direction. 'Ourselves a living sacrifice, we
freely offer up to God', asking Christ our 'Saviour' and 'triumphant Head' to 'Our meanest sacrifice receive, and to Thine
own oblation join'. Evangelically, it is surprising to see the response to the cross so clearly defined in sacrificial terms, and
then, what is more, to see it so intimately related to Christ's sacrifice and to the sacramental commemoration of the cross. Why
did the Wesleys put it this way, and were they right to do so?

In Daniel Stevick's excellent study of the Preface and the
Hymns he identifies one of the Wesleyan theological principles:

When both Brevint and Wesley say that Christians at the
Holy Communion freely give themselves to God in response
to grace, they describe this giving in terms of spiritual
sacrifice.[54]

This is made abundantly clear in the Preface, which says that 'though the sacrifice of ourselves cannot *procure* salvation, yet it is altogether needful to our receiving it'.[55] There are some interesting and fruitful theological dynamics at play here which take us back to some of the discussions in Chapter 3 on the doctrine of justification. First, we can see that in the *practice* of Christian life, *faith* and *obedience* cannot be held apart. Faith does, 'th'atoning blood apply'. But the act of faith involves a giving over of oneself to the mercy and the way of God, for, as Donald Baillie once said, 'There is no other way of receiving [Christ] except by giving ourselves to him: and there is no other way of giving ourselves to him except by receiving him.'[56] This is the reality Bonhoeffer described (and which we applied to Mary's 'Yes' to God in Chapter 5): '*Only the believers obey*, and *only the obedient believe*.'[57] It explains why evangelicals often talk about the time when people *commit* themselves to Christ as the moment of conversion and insist that one cannot have Christ as one's Saviour without at the same time having him as one's Lord.

John Wesley's distinction between justification and the new birth that we encountered in Chapter 3 may lie behind the close connection between personal faith and personal sacrifice that he and Charles make here. Although theologically, the two are distinct – 'God is justifying us does something *for* us: in begetting us again he does the work *in* us' – the one, in fact, leads to the other.[58] As we are justified by faith in the grace of God, so the same grace reconstitutes our fundamental characteristics by restoring us into relationship with the triune God. By grace we are then able to 'live in the grace of God' (Acts 13.43) and faith is able to 'work through love' (Galatians 5.6). The trinitarian basis of Christian life undergirds all of the Wesleys' thought, not least in these sections. Salvation is *communion* with Christ. It is participation in his life, and, therefore, involves *conformity* with Christ. The characteristics of Christ's life are to be replicated in the lives of his followers as they share in his life *through the Spirit*. This includes, pre-eminently, his life given over to death:

But of all these duties, the most necessary is the bearing of His Cross, and dying with Him in *Sacrifice*.[59]

By this the Wesleys' mean two things. First, that we must 'cast our sins'[60] onto Christ's sacrifice for forgiveness (more of that in a moment), and second, that we should put our sinful intentions to death in obedience, 'Crying in the Spirit's cry':[61]

Grant us full conformity,
Plunge us deep into Thy death.

Now inflict the mortal pain,
Now exert Thy passion's power,
Let the Man of Sin be slain;
Die the flesh, to live no more. (154)

Determining the Wesleys' understanding of the Spirit's work is the description in the book of Hebrews of Christ offering himself to the Father 'through the eternal Spirit' so that we can be purified and qualified 'to worship the living God' (9.14). We are able to give ourselves in obedient response because the same Spirit that filled Jesus is, through him, given to us. By this same Spirit we are empowered to offer ourselves in Christ. All of this comes to vivid expression in the Eucharist. As, by the Spirit, we commemorate the *event* of Christ's sacrifice for us, and as we have communion with him, the *attitude* that drove him to the cross is shaped within us by the Spirit, and we are able, in the words of the Prayer Book liturgy that would have been so familiar to the Wesleys, to 'offer and present unto [the] Lord, ourselves, our soul and bodies, to be a reasonable, holy and lively sacrifice':

Father, on us the Spirit bestow,
Through which Thine everlasting Son
Offer'd Himself for man below,
That *we*, even *we*, before Thy throne
Our souls and bodies may present,
And pay Thee all Thy grace hath lent.

O let Thy Spirit sanctify
Whate'er to Thee we now restore,
And make us with Thy will comply;
With all our mind, and soul, and power
Obey Thee, as Thy saints above,
In perfect innocence and love.   (150)

As we saw in hymn 128, as well as defining our response to Christ's sacrifice in sacrificial terms, the Wesleys also describe the joining of our sacrifice to Christ's in such a way that they can be seen as 'one and the same Sacrifice'.[62] At first sight this looks like dangerously dubious language that risks confusing the work of the church with the work of Christ, implying – exactly as the Wesleys did not want to – that we contribute to our salvation. There are points at which some of the hymns could easily be misconstrued in this way, and it would no doubt have been better if at times Charles had used more circumspect language. Nevertheless, the Wesleys' driving principles were thoroughly evangelical. They wanted to show that whatever responsive sacrifices we make to Christ's one sacrifice, they are only acceptable to God because of Christ's atoning work on the cross. Just as God's people of old threw their grain and drink offerings on the meat sacrifice of the sin-bearing lamb, so are we, they argued, to cast all our offerings on Christ, for 'this Great Sacrifice sustains and sanctifies only those things that are thrown into this fire, hallowed upon this Altar, and together with Christ consecrated to God'.[63] When we come to Christ, we come with the whole of ourselves, and all that we have. Yet at the same time, as Augustus Toplady was to write later in the century, 'nothing in our hands we bring, simply to the cross we cling'.[64] All that we are and all that we have we cast upon the crucified Christ and find, in Charles Wesley's distinctive language, that 'the altar sanctifies the gift'.[65]

As well as a gospel-emphasis on our inability to relate to God except through Christ and his sacrifice, the Wesleys' understanding of the integration of our sacrifice into Christ's sacrifice was also influenced by their strong view of the church

as the body of Christ, and of Christ as the representative human
being.

> Would the Saviour of mankind
> Without His people die?
> No, to Him we all are join'd
> As more than standers by.
> Freely as the Victim came
> To the altar of His cross,
> We attend the slaughter'd Lamb,
> And suffer for His cause.
>
> Him even now by faith we see;
> Before our eyes He stands!
> On the suffering Deity
> We lay our trembling hands,
> Lay our sins upon His head,
> Wait on the dread Sacrifice,
> Feel the lovely Victim bleed,
> And die while Jesus dies!   (131)

The 'suffering Deity' dies our death as one of us. God takes
on human life and dies human death, deliberately bearing his
own judgement on our sin and suffering the consequences – the
penalty – that evil brings upon itself. By faith we identify with
his sacrifice made for us as we acknowledge that it was 'our
sins which murder'd God' and that,[66] as Christ bears our sins,
he takes our sinful nature to death so that in *him* 'I who on His
cross have died' may, *through him*, 'To God for ever live'.[67]
The Eucharist is the appointed place of sacramental proclamation of the cross. It shows the cross to us through broken bread
and poured out wine so that spiritually we may *see the sacrifice*. It is a God-given opportunity for the *exercise of faith* in the
saving event of the cross, the *expression of faithful following*
of Christ in obedient living, patterned on his life and death,
and the *offering of praise and thanks* as the redeemed people of
God qualified, as the ancient liturgy of Hippolytus puts it, 'to
stand before God and minister to him'.[68]

9

Making Disciples

We only understand life backwards, but we must live forwards.[1]
Søren Kierkegaard

Introduction

This final chapter takes some of the insights of the previous chapters and applies them to the ministry and the mission of the church. It considers the form that the ministry and mission of the church will take when the gospel, the church and the Spirit are consciously and determinedly held together in the practice of the church. To put it in the shape of a question, it will ask, What will the ministry and mission of the church look like when they are gospel-driven, church-based and Spirit-led?[1] To attempt an answer I will be examining the *proclamation* of the gospel, the *signification* of the church and the *anticipation* of the Spirit. I will then move on to explore three missiological themes that emerge from the book as a whole and from this analysis in particular: evangelical catholicity of mission in the Spirit, ecclesiological imagination and renewed apostolicity. Along the way I will be drawing on three examples of God's work beyond this land that I have encountered in recent years among Coptic monks in Egypt's desert, new converts in India's slums and faithful Christians preserving a very ancient expression of the faith in the Syrian Orthodox Church. Closer to home – but not so far from the Egyptian desert or Syrian spirituality as might first be imagined – will be the inspiration I have found in the missionary monks and bishops from the edges of the British Isles who evangelized and re-evangelized not only these islands but also a good deal of mainland Europe around the collapse of the Roman Empire.

The *proclamation* of the gospel

The first thing to say about a gospel-driven, church-based and Spirit-led ministry and mission of the church is that it will be orientated towards the future, to the *eschaton*. It will look to the end and completion of God's perfecting purpose for the world, and the beginning of the age that is to come: the fulfilment of God's purposes in the new creation. Jesus is Israel's – and therefore the world's – messiah. He is the one anointed with the Spirit to establish the messianic community and to bring the kingdom of God, which is nothing less than the remaking of the created order, so that the earth, as well as heaven, is a place fit for God to dwell in. Although (using Kierkegaard's image) the church lives its life *forwards*, we – as the church – understand ourselves, our life and our work, *backwards*. The future will be *this* future, *the future of the kingdom of God*, because of God's decisive action through Jesus Christ *in the past*.

In Chapter 2 we saw that the fundamental *paradosis* – the tradition – of Christian faith is Jesus Christ who handed himself over to death for our sake, and who hands himself to the world through the life and ministry of the church. Paul explains how the truth about Christ was handed on to him in both the credal form of the one who died and rose again in accordance with scriptures, and in the sacramental form of the one who gave instructions about a meal to proclaim his death 'until he comes' in the future (1 Corinthians 15.3–5; 11.23–26). The Messiah who makes himself known in and through the life of the church – who is passed on, handed over, given to the world by the ministry of the church in creed and meal, word and sacrament – is the Christ received, interpreted and understood *according to the scriptures* within the life of the church. As we saw, this was a vital principle in the mission of the church in the early centuries. It is not *any* idea about Jesus of Nazareth that is communicated by the church. It is not *any* concept of a saving figure that lies at the heart of the church's claims. It is the Christ confessed by scripture as discerned by his people through the guidance of the Spirit who first inspired scripture: and that is the Christ who died and is risen.

Luke spells out this first principle of Christian theology and hermeneutics in the story of the disciples on the way to Emmaus in chapter 24. In one sense, these two followers of Christ were in a very privileged position. They had known, seen and heard Jesus during his ministry. They had witnessed the momentous events in Jerusalem during his last days. They had heard rumours about his body's disappearance from the tomb and of supernatural occurrences around it. Nevertheless, they were confused, perplexed, disheartened. What they needed was Jesus to say to them, 'Thus it was written, that the Messiah is to suffer and to rise from the dead on the third day, and that repentance is to be proclaimed in his name to the nations, beginning in Jerusalem' (vv. 46–47). They needed him to 'open their minds to understand the scriptures' (v. 45). They needed to see that the 'law of Moses, the prophets, and the psalms' were fulfilled in Jesus Christ (v. 44) *and* – the 'and' they could only understand after his death, as they looked back *with the scriptures* – that it was '*necessary that the Messiah should suffer* these things and then enter into his glory' (v. 26). Only then would their eyes be ready to recognize him in the breaking of the bread (vv. 31, 35) and their lips able to say that 'the Lord has risen indeed' (v. 34).

To summarize, then: first, the content of Christian faith is Jesus Christ himself. Jesus is God's news for the world. Knowing Christ as the present Lord and proclaiming him 'to all the nations' (Luke 24.47; Matthew 28.16–20) lies at the heart of evangelical ministry. Second, the understanding of this Christ is determined by scripture. For us, 'scripture' is not only the Jewish 'sacred writings' (2 Timothy 3.15) that Luke and Paul used, but the authentic apostolic interpretation of those writings by Luke, Paul and others in the New Testament. Third, because of this, the Christ we proclaim is the *coming Christ*, Israel's Messiah who came to bring the kingdom and who will come again to establish the kingdom throughout the world. We 'strain forward' to meet and greet this Christ (Philippians 3.14,

20–21) and, with the church in heaven and the Spirit of God's future, we say to all the nations, 'Come . . . let everyone who is thirsty come; let anyone who wishes take the water of life as a gift' (Revelation 22.17). Fourth, according to the scriptures as first interpreted by the Spirit-filled Messiah, we proclaim him as the Lord who will come to bring salvation because he is the one who died to secure salvation:

> Oh, how foolish you are, and how slow of heart to believe all that the prophets have declared! *Was it not necessary* that the Messiah should suffer these things and then enter into his glory (Luke 24.25–26).

Hence, the death of Christ and its meaning for the world will always be the heart of evangelical life and mission. Lesslie Newbigin, the missionary bishop and theologian, made this very clear to the village preachers of Madurai when he was Bishop of Madras in a book originally written in Tamil in 1956:

> Of course the cross must not be isolated from the whole work of Christ. Without his incarnation there could be no cross and no salvation. Without his words and works we should not know who it was that died for us there. Without his resurrection the cross would not be known to us as victory but as defeat. Without his ascension to the Father and the gift of the Spirit, we who live at other times and places could have no share in Christ. All these things are parts of the one complete work of Christ for the salvation of the whole world. But the centre and focus of that work is the cross.[2]

Concentration on Christ and his cross is as true for traditional catholic spirituality as it is for evangelical. This is made very clear in the contemplation of the cross on Good Friday when Isaiah's most poignant and powerful servant song is read or sung in the Liturgy of the Cross. Isaiah 53 has long been one of the determinative texts of the evangelical hermeneutic of scripture, the validity of which has been recently demonstrated by Tom Wright's studies of Jesus and his mission where he shows how Isaiah's songs of the suffering servant were a determining narrative for Jesus himself. The catholic liturgy of the church has spoken with the same voice in its remembrance of the passion where the solemn reading of Isaiah 52.13—53.12 acts as the interpretive key unlocking the meaning of the events that the dramatic ceremonies of the liturgy will display. Here is the heart of the gospel: the eternal God, 'despised and rejected', who has become 'a man of sorrows acquainted with grief' (AV), 'bears our infirmities' and 'carries our diseases'. God allows himself, in the person of the beloved Son, to be 'wounded for our transgressions, crushed for our iniquities' and to experience *in his own self* the punishment of our death so that we might be healed by his life (53.3–5). This is the death of the representative of God's people who takes their place in death as one of them, so that the kingdom that they were to proclaim to the nations would come. Therefore, this gospel, with Christ's death at its heart, cannot be separated from the church and the kingdom that are its consequence. This is why the Orthodox liturgy for Good Friday carries the Old Testament reading into Isaiah 54.1:

> Sing, O barren one who did not bear;
> > burst into song and shout,
> > you who have not been in labour!
> For the children of the desolate woman will be more
> > than the children of her that is married, says the Lord.

Here the liturgy connects the death of the Messiah with the great messianic prophecies of the Spirit to Israel and, through Israel, to the nations. The cross is an ecclesial, missional and cosmic event. God's people, his Israel, his church, barren no longer, will sing in praise and shout in proclamation, 'Come, buy wine and milk without money and without price . . . and all the trees of the field shall clap their hands' (54.1; 55.2; 55.12). We will return to the themes of the church and the kingdom in the next section. Now, we turn to some of the implications of all of this for the ministry of the church.

The minister as the preacher of the gospel.

Paul said to the church in Rome: 'I am not ashamed of the gospel; it is the power of God for salvation to everyone who has faith, to the Jew first and also to the Greek. For in it the righteousness of God is revealed through faith for faith; as it is written, "The one who is righteous will live by faith"' (Romans 1.16–17). The gospel of Christ's death reveals the righteousness of God, both in judging sin and in establishing righteousness for and in us. In fact, both happen in and through one and the same act. At the same time – as we have seen at other points – in order for this gift of God's grace to fulfil its work, it requires apprehension and acceptance by faith in its personal application through the Spirit. In turn, this, as Paul shows and as we have seen earlier, relies on the ministry of the church. The immediacy of God's saving presence is mediated through the ministry of God's people:

> But how are they to call on one in whom they have not believed? And how are they to believe in one of whom they have never heard? And how are they to hear without someone to proclaim him? And how are they to proclaim him unless they are sent? As it is written, 'How beautiful are the feet of those who bring good news!' But not all have obeyed the good news; for Isaiah says, 'Lord who has believed in our message?'. So faith comes from what is heard, and what is heard comes through the word of Christ. (Romans 10.14–17)

This is why P. T. Forsyth said that 'with preaching Christianity stands or falls because it is the declaration of a Gospel. Nay – far more – it is the Gospel prolonging and declaring itself'.[3] Preaching is the act of the church by which the act of God in Christ is made known, and through which the world is able to hear the word of grace and to respond in faith. This claim for preaching has to be supported by the sort of understanding of the church we arrived at in Chapter 4. The church is indeed the body of Christ, the form in which Christ's presence takes in the world and the means by which Christ expresses himself. This is why Paul describes the words of the preacher as 'the word of Christ' and why Bonhoeffer was able to say, 'The preacher should be assured that Christ enters the congregation through those words he proclaims from the Scriptures.'[4] Therefore, in Forsyth's words, 'The great, the fundamental, sacrament is the sacrament of the Word.'[5] Here, Christ not only speaks to his people about himself and his gospel, but comes to them in the gospel, presenting himself to them and making himself available, waiting to be welcomed and received by their faith.

All this means that the preacher of the gospel has an immensely high calling. The preacher is called to bring 'the word of Christ' (Romans 10.17) to the people, and, in so doing, to mediate not only Christ's word, but Christ speaking his word. Through the preacher's ministry Jesus Christ is present to his people and to the world, declaring himself as the saviour who suffered for them and as Lord who reigns over them. To begin to explore the implications of this for the preacher I am going to make use of some ancient principles of communication first presented by Aristotle, which form the basis of contemporary communication theory.[6] In his *Rhetoric*, dating from the fourth century BCE, Aristotle shows how effective communication relies on the interaction of *logos* (the *content* of what is said), *pathos* (the *situation* of those who hear what is said) and *ethos* (the *person* who saying it).

We have seen that the *logos* of Christian preaching is *the Logos*, the word of God 'incarnate of the Holy Spirit and of Mary, and made flesh in Jesus Christ, and crucified for us under Pontius Pilate', as the Nicene Creed puts it. This is why Paul told the Corinthian Christians that he 'decided to know nothing among [them] except Jesus Christ and him crucified' (1 Corinthians 2.2). This is the deep wisdom that preachers are called to search out and to shine upon the world as its source of meaning and hope. As we do so we find that we are being taken into the very 'depths of God' (1 Corinthians 2.10) and discovering the most fundamental truths about God and his purposes for the world. To enter into this sort of wisdom is the most demanding intellectual task a human being can face. Little wonder that it has captivated some of the greatest minds of world history for two millennia. Thomas Traherne in the seventeenth century said that, 'As nothing is more easy than to think, so nothing is more difficult than to think well.'[7] Nothing is so hard as to think the truth, truth as it is ultimately and finally: truth as it is in God. Yet the Christian *logos* – and here we meet the difference between the world's rhetoricians and the church's preachers, between the many and varied *logoi* of political persuaders and the one *Logos* of the Christian communicator – is not a theory that we try to reach but a revelation that we receive, not words that we find but the word that finds us and finds our hearers as we and they yield to the dynamic of Spirit and scripture. As we immerse ourselves in the 'sacred writings' we become *'wise unto salvation'* (2 Timothy 3.15 AV). And as we preach the Christ of whom the Spirit speaks in scripture – or, in Paul's language, as we 'speak of these things in words not taught by human wisdom but *taught by the Spirit'* (1 Corinthians 2.13) – this same Spirit of God opens the minds of unbelievers to receive what 2 Peter 1.3 calls 'the knowledge of him who called us by his own glory and goodness', and leads the minds of believers further into what Paul calls 'the mind of Christ' (1 Corinthians 2.16).

There is no fundamental tension between attention to the *logos* of Christian faith and the *pathos* of their hearers. Paul is a skilled example of someone who can discern the dynamics of different contexts, whether Jewish synagogue, Roman court or Athenian Areopagus, and proclaim the crucified and risen Christ consistently. However, there are dangers to avoid. Ian Stackhouse is impatient with some forms of contemporary preaching in some circles, essentially for letting *pathos* override *logos*.

The present antipathy towards preaching in certain sections of the renewal – particularly where accessibility has become the dominant concern – is derived, in our opinion, from this same failure of imagination: a preference for mood rather than the moral; apologetic rather than apostolic; theosophic rather than theological; and practical rather than doxological . . . In effect, it represents a loss of nerve in the gospel's ability to create its own agenda, to pose its own questions. Driven by the urgency of the evangelistic challenge, preaching has accommodated itself apologetically to the questions posed by the culture rather than to the crisis posed by the gospel.[8]

Stackhouse rightly warns against the sort of pragmatism of panic that, in a desperate attempt to communicate to the culture, actually loses confidence in the power of the gospel to address the deepest human needs with the 'foolishness of God' as opposed to 'wisdom of the world'.[9] Authentic preaching of the cross will produce what Stackhouse calls 'an evangelical crisis' (essentially, a recognition of the judgement of the cross leading to reliance on the promise of the cross) that will affect the emotions and will be deeply practical, for it contains 'everything needed for life and godliness' (2 Peter 1.3). At the same time, preaching of the crucified Christ can only be authentic if it is faithful to the incarnational way in which God acts through Jesus Christ, embedding himself in the human situation and relating to people of a particular time, place, language, thought form and so on. God comes to the world in this way because he 'so loves the world' (John 3.16) and will do all that is necessary to be heard by the world. The preacher who preaches this God will reflect this attention to the world and to the processes by which 'the word of Christ' can be heard by the world. Martyn Percy uses a very helpful analogy for this sort of pastoral attentiveness to context and circumstances that ministry in Christ's name requires. He refers to what viticulturists call the *terroir*, 'a word that describes the combination of climate, geography, local knowledge and instinct that goes into the making of wine'.[10] Preaching the *Logos who became flesh* involves this sort of patient attention to everything that shapes the *pathos* of the hearers. As well as being *theologians* who have a 'firm grasp of the word' (Titus 1.9), we are *anthropologists* who learn how human beings function, and *sociologists* who see how communities and societies operate. This does not mean that we have to relativize the Christian story, but it does mean we have to relate it to the conditions and context in which we find ourselves telling it, learning how the connections with people's capacity to hear can be made.

This capacity to hear is significantly affected by the *ethos* of the preacher. 'And how are they to hear without someone to proclaim him?', as Paul asks (Romans 10.14). The preacher, as we have said, communicates the heart of the Christian tradition – Jesus Christ, *the paradosis*, the one who allows himself to be handed over, in the words of the preacher. The correspondence that Christian preaching claims between the words of the preacher and the words of Christ, implies a correspondence, or connection at least, between the person of the preacher and the person of Christ. In George Hunter's discussion of effective Christian communication he quotes Ralph Waldo Emerson's definition of eloquence as 'the art of speaking what you mean and are'. Emerson explained that 'the reason why anyone refuses his assent to your opinion . . . is in you. He refuses to accept you as a bringer of truth, because, though you think you have it, he feels you have it not. You have not given him the authentic sign.'[11] If we are preaching Jesus Christ, people will expect us to display something of the transformative effect of Christ that we claim for him, to be *authentic signs* of the power of his presence on a human life, even to be a sign of his presence itself.

The most memorable sermons I have heard have been from elderly Christians – people who have followed Christ for decades and speak of him with the sort of closeness that can only come after years of walking together and facing with him all that life can throw at you. It is the sort of knowledge of the love of God in Christ that leads to the extraordinary influence on a person's life that Paul describes in 2 Corinthians 4: as 'we proclaim Jesus Christ as Lord and ourselves as your slaves for Jesus' sake' (v. 5) says Paul, 'the life of Jesus is made visible in our mortal bodies' (v. 11). One such occasion when this was particularly evident for me was when John Stott was preaching in the chapel of Ridley Hall where he had worshipped as a student 60 years earlier. It was a characteristically clear sermon full of deep Christian wisdom, but what drove its message home to the chapel packed with ordinands was the sight of a man in his eighties, suddenly looking quite frail, being led back to his seat and then falling to his knees in prayer. There was something in his dependence on the grace of God that had a Christlike character that was convicting and renewed our determination to grow in the knowledge of Christ.[12]

Of course age is by no means a guarantee of the authenticity of the preacher. We have all heard powerful testimonies from young people who have only recently found faith in Christ or who have followed him all their lives. What is critical for the preacher, whether a relatively new convert or an established disciple, is that our preaching grows out of our first-hand knowledge of Christ *according to the scriptures* and the practice of following his way. The Eastern monastic tradition has something to teach us about the discipline involved in shaping the theological mind and qualifying it to speak truthfully of God. First, the monks must submit themselves to the rigours of the ascetic life, not out of some sort of masochistic desire to punish the body, but so as to arrive at the recognition of their human fragility and their inability to serve and know God in their own strength. They are to come to the point of *humility* where they acknowledge their intellectual and spiritual poverty so that they can receive the truth that God gives. Then the monks are to attend to the spiritual practices (literally, what the Spirit practises in us) of 'un-distracted prayer and intensive reading of the Scriptures'.[13] As they do so under the Spirit's leading they will be given the grace to apprehend the reality of God and see his face in the face of Jesus Christ for, as the psalmist says, 'In your light, shall we see light' (36.9). The same method is commended to those about to be ordained priest in the Church of England's *Common Worship* ordinal:

In the name of our Lord we bid you remember the greatness of the trust that is now to be committed to your charge.
Remember always with thanksgiving that the treasure now
to be entrusted to you is Christ's own flock, bought by the
shedding of his blood on the cross. It is to him that you will
render account for your stewardship of his people.

You cannot bear the weight of this calling in your own
strength, but only by the grace and power of God. Pray
therefore that your heart may daily be enlarged and your
understanding of the Scriptures enlightened.[14]

The method of the monks and the ordinal is not far from
Karl Barth's understanding of the nature of theology and the
calling of the preacher. Like the Eastern monks, Barth described
theology as an act of 'repentant humility'. He kept himself
vividly reminded of this as he worked with a copy of Matthias
Grunewald's Isenheim altarpiece hung over his desk in Basle,
where it still remains. Grunewald's forceful rendering of the
crucifixion, with the tortured body of Christ in the central
foreground, the distraught Mary on the one side, has John the
Baptist on the other with a copy of the scriptures in one hand
and an elongated finger of the other hand pointing to Christ on
the cross. Barth believed that the figure of John pointing, not
to himself or to anyone else, but to Christ alone, was the ideal
prototype for all preachers and theologians whose calling is to
say with the Baptist, 'Behold, the Lamb of God who takes away
the sin of the world' (John 1.29). With John they are also to say
the words that appear in faded red Latin in the background of
the altarpiece, 'He must increase, I must decrease'.

The *signification* of the church

The renewal of creation through the life, death and resurrection of Jesus Christ that the church *proclaims* in its ministry of
the word, is *signified* in the identity and activity of the church.
The necessity of the church to God's mission for the created

order is made very clear by Paul when he delves into the full implications of his ministry to the Gentiles.

> Although I am the very least of all the saints, this grace was given to me to bring to the Gentiles the news of the boundless riches of Christ, and to make everyone see what is the plan of the mystery hidden for ages in God who created all things; so that *through the church the wisdom of God in its rich variety might now be made known to the rulers and authorities in the heavenly places.* This was in accordance with the eternal purpose that he has carried out in Christ Jesus our Lord, in whom we have access to God in boldness and confidence through faith in him. (Ephesians 3.8–12)

The *mysterion*, the plan and will of God 'hidden for ages in God', is manifested to the world and to 'the rulers and authorities in the heavenly places' *'through the church'* by what the church is and by what the church does. Notice how Paul talks about 'wisdom of God in its *rich variety*' being made known through the church. The reconciliation of Jew and Gentile, and the sheer breadth of humanity that they represent together, are a sign of the sort of future that God intends for the creation. In this sense, the catholicity of the church – our being with the whole of God's people – is a reflection of the coming kingdom where, according to John's vision, 'saints from every tribe and language and people and nation' will have been made into 'a kingdom and priests serving our God' (Revelation 5.10). As we saw in Chapter 4, the church is not a passive sign that simply *points* to the eschatological salvation of Christ. It *provides* this salvation in the sense that it is God's means of making this eschatological salvation available and accessible, visible and present, albeit it in a provisional, anticipatory way. In this sense it is an active sign, an *effectual sign* of the kingdom. It is an agent of God's mission proclaiming (through its words), embodying (through its life) and demonstrating (through its actions) the coming kingdom of God.

The church *lives forwards* to this kingdom because it *under-*

stands itself backwards. The church is the messianic community born, as Isaiah has shown us, out of the birth-pangs of the cross. We are, in Lesslie Newbigin's powerful expression, the 'hermeneutic of the gospel'. We are to show that the extraordinary claims of the Christian faith that 'the last words in human affairs are represented by a man hanging on the cross' make sense and that they provide a new way of ordering human life that works, and is built to last.[15] We are to embody the gospel by our *koinōnia*, our common life, our life lived *together towards the future.* It is life lived according to the needs of the whole of God's people – *catholic life* – and it is life lived according to the principles and values of the kingdom – *eschatological, Spirit-filled life.*

This is a high calling, though it would be surprising if God had any lesser purpose for the body of his Son. One period in the life of the church of this land from which many people today are drawing inspiration is the fourth to the seventh century when, with the Roman Empire collapsing around it, Christianity was forced to the Celtic edges of Britain. Here Christians regrouped and began a momentous mission that eventually claimed not only Ireland, Scotland and the north of England, but reclaimed much of the rest of England and Europe where the dispirited remnants of the church remained. My favourite among the Celtic missionaries is Aidan, sent by the Columban monks of Iona at King Oswald's request to evangelize his kingdom of Northumbria. Aidan's conversational evangelism was affirming and challenging at the same time. 'Do you love God?', he would ask the pagan poor he met on his travels. If they answered 'Yes, we love God', he would say, 'Then let me tell you more about the love of God in Jesus Christ.' If they said, 'No, we don't love God', he would respond, 'Then let me tell you about Jesus Christ and you'll hear how much God loves you.' His preaching of the gospel of Christ was undergirded by a simplicity of lifestyle and an integrity of missionary style that proved compelling to many of those he evangelized. He liked to travel on foot so that he was literally on the same level as them and able to relate to them as a genuine ambassador of the poor Christ rather than a representative of the powerful Northumberland king. Once, much to Oswald's consternation, Aidan gave away to a beggar he met along the way a horse that the king had given him. The king, who was in fact a deeply godly person, had actually given the horse to Aidan not as a status symbol but as a missionary resource, so that, as Bede says, he could 'undertake difficult or urgent journeys'. But for Aidan it was better used as a sign of the compassion and generosity of the gospel to the poor, and as a lesson to Oswald that 'this child of God' is 'more valuable than the child of a mare'.[16]

Although an effective evangelist, Aidan did not operate alone. His whole strategy, in line with the Celtic mission generally, was deeply ecclesial. He was sent by the Columban community on Iona to be a missionary bishop, and the first thing he did was to establish a community on Lindisfarne. This became a powerhouse of prayer which sustained the mission, and a place where the evangelizing monks would return to be nourished by the common life and to be spiritually renewed for their next evangelistic adventure. From this mother house, other communities were established throughout Northumberland, forming a *parochia*, a network of houses bound together by a common origin and discipline, by relationality rather than geography. Beginning very small, they would be an outpost of the kingdom of God established on the edge of a settlement. Here the monks, and in many cases nuns, as often they were 'double communities' of men and women, would model what it means to be Christian. Most of the monks were lay and so would bring their trades and skills with them, making them available to the local people. Gradually others would join them and the community would grow into a sizable settlement in its own right. From the monastic houses the *peregrinati*, the wandering missionaries, would travel around Oswald's kingdom, proclaiming the gospel, demonstrating the power and authority of the kingdom of God, and, as we hear from Bede, establishing new communities, local churches and monasteries:

Churches were built in several places, and the people flocked gladly to hear the word of God, while the king of his bounty gave lands and endowments to establish monasteries, and the English, both noble and simple, were instructed by their Irish teachers to observe a monastic life.[17]

Even though there are interesting parallels between Britain then and now, and the place of the church in society, we are in a very different cultural context from our Celtic forebears. We cannot replicate their missionary strategies in any sort of exact form. For example, as Michelle Brown notes in her detailed study of the evangelization of Britain and Ireland, the structure of a Celtic monastic community 'mapped well' onto the rural tribal society of the time, making it a particularly effective missionary tool in a way that is simply not the case today.[18] It is true that there are some important and imaginative initiatives directly inspired by the Celtic monastic movement that deserve every encouragement, but it is the underlying principles of its mission that are more likely to be transferable than the exact shape of their practice.[19] The missional value of a Christian community living out the principles of the kingdom of God and the ecclesial character of evangelism are the ones I want to highlight here. Brown shows how these early monastic communities 'presented a mirror to secular society' of God's kingdom, reflecting an enhanced, better way of organizing human life, one that was more just, more true and attractive: 'an alternative social model in which the poorest, in background and spirit, could rise to the highest position by virtue of their vocation'.[20] Contemporary culture places a high value on networks of relationships and yet is deeply fragmented, internally struggling with apparently inexorable pressures towards individualism which deny all its best instincts. Providing a local, visible and tangible example of committed, trusting and accepting community is a missionary imperative for the contemporary church. These will be generous communities that will be seen to be a *blessing* to those around them, adding value to the local community. They will offer a place of *belonging*, welcoming people into distinctive patterns of living. They will provide opportunities for learning the Christian story and *believing* its truth. They will be *Christlike* communities of grace and truth.

As well as the characteristics of the kingdom of God being modelled in the life of local churches and other forms of Christian community, the extension of the kingdom of God through evangelism is an ecclesial activity. The Celtic mission involved the strategic use of bishops such as Patrick, Aidan and Cuthbert as missionary leaders. At the same time it was a predominantly lay initiative using the gifts of committed Christian monks who made a virtue out of the fact they were not ordained. It combined the preaching of the gospel with processes by which converts could be initiated into the life of the church and discipled effectively. It faced the traumas of evangelistic disappointment and cultural persecution communally. Similarly, the evangelistic strategies that are most effective in the contemporary culture are ecclesially based, whether staged, catechumenate-style courses of initiation such as Alpha, Emmaus, or Christianity Explored, or the planting of new congregations, communities and churches in the 'Fresh expressions' and church planting movement (the latter relying very much on the missionary leadership of bishops). The way in which evangelicals have embraced these developments, often leading the way in them, is a welcome sign of the more ecclesial form of evangelicalism that I have been proposing in this book. Their long-term success depends on fostering the sort of ecclesiological imagination that we can see in the Celtic mission and which I will say more about later. It will also involve evangelicals learning more lessons from the life of the church in the third and fourth centuries in Jerusalem, Alexandria and Rome about the integration of stages to faith with the sacramental processes of the church. Robert Webber in the USA has done a great deal to relate the catechetical categories of the early church, which have been adopted into more formal systems of initiation such as the Roman Catholic *Rite of Initiation of Christian Adults*, to patterns of evangelism and discipleship more familiar to evangelicals.[21] Regrettably, his work has not received much attention in the UK and so there is more to be done to recover the originating missionary mandate of the church to make disciples through combined sacramental and didactic processes (Matthew 28.19–20).

The minister as a sign of the priestly people.

The calling of those ordained as presbyters is to serve the community of faith by presiding among its people, as Columba, who like many leaders of Celtic communities remained in presbyters orders, did in the community of Iona. Leadership in communities that are called to be Christlike brings the mandate of Christlikeness to the presider just as much as it does to the preacher. 1 Peter 5, almost an ordination charge in its quality, exhorts presbyters to be 'examples to the flock'. They are *signs within a sign.* Just as the church, the messianic community, is called to be a sign of the kingdom of the Messiah, presbyters are called to be signs of the life and health of the church – embodiments of what it means to be the church, indicators of its priestly identity, 'sacramental personalities' as Oswald Chambers puts it, of its missionary character.[22] Similarly, just as the church is to be an active sign of the kingdom, effecting what it signifies, so presbyters are to be effectual signs of the church's nature and mission, serving and leading the church in such a way that its 'inner nature' is more fully realized.

I have written at length about ordained ministry along these lines elsewhere, so there is no need to repeat here what is said there.[23] The point I want to make now is the relationship between the mission of the church and the priestly character of ministry hinted at by Paul in Romans 15.15–16:

> Nevertheless on some points I have written to you rather boldly by way of reminder, because of the grace given to me by God to be a minister of Christ Jesus to the Gentiles in the priestly service of the gospel of God, so that the offering of the Gentiles may be acceptable, sanctified by the Holy Spirit.

This is the only occasion where Paul explicitly connects Christian ministry to priestly activity. It is significant that he does so in the context of his fundamental calling to preach the gospel to the Gentiles. Making the God of the covenant and his just rule known to the nations was the ultimate calling of Israel. This was how God's people were to fulfil their charge to be a blessing to the nations. This was why they were chosen. This would be the purest sacrifice of obedience and praise that they would offer to God. All of this Paul saw fulfilled in the mission of the church to the Gentiles as it proclaimed that all – Jews and Gentiles – 'are one in Christ Jesus' and thus all are heirs to the promise the kingdom (Galatians 3.28–29). As we saw in Chapter 8, the missionary calling and priestly vocation of the church are inextricably bound together. Indeed, the missionary activity of the church is the most complete expression of its priestly identity. Similarly, those called to be signs of the messianic life of the church and leaders in its mission are called to 'the priestly service of the gospel', desiring above all to see 'Christ formed' in his people (Galatians 4.19) and the Gentiles become an 'acceptable offering, sanctified by the Holy Spirit' (Romans 15.16).

The *anticipation* of the Spirit

We have already said a good deal about the Spirit in this chapter: how the Spirit is the Spirit of God's future; how the Spirit anointed Christ as the bringer of the future reign of God; how the Spirit anoints us as the messianic community of Christ to proclaim, embody and demonstrate the kingdom of God's love, his shalom of reconciliation, justice and peace where the whole creation is renewed. The Spirit is given to us as the *arrabōn*, the down-payment of this future (2 Corinthians 1.22), bringing us the *aparchē*, the first-fruit of all that is to come (Romans 8.23). So the Spirit enables us to *live forwards*, even groaning within us, sharing our sighs, as we long for the kingdom to come fully (Romans 8.18–27). At the same time the

Spirit helps us to *understand ourselves backwards* by teaching us about the messianic ministry of Christ, reminding us of all that he did, taking what is his, and declaring it to us, incorporating us into his ministry (John 15.15).

What does this look like in practice? What does this sort of kingdom ministry look like, and what does it achieve? What, for example, does the kingdom of God look like in the slums of Delhi in the twenty-first century? That is exactly the question that Kiran Martin asked and answers in the following remarkable letter. Kiran is an irrepressible medical doctor who founded a charity called Asha, a Hindi word meaning hope. I had a brief opportunity to work with Asha in one of the slums where it works. I have seen what she describes.

What does the kingdom of God look like in the slums, where little children play with excrement, fall into dirty drains, where waste rots, pigs feed, flies feast, pollution lingers, odours ferment and diseases mock? Where children live in tents stitched with rags, neglected and abused, where the joy of childhood is never experienced? Where women are suppressed and beaten, stripped of their rights, voiceless?

I began my spiritual quest nearly twenty years ago through sitting outside a tiny slum hut, one among hundreds of huts squeezed together along a filthy drain. I treated the sick all day, listening to them and comforting them. Today, nearly two decades later, as I see the beautiful women holding their heads high, empowered and confident, healthy children living in safe and secure homes, and playing happily on the clean paved streets, perhaps I have had a glimpse of what the kingdom of God looks like in the slums.

In this kingdom, the slums become a place where the poor, created in the image of God, become possessors of a dignity, their inherent worthiness, which is inalienable and inviolable. Where they are empowered to live full and meaningful lives. Where God's justice and impartiality are consistently expressed. Where the oppressed and exploited, those treated with scorn, exclusion and contempt, are defended and comforted. Where the fainthearted are encouraged, where the dimly burning flame is never quenched, where fairness and truth reign.

It is a place where we respond to injustice through non-violent resistance and active peacemaking, thus showing ourselves not violent or weak, but rather courageous and dignified and strong, exposing the naked greed and cruelty of our oppressors.

It is a place where compassion and love is the fundamental thing. And it is not just about loving friends and hating enemies, but about loving our enemies. About pursuing forgiveness and reconciliation, not retaliation and revenge.

It is a place where we practise a liberating generosity toward the poor, to dethrone greed that clouds our outlook, and topple the regime of money.

It is a place where joyful, worshipping communities of the poor and the outcasts experience God's forgiveness and blessing, healing and restoration.

Those belonging to this kingdom refuse to respect economic, class or social barriers, but rather treat everyone with kindness and respect. They enjoy the company of the poor, the homeless, the disadvantaged, the social outcasts and the marginalized women and children, eating and drinking with them.

This kingdom advances not through those who are preoccupied with money, power, status and control, but through those who are preoccupied with service and love, justice and mercy, humility and hope. With those who are fired up to sacrifice their time, intelligence, money and energy in the advancement of this kingdom. And once we get a glimpse of this kingdom, nothing else will fully satisfy us.

It is my prayer that my slums will become a place God is at home in, a place that God takes pride and pleasure in, a place where God's dreams come true.

This is powerful example of Christian ministry actually demonstrating the way and rule of God. It is making a difference to lives – hundreds of them. It is changing communities, slowly but very surely. It is influencing politicians and officials, persuading them to act justly. It also draws people to Christ, the bringer of the kingdom – two men and many women come to mind. There is the teacher employed to give the slum children a basic education and to help them to access the state education system. A Hindu by background, he joined in the prayer meetings of the Christian staff in the slum where he worked. As some of the slum dwellers began to take a more active part in the meetings, he took a particular interest in the Bible readings. Being one of the few who could read, he offered to read the reading and then to give the short talk that usually followed it. Although at this stage he would have still called himself a Hindu, the influence of the embryonic Christian community which was emerging in the slum, and the self-authenticating character of scripture, had their effect and he gradually moved into Christian faith. Then there is a very sophisticated Hindu, an impressive intellectual and a prominent journalist with the *Hindi Times*. He was attracted to Asha because of the integrity of its founder and staff and its long-term commitment to the improvement of conditions in the slums. He offered to become its Treasurer and to use his influence in Delhi society to further its ends. He remains a Hindu but is clearly 'not far from the kingdom of God' and deeply attracted to its Messiah.

The women I met in the slums had the most moving stories to tell. They certainly were 'the joyful, worshipping communities of the poor and the outcasts experiencing God's forgiveness and blessing, healing and restoration' that Kiran Martin describes. Their movement towards Christ was fascinating. As they trusted the Christian staff who came to serve them, they joined with them in their daily prayer meetings. After some time they began praying to Christ themselves. They found that their prayers were answered when they prayed to Jesus in a way that they had never known in their prayers to the Hindu gods. Gradually they moved from adopting Jesus as their personal God (quite an acceptable thing to do in Hindu religion) to confessing him as Lord of Lords.

The 'healing and restoration' experienced in the slums involved political engagement with the local and national government, radical improvement of the child mortality rate, confidence to step out of one's slum dwelling, the joy of seeing one's children fulfil their ability in school, the healing of bodies, the forgiveness of sins and a good deal else. And their prayers ranged across all these dimensions of life – social, political, spiritual, bodily, relational – with some remarkable answers to their prayers on every level of life that one could only describe as miraculous. Their understanding of the scope and reality of God's present activity fits almost exactly with the Hebrew expectation about the coming kingdom of God described by the Old Testament scholar and missiologist Chris Wright in his classic study, *The Mission of God*.

> The reign of YHWH, when it would finally come, would mean justice for the oppressed and the overthrow of the wicked. It would bring true peace to the nations and the abolition of war, the means of war, and training for war. It would put an end to poverty, want and need, and provide everyone with economic viability . . . It would mean satisfying and fulfilling life for human families, safety for children, and fulfilment for the elderly, without danger from enemies, and all of this within a renewed creation free from harm and threat. It would mean the inversion of the moral values that dominate the current world order, for in the kingdom of God the upside down priorities of the beatitudes operate and the Magnificat is not just wishful thinking.[24]

As Kiran Martin says about the work of the Spirit in the slums of Delhi, 'once we get a glimpse of this kingdom, nothing else will fully satisfy us'.

The minister and the ministry of the Spirit.

If the church is to be an agent of the coming kingdom of God, those ordained to its ministry are to lead the church in the fullness of the Spirit's ministry: the proclamation of Christ as Lord; the building up of the church as the community of the Messiah; the work of the kingdom of God in all its breadth, with the same signs that accompanied Jesus and his disciples, and have been evident throughout the history of the church, especially in the front line of mission. This is the eschatological breadth of ministry that Paul is able to boast of because of the messianic work of Christ at work through him.

> In Christ Jesus, then, I have good reason to boast of my work for God. For I will not venture to speak of anything except what Christ has accomplished through me to win obedience from the Gentiles, by word and deed, by the power of signs and wonders, by the power of the Spirit of God, so that from Jerusalem and as far around as Illyricum I have fully proclaimed the good news of Christ. (Romans 15.17–19)

I had an encounter with this Pauline breadth of ministry in a place where I had not expected to find it.[25] I made a retreat in a Coptic monastery in the Wadi el-Natroum between Cairo and Alexandria in northern Egypt. It was founded in the desert by St Macarius, a contemporary of St Antony in the fourth century. Like Antony, Macarius went into the Egyptian desert seeking space and solitude in which to pray. He was followed by other Christians who felt that commitment to faith had been diluted by the legalization of Christianity and the ensuing influx into the churches. They were searching for a more serious form of faith, and they looked for it in the desert. In time, Macarius wove these eremitic monks into a loose-knit community, eventually building a chapel large enough for 400 monks to gather in. The monastery still remains. Restored in the 1970s during a revival in the Coptic Church, it is a large, vibrant community – literally an oasis in the desert and an enduring witness to the power of the faith to survive the vicissitudes of the centuries.

Among the many monks I met at Macarius was the librarian, Father Philemon. He looked the part: small and thin, face hidden by a long, grey beard, body shrouded by a long, black cassock. I had asked him to talk me through the liturgy of St Basil used in the daily Eucharist. But Philemon had other ideas. 'Tell me about Reinhard Bonnke!', he said. I was completely taken aback. The last person I expected this elderly monk from one of the most ancient Christian traditions in the world to be interested in was a free-church German evangelist whose pentecostal style even I found somewhat off-putting. 'I know he's not an Orthodox', said Philemon, 'but he's bringing many people to Christ, and that's wonderful.' 'I want to hear about these people who have come to know Jesus!' Philemon wanted people to know Jesus Christ. This is the heart of evangelical ministry, the core of the gospel, the heart of the tradition, the centre of scripture.

Philemon's love of the gospel was set within a very strong commitment to the life of the church. This is simply a given in the monastic life of Macarius, an assumption around which the whole life of the community is based. The monks have their own cells and much more freedom to order their disciplines than in a Western monastery. Some of them live in hermitages outside the main enclosure of the monastery, on the edge of the wildness of the desert. But their lives are bound together, *for life*. They worship in the church where the bones of Macarius and his two successors with the same name rest, rolled in velvet shrouds and placed in a niche of the chapel. They have no doubt that they belong to an unbroken tradition of the community where Christ is present with his people. They believe that he is present as they worship, and their celebration of the Eucharist comes to a dramatic climax with the bringing of the consecrated elements into the body of the congregation and a palpable sense of the inbreaking presence of God among his people.

Convictions about the power of the gospel and the presence of Christ in the church, as well as centuries of evidence, leave the monks with no doubt about the charismatic, kingdom-bringing activity of God's Spirit. In my early conversations with Philemon I tentatively asked him whether he believed in the healing ministry of the church. He looked at me in astonishment. How could I not believe that God heals through the ministry of the church? Then he went on to recount stories of other miraculous works of God – healings, words, visions, extraordinary provision of money when the monastery was being rebuilt and the community purse and larder were empty, with workers needing to be paid and stomachs to be fed the next day. Each of these commitments to the gospel, the church and the kingdom life of the Spirit were entirely familiar to me. I had friends across the Christian spectrum who had built their whole lives on one, and sometimes on two of them. What I found so inspiring in Philemon and the other monks I met was the way this ancient tradition *held them together*.

It will come as no surprise that there are several historical connections between the movement of the Spirit in the fourth century in the Egyptian desert and that other source of inspiration to this chapter – the movement of the Spirit in the fifth to seventh centuries on the edges of the British Isles. The Celts were by nature a wandering people, and there is a good deal of evidence that the Celtic monks may have found their way to the Egyptian desert. Certainly they knew of the writings about the desert fathers by Cassian and Pachomios, and there are obvious similarities between the Coptic and Celtic art forms still evident today in the intricate patterns on the woodwork of the church of St Macarius. Perhaps the most obvious example of interplay between the two traditions is the church of St Brigid at Kildare in Ireland built in an early Coptic style. Most interesting though, from my point of view, is the way that both Copts (ancient and modern) and Celts had a holistic, integrated understanding of Christian life and mission.

The most influential figure in the early stages of the Celtic mission was Patrick, born in Britain in a Christian home around 398 CE but converted 16 years later ('with all [his] heart to the Lord') in Ireland after he had been abducted from his home land and forced into slavery.[26] Patrick said, 'I cannot be silent . . . about the great grace' that he had encountered on the Irish moors when he came to faith in Christ. He became an ardent evangelist, preaching and baptizing thousands. He gathered followers around him and formed communities of prayer and spiritual training from which the Irish monks went to Iona, Lindisfarne, Paris, Berne, Salzburg and as far south as Naples, reclaiming Europe for Christ.[27] He designed institutional structures for the church to serve its mission, and hundreds of local churches were established. As well as preaching to convert, Patrick saw the social implications of the gospel. He was perhaps the earliest campaigner against the slave trade of which he had been a victim, and his whole evangelistic strategy aimed to bring Ireland, and surrounding nations, closer to the kingdom of God. The presence of the coming kingdom was experienced by Patrick through various other workings of the Spirit. Like the desert fathers, Patrick heard God speaking to him through visions and words, he experienced God answering prayers with remarkable timing, he saw God prove himself stronger than the powers of Druid religion, and healings and other miracles were commonplace in his ministry as they were right through to Cuthbert's ministry in the seventh century. For example, Adomnán's *Life of Columba* (Columba carried the Irish mission to the Picts in the north of Scotland) is full of stories of dramatic miracles, the appearance of angels and experiences of the uncreated light of heaven that plays an important part in Eastern monastic spirituality. Scholars have tended to dismiss Adomnán's work as a piece of blatant hagiography modelled on pagan works that have the sole purpose of authenticating the life of a holy person by recounting tales of the miraculous that the modern reader will instinctively dismiss as pure fabrication. However, James Bruce's careful study of Adomnán's *Life of Cuthbert* has shown that his work is based on biblical and traditional Christian precedents and is designed not to prove Columba's sanctity but to authenticate the Columban mission by showing how, through the messianic and apostolic ministry of Columba and those supporting him, the eschatological kingdom was breaking in through the Spirit's power. Bruce concludes his study in this way:

Adomnán presents himself, and his subject, as Christians fully conversant with, and expectant of the present reality of, a tradition of Christian practice as recorded in the canonical and patristic record. The evidence points us to the conclusion that for Adomnán, in his contemporary culture, these phenomena are both real, and to be expected, as the kingdom of God is promulgated.[28]

I hope that these contemporary and historical examples of a holistic approach to Christian life and ministry will support and illustrate the theological case I have been making throughout this study, which is that evangelical ministry is most true to the gospel, and therefore to itself, when its underlying theology and its missionary practice keep the gospel of Christ's saving work in the closest connection with the life of his church and the dynamic presence of the Spirit. This is what I mean by *evangelical catholicity in the Spirit*. Essentially, it is about the wholeness of the gospel for the wholeness of life and for the whole of the world.

Ecclesiological imagination

My one disappointment during my short time in India was seeing the Church of North India's (CNI) reluctance to involve itself in some of the new forms of church life that were springing up in Delhi and no doubt beyond. Several of the people who worked with Asha were from CNI, and they found themselves in a dilemma. They had not intended to grow churches. They were a medical charity. But, as Christians served the kingdom of God and witnessed to Christ by their compassion, the church was coming to be, emerging from the ground that the Spirit was reclaiming. People were coming to faith in Christ and needing to be nurtured in discipleship and organized into patterns of common life. However, this raw and untidy emergence of the church as an apparently spontaneous propagation of a gospel-driven and Spirit-filled ministry, did not fit the established ecclesial systems and structures of the denomination. And that is exactly how it seemed to me that CNI understood itself in this situation – as *one denomination among others*, built to operate reasonably successfully in some situations and among existing Christians of a certain sort, but not suitable for many others.

All of this gave me a renewed appreciation of contemporary English Anglican ecclesiology. Because of its self-understanding as 'the ancient Church of this land' and its commitment to the whole nation, the Church of England is uncomfortable with denominational ecclesiology, and even less with a denominational missiology.[29] It is committed to a mission to the whole nation and, at least in principle, does not allow itself the luxury of abdicating responsibility to serve everyone everywhere. Over recent years there have been several signs that this ecclesiological principle is being turned into missional practice through a renewal of ecclesiological imagination. Times of missionary challenge and opportunity require hard thinking about the shape of the church and the way it manages its life, asking the fundamental question of how far its systems and structures arise from and serve the gospel. It is not, as we saw in Chapter 4, simply a case of throwing out everything associated with the church in favour of everything associated with the gospel, as if such a neat distinction could be made. The church belongs to the gospel and so do the deepest characteristics of its order. It is a case, though, of trying to discern the *Rule* of the church – that which makes it what it is, and without which it would not be the church – from the *rules* of the church, those culturally and historically conditioned expressions and applications of the *Rule* to particular times and places. In the terms we were using in Chapter 2, it is about distinguishing the *paradosis*, and all that intrinsically arises from it, from the *paradoseis*, the Tradition of the gospel, from the traditions that attempt to live out the Tradition at different times.

I have tried elsewhere to identify the *Rule* of the church and all that necessarily follows from it. I offer the following adapted version as an example of the sort of process we need if we are to reshape the church effectively, and not to damage it in the process.

> The deepest Rule of the Church is the gospel of grace that generates communities *organised* around 'the apostolic teaching and fellowship' and 'the breaking of the bread and prayers' (Acts 2.42). They are *ordered* towards mutual responsibility expressed through a network of interrelated and interdependent gifts and ministries and gifts that promote its growth in love (Philippians 2.4; Ephesians 4.7–16), and that include the equipping and animating ministries of apostolic overseers, congregational leaders and servants of the kingdom (Acts 20.28; 2 Timothy 3.1–13; Titus 1.5–9; 1 Peter 5.1–2). And they are *orientated* towards those who do not confess Christ as the Messiah by proclaiming him as Lord and by baptising those who 'welcome the message' with the result that 'the Lord adds to their number'. (Acts 2.36–47)[30]

An interesting example of the church re-examining its *rules* to see how far they served the messianic *Rule* to proclaim Christ and his kingdom, and then adjusting them as necessary, stems from the early sixteenth century when Pope Leo X promulgated the *Apostolic Faculties*. The *Faculties* were a set of permissions that freed the local bishop to adapt the church's common, or canon law, to meet the needs of the new missionary situations opening up in different parts of the world. It is 'realized', they said, 'that missionaries have to be furnished with special faculties in order to be able to establish the Church and to exercise their holy calling among newly converted Christians'.[31] The Mission Orders of the Church of England are a contemporary example of the same attempt. They allow the bishop directly to promote new missional endeavours that will 'foster or develop a form of Christian community'.[32] They are a new departure on a number of levels. *Geographically*, they reduce the autonomy of the parish system. They allow for new forms of church to be formed within a geographical parish but independently of the parish church itself. They give the bishop freedom to be *apostolic*, to send workers into the harvest to work in parallel alongside traditional parish ministry. *Institutionally*, they recognize that the church is an ecosystem able to sustain various forms of mutually supporting life within it. (To change the analogy, they see that the church has a large enough hard-drive and a powerful enough operating environment to allow it to run several programs at the same time without crashing.) *Ecclesially*, they give the congregation space in which to develop in ways that are appropriate to the context and faithful to the Anglican tradition. *Liturgically*, they encourage worship that is appropriate to the people and place but consistent with Anglican principles and values. Of course, it will be some time before we can judge the success of the Orders and, of themselves, they are not an end to the challenge to think imaginatively about the structure and shape of the church, but they are a significant step along the way.

Renewal of apostolicity

The Syrian Orthodox Church has a very ancient feel to it. It is something to do with the land itself where the Euphrates runs and where Paul was converted. It is something to do with the language, a dialect of Aramaic, the language of Jesus. It is something to do with the Christians themselves who think in long historical terms. The antiquity of the Church is palpable, but so is its present vitality as it faces the familiar pressures on Christians in the Middle East and somehow manages to thrive. When one of the friends I met on my travels to the Syrian church visited the UK for a few months he asked me to explain the Church of England to him. His first question was, 'And which Apostle founded your Church?' He was not trying to score any ecumenical points. It was an entirely natural question for someone from a semitic church 150 miles from Jerusalem that traces its leaders back from the present Patriarch to Peter himself. It was also an important question because the church is 'built upon the foundation of the apostles and prophets, with Christ Jesus himself as the chief cornerstone' (Ephesians 2.20).[33] The apostles were sent by Jesus who in turn was sent by the Father (Mark 3.13–15). The church is apostolic because it participates in the originating sending of the apostles by the Son, and in so doing is drawn by the Son into his sending by the Father, through the Holy Spirit, to proclaim the kingdom and redeem the world: 'As the Father has sent me, so I send you' (John 20.21). We are only the church inasmuch as we share in this apostolic mission and proclaim this apostolic faith.

How is the *sentness*, the apostolicity of the church, to be preserved and promoted? How is it to be renewed and released? Again we can appeal to the eschatological dynamic of living *forwards* and understanding ourselves *backwards*. The apostolic faith is the DNA, the genetic code of the church in which it lives and grows, speaks and acts. If this code is distorted the church mutates into a body that cannot fully live towards the future of the kingdom or play its part in its coming. The necessity of passing on this code and preserving its integrity is why I have maintained that the gospel of grace gives rise to apostolic overseers who guard the transmission and expression of the apostolic faith and its core practices: the teaching and fellowship, the breaking of the bread and the prayers (Acts 2.42). I have also argued that the gospel gives rise to these ministries because they not only preserve the essential characteristics of the sent church, but also because they promote its *sentness* by structuring its life and reordering its rules to ensure that the church is truly able to be apostolic. As we saw in Chapter 4, this is the ministry that bishops are called to exercise in the church. They are ordained to signify the apostolic mission of the church by their historical connection to the ministry of the originating apostles, and to enable the church to be effective in mission by fulfilling the apostolic functions handed over to them at their ordinations. With their oversight of multiple congregations, their authority to ordain, their capacity to inspire and encourage, their ability to adapt the rules and conventions of the church and their responsibility as guardians and interpreters of the faith and their powers to establish new congregations, bishops have a unique gospel-driven opportunity to release the apostolicity of the church for the sake of the kingdom of God. We need that ministry as much in our day as they did in Patrick's.

Epilogue

Concluding with some pictures, a prayer and a person.

As well as being remarkably effective in mission, the early British monastic movement that we met in the previous chapter was also extraordinarily creative in its art. Just as its mission was notable for the way it held together gospel, church and Spirit in a holistic commitment to convicting word, powerful sign and dynamic community, so its art forms were structured around careful systems that deliberately brought together that which appeared to be different. The Lindisfarne Gospels are, perhaps, the most glorious example.[1] Aidan's monks – now half a century on – took the saving words of Jesus (the *gospel*) addressed to his people (the *church*) through the *Holy Spirit*, and crafted them onto the best vellum with exquisite calligraphy, decorating them with vibrant images. Word and image belonged together in the minds of the monks. At one moment the word becomes image, at another the image becomes word. Both speak to heart and mind. 'In images, the illiterate read,' said Pope Gregory the Great, 'each word written as a wound on Satan's body.' And so the monks inscribed their scripture not only as a ministry of love to the person behind the text, but as a share in his missionary work. These were the books that would present the *Godspell* (the old English word for gospel) to the English people. They would make Jesus known.

Cuthbert, Aidan's successor, also embodied the evangelistic zeal, charismatic expectation and catholic commitment to the life of the church typical of the Celtic mission. But times had moved on since Aidan's day, and now the challenge was to find a way of holding the Celtic energy that had come from the west via the north together with the more Roman, and somewhat more settled, patterns of church life that had grown out of Augustine's mission in the south. The magnanimity that Cuthbert displayed at the Council of Whitby in 664, where his great aim was the unity of the church, with its richness of life lived together for the sake of Christ's one gospel, is demonstrated artistically in the Lindisfarne Gospels. Each gospel is prefaced by a 'cross-carpet' page with an intricately swirling design, full of colour and life, into which a different form of the cross is set for each gospel – not only the Roman and Celtic crosses of the West but also two different versions of Eastern style crosses. Here the church across the known world was held together in the covers of the book about the one who holds his people together in his own body. Here also was an instinctive understanding of the character of scripture centuries before the rise of biblical criticism as we know it. They knew that each of the Gospels told the story of Jesus in a different way; but they knew that it is same story about the same person with the same ending in the cross and resurrection – and that it was this story that binds together the different gospel accounts and the different books of the Bible into one sacred text. Running alongside the theological and ecclesiastical concerns of the Lindisfarne monks was the desire (itself driven by the ways of the kingdom of God) to bring the diverse cultures that now inhabited the islands of Britain and Ireland into some sort of common life. Theirs was a vision that wove the indigenous Celtic and Anglo-Saxon traditions into a vibrant fabric of national life shot through with colourful threads of life from Mediterranean, North African and Byzantine church and culture. It was a missionary strategy that encompassed the whole of society.

All of this activity was centred on the words of the person described in the first chapter of this book as 'the principle of cohesion in the universe [who] impresses upon creation that unity which makes it a cosmos rather than a chaos'.[2] There is an ancient prayer that has its origins in the cry of a blind Jewish man to the wandering Jewish sage and miracle-worker who was none other than this eternal principle of cohesion embodied in the contingencies of human life. The Jesus Prayer, as it has become known, has developed into a slightly fuller form since Bartimaeus' day, but it remains very simple: 'Lord Jesus Christ, Son of God, have mercy on me a sinner'.[3] It is a prayer that grew out of the semitic soil of Israel, the ground that Jesus trod, and from the people who were his own. It took root in far-off places among the monks and mystics of Egyptian deserts, Greek monasteries, and hermits and pilgrims across the plains of Russia. After many years of being somewhat hidden in the spiritual treasuries of the East, it has become increasingly popular in the Western church. Perhaps its appeal lies also in its juxtaposition of the humanity and divinity of Christ (who is at the same time *Jesus of Nazareth* and *eternal Son of God*), or in its tension between the unending graciousness of God, with its unwavering invitation to follow Christ, and the pervasive sinfulness of those of us who try to do so. I find it a helpful prayer because, like any prayer to Jesus Christ, its function is to lead us into his presence so that there – *in Christ* – we can begin to discover his 'boundless riches' and there find our place in the life of God. These are the boundless riches of the one anointed by the Spirit to proclaim the gospel of the kingdom of God, and to form a community around him through which 'the wisdom of God in its rich variety may be made known to the rulers and the authorities in the heavenly places', so that 'everyone can see what is the plan of the mystery hidden for ages in God who created all things' (Ephesians 3.8–10). When Jesus' first followers lived out his calling to go out in his name, anointed with his Spirit to proclaim the kingdom of God and to confront evil, we are told that he 'rejoiced in the Holy Spirit and said, "I thank you, Father, Lord of heaven and earth"' (Luke 10.21). The prayer of those who follow him is that we too may cause this prayer to resound in the triune life of the one God where the Father, the Son and the Holy Spirit are held together in one communion of love.

Notes

Preface

1 Charles Simeon's preface to *Horae Homilecticae*, quoted in Handley C. G. Moule, *Charles Simeon: Biography of a Same Saint*, London: InterVarsity Press, 1965, p. 79.

2 Amos Yong, *Spirit–Word–Community*, Aldershot: Ashgate, 2002, p. 14.

3 For a study that bears some relationship to this one, but that works with a somewhat different methodology, see Alan Bartlett, *A Passionate Balance: The Anglican Tradition*, London: DLT, 2007.

4 I am grateful to the Harold Buxton Trust and the Philip Usher Memorial Fund for funding my time in Egypt and Syria, and to friends and family for sponsoring my visit to India.

Chapter 1

1 For a thorough analysis of the dating of Colossians, see Peter T. O'Brien, *Colossians, Philemon*, 'Word Biblical Commentary', vol. 44, Waco: Word Books, 1982, pp. xlix–liv.

2 Although I find nothing unreasonable in the letter's claim that Paul is its author, for our purposes it does not matter a great deal whether it was written by Paul or by someone in his school of thought, perhaps a person who had travelled and ministered with him. It is generally agreed that the letter works with the principles and priorities of Pauline thought while at the same time digging deeper into the 'mystery that has been hidden throughout the ages and generations but has now been revealed to his saints' (Colossians 1.26). The same applies to the letter to the Ephesians.

3 Cited in Eduard Lohse, *Colossians and Philemon*, Philadelphia: Fortress Press, 1971, p. 52.

4 Joseph B. Lightfoot, *Epistles to the Colossians and to Philemon*, London: Macmillan, 1890, p. 154.

5 O'Brien, *Colossians, Philemon*, p. 47.

6 See Ezekiel 1.15–26.

7 Frederick F. Bruce, *The Epistles to the Colossians, to Philemon and to the Ephesians*, 'The New International Commentary on the New Testament', Grand Rapids: Eerdmans, 1984, p. 29.

8 Lightfoot, *Epistles to the Colossians and to Philemon*, p. 164.

9 Clark H. Pinnock, *The Concept of Spirit in the Epistles of Paul*, unpublished thesis: Manchester, 1963, p. 105, quoted in Bruce, *The Epistles to the Colossians, to Philemon and to the Ephesians*, p. 28.

10 Bruce, *The Epistles to the Colossians, to Philemon and to the Ephesians*, p. 28.

11 Paul Avis, *The Church in the Theology of the Reformers*, London: Marshall, Morgan & Scott, 1981, p. 3.

12 Ignatius, *Epistle to the Smyrnaeans*, 8.2.

13 Irenaeus, *Adversus Haereses*, New York: Paulist Press, 1992, 3.24.1.

14 The full text of the exchange between Sadoleto and Calvin can be found in John C. Olin (ed.), *A Reformation Debate: Sadoleto's Letter to the Genevans and Calvin's Reply*, New York: Harper & Row, 1966, p. 62. Hereafter, cited as *Sadoleto's Letter to the Genevans and Calvin's Reply*.

15 *Sadoleto's Letter to the Genevans and Calvin's Reply*, p. 62.

16 Cited in Alister E. McGrath, *Roots That Refresh: A Celebration of Reformed Spirituality*, London: Hodder & Stoughton, 1992, p. 15. See also Jaroslav Pelikan, *Catholic Substance and Protestant Principle in Luther's Reformation*, London: SCM Press, 1964. Note particularly his comment on the (Lutheran) Augsburg Confession: 'It refused to be identified with those movements, past and present, which accepted the identification between Roman and Catholic and then proceeded to reject both. Rather, the Augsburg Confession sought to root its protest against Rome in the Catholic Tradition' (p.45).

17 From 'The Author to the Christian Reader', William Perkins, *A Reformed Catholike*, London: John Legat, 1598.

18 'The Author to the Christian Reader' in Perkins, *A Reformed Catholike*.

19 Perkins, *A Reformed Catholike*, p. 354. Perkins was being deliberately evocative of Vincent of Lerin's famous definition of catholic truth as 'what has been believed everywhere, always and by all'.

20 See 'A Letter to a Roman Catholic' (1749) in *The Works of John Wesley*, vol. 10, Grand Rapids: Zondervan Publishing House, 1872, p. 81; and 'Catholic Spirit' in John Wesley, 'Sermons II: 43–70', ed. Albert C. Outler, *The Works of John Wesley*, vol. 2, Nashville: Abingdon Press, 1984, III.4, p. 94.

21 Dieter Voll, *Catholic Evangelicalism: The Acceptance of Evangeli-*

cal Traditions by the Oxford Movement During the Second Half of the Nineteenth Century, London: Faith Press, 1963, p. 71.

22 Henry Scott Holland, *A Bundle of Memories*, London: Wells, Gardner, Darton & Co., 1915, p. 77. For Wilkinson's theology, see *The Invisible Glory: Selected Sermons Preached by George Howard Wilkinson*, London: A. R. Mowbray, 1908.

23 Charles W. Colson and Richard John Neuhaus (eds), *Evangelicals and Catholics Together: Toward A Common Mission*, London: Hodder & Stoughton, 1996; and James S. Cutsinger (ed.), *Reclaiming the Great Tradition: Evangelicals, Catholics and Orthodox in Dialogue*, Downers Grove: InterVarsity Press, 1997. For various examples of attempts within the wider world of Protestantism to develop a theology which is genuinely evangelical *and* catholic, see James J. Buckley and David S. Yeago, 'Introduction: A Catholic and Evangelical Theology', in *Knowing the Triune God: The Work of the Spirit in the Practices of the Church*, ed. James J. Buckley and David S. Yeago, Grand Rapids: Eerdmans, 2001; and Simon Chan, *Pentecostal Theology and the Spiritual Tradition*, Sheffield: SAP, 2000; also Simon Chan, *Liturgical Theology: The Church as a Worshipping Community*, Downers Grove: InterVarsity Press, 2006.

24 Quoted in Robert Webber, *Ancient-Future Faith: Rethinking Evangelicalism for a Postmodern World*, Grand Rapids: Baker Books, 2004, p. 26.

25 Webber, *Ancient-Future Faith*, p. 204.

26 Webber, *Ancient-Future Faith*, p. 204.

27 'Windows' in Christopher Ricks (ed.), *George Herbert: The Complete English Poems*, Middlesex: Penguin Books, 1991, p. 61. For a fuller presentation of the imagery in Ridley's Chapel see my 'Windows of Grace and Truth: Envisaging Anglican-Evangelical Methodology through the Iconography of a Chapel', *Theology* 104 (2003).

28 Charles Wesley and John Wesley, *The Poetical Works of John and Charles Wesley*, ed. G. Osborn, vol. 6, London: Wesleyan-Methodist Conference Office, 1870, pp. 71–2.

29 Charles H. Spurgeon, *Lectures To My Students*, London: Marshall, Morgan & Scott, 1954, p. 188.

30 Michael Ramsey, *The Gospel and the Catholic Church*, London: SPCK, 1990, p. 180.

Chapter 2

1 David S. Yeago, 'The New Testament and the Nicene Dogma: A Contribution to the Recovery of Theological Exegesis', in *The Theological Interpretation of Scripture*, ed. Stephen E. Fowl, London: Blackwell, 1997, p. 97.

2 David S. Yeago, 'The Bible: The Spirit, the Church and the Scriptures: Biblical Inspiration and Interpretation Revisited' in *Knowing the Triune God: The Work of the Spirit in the Practices of the Church*, ed. Buckley and Yeago, p. 68.

3 *Sadoleto's Letter to the Genevans and Calvin's Reply*, p. 43.

4 *Sadoleto's Letter to the Genevans and Calvin's Reply*, p. 61.

5 *Sadoleto's Letter to the Genevans and Calvin's Reply*, p. 61, 62. See also Calvin's 'Prefatory Address to King Francis' in the 1536 edition of his *Institutes* where he argues that, because the theology of the Reformation is based on scripture, those who enquire of it 'will find nothing new among us'.

6 John Webster, *Holy Scripture*, Cambridge: Cambridge University Press, 2003; N. T. Wright, *Scripture and the Authority of God*, London: SPCK, 2005.

7 Webster, *Holy Scripture*, p. 13.

8 Webster, *Holy Scripture*, p. 21.

9 Webster, *Holy Scripture*, p. 26.

10 Webster, *Holy Scripture*, pp. 21, 26, 39.

11 2 Peter 1.21; 2 Timothy 3.16. The affirmation of the human and divine character of scripture, together with the recognition that the place of scripture in the divine economy involved the inspiration of communicative words, lay at the heart of B. B. Warfield's doctrine of scripture constructed in the nineteenth century and defended for much of the twentieth century by John Stott.

12 Webster, *Holy Scripture*, p. 39.

13 Wright, *Scripture and the Authority of God*, p. 48.

14 Wright, *Scripture and the Authority of God*, p. 84.

15 A quote from Weka Musuku (from the former Zaire), in *Word in Action*, Summer 2004 (celebrating 200 years of the Bible Society), p. 9.

16 Dietrich Bonhoeffer, *Meditating on the Word*, Cambridge, Massachusetts: Cowley, 1986, p. 43; cited in Webster, *Holy Scripture*, p. 84.

17 John Calvin, 'The True Method of Giving Peace to Christendom and of Reforming the Church', in *Tracts and Treatises in Defence of the Reformed Faith*, ed. T. F. Torrance, vol. 3, Edinburgh: Oliver & Boyd, 1958, p. 267; cited in Webster, *Holy Scripture*, p. 61.

18 Hilary, *The Trinity*, Washington: The Catholic University of America Press, 1954, Book 1.37–38.

19 Hilary, *The Trinity*, Book 1.37–38.

20 Hilary, *The Trinity*, Book 2.1.

21 The question echoes the VIth Article of Religion. The exact 1550 wording is: 'Are you persuaded that the holy Scriptures contain sufficiently all doctrine required of necessity for eternal salvation in Jesus Christ?'

22 For Athanasius, see *Contra Gentes* 1. For Calvin, see *Institutes of the Christian Religion*, ed. John T. McNeill, trans. Ford Lewis Battles, 'Library of Christian Classics', Philadelphia: Westminster Press, 1960, I.vi.1.

23 Richard Hooker, *Of the Lawes of Ecclesiastical Polity*, Massachusetts: Harvard University Press, 1981, 3.2.2, 1, pp. 208–9.

24 W. H. Vanstone, *The Stature of Waiting*, London: Darton, Longman & Todd, 1982. See especially pp. 1–32.

25 This is a consistent emphasis in Eastern Orthodox theology. For a classic statement, see Georges Florovsky, *Bible, Church, Tradition: An Eastern Orthodox View*, Belmont: Norland, 1972. For a very good analysis from an Orthodox perspective on the use of the Jewish scriptures by New Testament writers and by the early Fathers, see John Behr, *Formation of Christian Theology: The Way to Nicea*, Crestwood: St Vladimir's Seminary Press, 2001.

26 Cited in Yeago, 'The Bible: The Spirit, the Church and the Scriptures', p. 54.

27 Cited in Florovsky, *Bible, Church, Tradition*, p. 75.

28 Cited in Florovsky, *Bible, Church, Tradition*, p. 89.

29 'Dogmatic Constitution on Divine Revelation (*Dei Verbum*) 1965' in *The Documents of Vatican II*, ed. Walter M. Abbot, London: Geoffrey Chapman, 1967, III.12.

30 George Tavard, *Holy Writ or Holy Church: The Crisis of the Protestant Reformation*, London: Burns & Oates, 1959, p. 63.

31 Donald G. Bloesch, *A Theology of Word and Spirit*, Downers Grove: InterVarsity Press, 1992, p. 189.

32 Bloesch, *Theology of Word and Spirit*, p. 193.

33 Charles Colson and Richard John Neuhaus, 'Your Word is Truth Statement' in *Your Word is Truth: A Project of Evangelicals and Catholics Together*, ed. Charles Colson and Richard John Neuhaus, Grand Rapids, Michigan: Eerdmans, 2002, p. 4. For an eirenic discussion of the relationship between scripture and tradition, see Timothy George, 'An Evangelical Reflection on Scripture and Tradition', *Pro Ecclesia* 9, no. 2 (2000). On the 'reciprocal relation that necessarily existed between Scripture, Tradition and the church' in the early centuries of its life, see 'Sola Scriptura in the Early Church' in Daniel H. Williams, *Retrieving the Tradition and Renewing Evangelicalism*, Grand Rapids: Eerdmans, 1999, pp. 229–34.

34 Cited in Florovsky, *Bible, Church, Tradition*, p. 77.

35 Benjamin B. Warfield, 'Trinity' in *The International Standard Bible Encyclopedia*, ed. James Orr, Chicago: Howard-Severance Co., 1930, 5.3012; cited in Andrew Walker, 'Deep Church as *Paradosis*: On Relating Scripture and Tradition' in *Remembering Our Future: Explorations in Deep Church*, ed. Andrew Walker and Luke Bretherton, London: Paternoster, 1998, p. 75.

36 Handley C. G. Moule, *The Evangelical School in the Church of England*, London: James Nisbit, 1901, p. 16.

37 See Florovsky, *Bible, Church, Tradition*, in particular the chapters on 'The Lost Scriptural Mind' and 'The Function of Tradition in the Ancient Church'.

38 In a similar fashion, the Second Vatican Council described scripture as the word of God 'consigned to writing under the authority of the Holy Spirit', *Dei Verbum*, II.9.

39 '(Church of England) Article of Religion, 25'.

40 Tavard, *Holy Writ or Holy Church: The Crisis of the Protestant Reformation*, p. 5.

41 See 2 Thessalonians 2.15; Philippians 4.9.

42 Steven J. Land, *Pentecostal Spirituality: A Passion for the Kingdom*, Sheffield: SAP, 1993, p. 100. For a similar Pentecostal appraisal of the work of the Spirit in relation to scripture and for a positive assessment of the relationship between scripture and tradition, see Chan, *Pentecostal Theology and the Spiritual Tradition*.

43 Land, *Pentecostal Spirituality: A Passion for the Kingdom*, p. 100.

44 From the Church of England's 'Declaration of Assent'.

45 Augustine, *Confessions*, trans. Henry Chadwick, Oxford: Oxford University Press, 1991, VIII.vi.13; VIII.vii.17.

46 Augustine, *Confessions*, VIII.vi.15.

47 Augustine, *Confessions*, VIII.viii.19.

48 Augustine, *Confessions*, VIII.viii.19.

49 Augustine, *Confessions*, VIII.xii.29.

50 Augustine, *Confessions*, VIII.xii.29.

51 Augustine, *Confessions*, VIII.xii.29.

52 Augustine tells the story of his conversion in Book VIII.xiii–xxx of his *Confessions*. For an interesting philosophical analysis of Augustine's experience of God speaking, see Nicholas Wolterstorff, *Divine Disclosure: Philosophical Reflections on the Claim that God Speaks*, Cambridge: Cambridge University Press, 1995. I am grateful to my colleague Stephen Plant for leading me to Wolterstorff and to the relevance of Augustine's conversion.

53 Williams, *Retrieving the Tradition and Renewing Evangelicalism*, p. 36. As well as cohering with my understanding of tradition as used in this chapter, William's definition accords closely with Martin Chemnitz's

expansive version in his *Examen* of the Council of Trent; see Jaroslav Pelikan, *Obedient Rebels: Catholic Substance and Protestant Principle in Luther's Reformation*, London: SCM Press, 1964, pp. 49–53.

54 Williams, *Retrieving the Tradition and Renewing Evangelicalism*, p. 16.

55 Hilary, *The Trinity*, Book 2.1.

56 Eduardo Chillida, *Homage to Bach*, Weiss-Arenthon: Editions Edouard, 1997.

57 Thomas Jackson (ed.), *The Works of the Reverend John Wesley*, Grand Rapids: Baker Books, 1984, p. 484.

58 See the Report of the *First International Consultation of the Evangelical Fellowship in the Anglican Communion* in 1993 which affirms the importance of 'a historical and global perspective' reading of scripture 'so that we do not fall into indefensible private interpretations', John Stott (ed.), *The Anglican Communion and Scripture*, Oxford: Regnum, 1996, p. 4. There are a number of significant initiatives encouraging evangelicals to read scripture as participants in a living tradition which stretches back to the earliest centuries of the church. See for examples, Thomas C. Oden, *Systematic Theology*, three vols, San Francisco: Harper & Row, 1987; and the *Ancient Christian Commentary on Scripture*, a major undertaking that collects comments by the Fathers on the books of scripture, published by the InterVarsity Press, the flagship evangelical publisher.

59 Heiko A. Oberman, 'The Virgin Mary in Evangelical Perspective', *Journal of Ecumenical Studies* 1, no. 2 (1964), p. 289.

Chapter 3

1 Richard Hooker, 'A Learned Discourse of Justification, Works, and How the Foundation of Faith is Overthrown' in Richard Hooker, *The Works of Mr Richard Hooker*, ed. John Keble, vol. 2, Oxford: Clarendon Press, 1865–75, p. 603.

2 'Sermon 5: Justification by Faith' in John Wesley, 'Sermons I: 1–33', ed. Albert C. Outler, *The Works of John Wesley*, vol. 1, Grand Rapids: Zondervan, 1958, p. 195. Here Wesley is glossing the second sermon on the Passion from Homilies.

3 *Sadoleto's Letter to the Genevans and Calvin's Reply*, p. 35.

4 *Sadoleto's Letter to the Genevans and Calvin's Reply*, pp. 35–6.

5 *Sadoleto's Letter to the Genevans and Calvin's Reply*, pp. 35–6. My italics.

6 *Sadoleto's Letter to the Genevans and Calvin's Reply*, p. 69.

7 *Sadoleto's Letter to the Genevans and Calvin's Reply*, p. 67.

8 *Sadoleto's Letter to the Genevans and Calvin's Reply*, p. 68.

9 'Geneva Catechism, 1541' in Thomas. F. Torrance (ed.), *School of Faith: The Catechisms of the Reformed Church*, London: James Clarke, 1959, pp. 5–65 (p.22).

10 *Sadoleto's Letter to the Genevans and Calvin's Reply*, p. 68.

11 *Sadoleto's Letter to the Genevans and Calvin's Reply*, p. 66.

12 George Anderson, Austin Murphy and Joseph Burgess (eds), *Justification by Faith: Lutherans and Catholics in Dialogue*, Minneapolis: Augsburg Publishing House, 1985. For the text of the *Joint Declaration*, see Anthony N. S. Lane, *Justification by Faith in Catholic-Protestant Dialogue: An Evangelical Assessment*, London: T & T Clark, 2002, pp. 239–59.

13 Karl Lehmann and Wolfhart Pannenberg, *The Condemnations of the Reformation Era: Do They Still Divide?*, Minneapolis: Fortress Press, 1989, pp. 40–1.

14 For a detailed discussion of the Hebrew, Greek and Latin etymology, see Alister. E. McGrath, *Iustitia Dei: A History of the Christian Doctrine of Justification*, second edn, Cambridge: Cambridge University Press, 1998, pp. 4–16.

15 See Augustine, *The Spirit and the Letter* 26:45 in John Burnaby (ed.), *Augustine: Later Works*, London: SCM Press, 1955, p. 228, quoted by Lane, *Justification by Faith in Catholic–Protestant Dialogue*, p. 45.

16 McGrath, *Iustitia Dei*, p. 41.

17 *Evangelical Catholic Initiative, 'What is an Evangelical Catholic?'*, Dublin: ECI, 1990, p. 4.

18 This is Calvin's response to Canon XI of the 6th Session of the Council of Trent. See Lane, *Justification by Faith in Catholic–Protestant Dialogue*, p. 181.

19 Lehmann and Pannenberg, *The Condemnations of the Reformation Era*, p. 41.

20 Lehmann and Pannenberg, *The Condemnations of the Reformation Era*, pp. 52–3.

21 Wesley, *Works 1*, p. 103.

22 Wesley's testimony of the events leading to and following his Aldersgate experience is worth reading. The centrality of his passion for holiness is very evident throughout. See *The Works of John Wesley*, vol. 1, entries from 1 February to 7 June (pp. 83–106).

23 The most useful primary sources for Wesley's theology of salvation are as follows.

(1) Sermons: 'Sermon 1: Salvation by Faith' (1738); 'Sermon 5: Justification by Faith' (1746); 'Sermon 45: The New Birth' (1760); 'Sermon 17: The Circumcision of the Heart' (1733); 'Sermon 18: The Marks of the New Birth' (1748); 'Sermon 19: The Great Privilege of those that are Born of God' (1748); 'Sermon 85: On Working our own

Salvation' (1785); 'Sermon 40: Christian Perfection' (1741). All sermons are from Albert C. Outler (ed.), *The Works of John Wesley*, vols. 1–4, Nashville: Abingdon Press, 1987.

(2) **Letters**: 'Letter to Mr Horne' (1762); 'Thoughts on Imputed Righteousness' (1762); 'A Blow to the Root, or Christ stabbed in the House of his Friends' (1762). All letters are from *The Works of John Wesley*, 14 vols, Grand Rapids: Zondervan Publishing House, 1872.

(3) **His Journal**: particularly his entries around the period of his Aldersgate experience.

Useful secondary sources are Randy Maddox, *Responsible Grace: John Wesley's Practical Theology*, Nashville: Abingdon-Kingswood, 1994; David M. Chapman, *In Search of the Catholic Spirit: Methodists and Catholics in Dialogue*, Peterborough: Epworth, 2004; and Kenneth Collins, 'The Doctrine of Justification: Historic Wesleyan and Contemporary Understandings' in *Justification: What's at Stake in the Current Debates*, ed. Mark A. Husbands and Daniel J. Trier, Leicester: Apollos, 2004, pp. 177–202; Lorna Khoo, *Wesleyan Eucharistic Spirituality: Its Nature, Sources and Future*, Hindmarsh, South Australia: ATF Press, 2005.

24 'Sermon 85: On Working Out Our Own Salvation' in John Wesley, 'Sermons III: 71–114', ed. Albert C. Outler, *The Works of John Wesley*, vol. 3, Nashville: Abingdon Press, 1984, p. 208.

25 Lehmann and Pannenberg, *The Condemnations of the Reformation Era*, pp. 47–8.

26 'Sermon 1: Salvation by Faith' in Wesley, *Works 1*, p. 124.

27 'Sermon 5: Justification by Faith' in Wesley, *Works 1*, p. 186.

28 'Sermon 19: The Great Privilege of those that are Born of God' in Wesley, *Works 1*, pp. 413–32.

29 See 'Sermon 45: The New Birth' in Wesley, *Works 2*, pp. 187–201; 'Sermon 18: The Marks of the New Birth', Wesley, *Works 2*, pp. 417–30; 'Sermon 19: The Great Privilege of those that are Born of God' in Wesley, *Works 1*, pp. 431–43.

30 'Sermon 19: The Great Privilege of those that are Born of God' in Wesley, *Works 1*, p. 432.

31 For the text of Article 5 of Regensburg and for an analysis, see Anthony N. S. Lane, 'Twofold Righteousness: A Key to the Doctrine of Justification', in *Justification: What's at Stake in the Current Debates*, ed. Mark A. Husbands and Daniel J. Trier, Leicester: Apollos, 2004, pp. 205–24. See also Anthony N. S. Lane's larger work, *Justification by Faith in Catholic–Protestant Dialogue*; and 'Common Statement' in Anderson, Murphy and Burgess (eds), *Justification by Faith: Lutherans and Catholics in Dialogue*, paras. 47–8.

32 'The Regensburg Agreement' in Lane, *Justification by Faith*, p. 234.

33 'The Regensburg Agreement' in Lane, *Justification by Faith*, p. 234.

34 'The Regensburg Agreement' in Lane, *Justification by Faith*, p. 235.

35 'Letter 67: To Farel' in John Calvin, *Letters of John Calvin*, vol. 1, New York: Burt Franklin Reprints, 1972, p. 260.

36 Alister E. McGrath, *Iustitia Dei: A History of the Christian Doctrine of Justification*, first edn, vol. 2, Cambridge: Cambridge University Press, 1986, pp. 60–1; Lane, 'Twofold Righteousness: A Key to the Doctrine of Justification', p. 217.

37 'Common Statement' in Anderson, Murphy and Burgess (eds), *Justification by Faith*, paras 4 and 157.

38 'Common Statement' in Anderson, Murphy and Burgess (eds), *Justification by Faith*, paras 163–4.

39 'Common Statement' in Anderson, Murphy and Burgess (eds), *Justification by Faith*, para. 156. My italics.

40 'Common Statement' in Anderson, Murphy and Burgess (eds), *Justification by Faith*, para. 89.

41 'Joint Declaration' Preamble 5 in Lane, *Justification by Faith*, p. 242.

42 'Joint Declaration' 5 in Lane, *Justification by Faith*, p. 254.

43 'Joint Declaration' 4.2 in Lane, *Justification by Faith*, pp. 247–48. My italics.

44 'Joint Declaration' 4.3 in Lane, *Justification by Faith*, p. 249.

45 'Sermon 43: The Scripture Way of Salvation' in Wesley, *Works* 2, pp. 164–65.

46 'Sermon 18: The Marks of the New Birth' in Wesley, *Works 1*, p. 420.

47 'Joint Declaration' 4.4 in Lane, *Justification by Faith in Catholic–Protestant Dialogue*, p. 250. See also 'Sermon 5: Justification by Faith', Wesley, *Works 1*, pp. 182–99.

48 'Sermon 18: The Marks of the New Birth' in Wesley, *Works 1*, p. 420.

49 'Sermon 19: The Great Privilege of those that are Born of God' in Wesley, *Works 1*, p. 436.

50 The teaching of 1 John, and especially 3.9 ('Those who have been born again do not sin') was a great influence on Wesley, which he was determined to take seriously.

51 See 'Sermon 19: The Great Privilege of those that are Born of God' in Wesley, *Works 1*, p. 440.

52 'Sermon 19: The Great Privilege of those that are Born of God' in Wesley, *Works 1*, p. 441.

53 'Sermon 19: The Great Privilege of those that are Born of God' in Wesley, *Works 1*, p. 442.

54 William Law, *A Serious Call to a Devout and Holy Life, The Spirit of Love*, ed. Paul G. Stanwood, 'The Classics of Western Spirituality', Mahwah, New Jersey: Paulist Press, 1978.

55 'Collect of 19th Sunday after Trinity' in *Common Worship: Daily Prayer*, London: Church House Publishing, 2005, p. 441.

56 'Sermon 19: The Great Privilege of those that are Born of God' in Wesley, *Works 1*, p. 442.

57 'Sermon 19: The Great Privilege of those that are Born of God' in Wesley, *Works 1*, p. 442.

58 'Sermon 85: On Working Out Our Own Salvation' in Wesley, *Works 3*, p. 208.

59 'Sermon 43: The Scripture Way of Salvation' in Wesley, *Works 2*, p. 165.

60 Wesley describes love as 'the proof that we are born again', see 'Sermon 18: The Marks of the New Birth' in Wesley, *Works 1*, p. 424.

61 'A Letter to the Rev. Mr Horne', John Wesley, 'The Appeals to Men of Reason and Religion', ed. Gerald R. Cragg, *The Works of John Wesley*, vol. 11, Oxford: Clarendon Press, 1975, p. 456 – quoting Romans 8.1, Colossians 2.6 and Romans 8.1.

62 John Wesley, *A Plain Account of Christian Perfection*, London: Epworth, 1960, p. 52.

63 Quoted by John Ernest Rattenbury, *The Eucharistic Hymns of John and Charles Wesley*, London: Epworth, 1948, p. 49.

64 Hymn 54 from 'The Hymns of the Lord's Supper' in Rattenbury, *Eucharistic Hymns*, p. 212.

65 'Sermon 18: The Marks of the New Birth' in Wesley, *Works 1*, p. 430.

66 Martin Luther, 'On the Councils and the Church', Church and Ministry 3', ed. Eric W. Gritsch, *Luther's Works*, vol. 41, Philadelphia: Fortress Press, 1970, p. 172.

67 N. T. Wright, *What Saint Paul Really Said*, Grand Rapids: Eerdmans, 1997, p. 132. In addition to this book, helpful ways into the New Perspective are Michael Thompson, *New Perspective*, Cambridge: Grove Books, 2002; and the Paul Page website, <www.thepaulpage.com>.

68 These words, which Wesley once overheard casually said, had a profound effect upon him and convinced him at an early stage of his ministry that Christianity is a 'social religion'. See John Ernest Rattenbury, *The Conversion of the Wesleys: A Critical Study*, London: Epworth, 1938, p. 45.

Chapter 4

1 Calvin, *Institutes*, IV.i.3.

2 John Wesley, 'The Doctrine of Original Sin' in Thomas Jackson (ed.), *The Works of the Reverend John Wesley*, Grand Rapids: Baker Books, 1984, p. 221. Both quoted in a shrewd article by Bruce Hindmarsh, 'Is Evangelical Ecclesiology an Oxymoron?' in *Evangelical Ecclesiology: Reality or Illusion?*, ed. John G. Stackhouse, Grand Rapids: Baker Books, 2003, pp. 22–3.

3 George R. Hunsberger, 'Evangelical Conversion toward a Missional Ecclesiology' in *Evangelical Ecclesiology: Reality or Illusion?*, p. 118.

4 Hunsberger, 'Evangelical Conversion toward a Missional Ecclesiology', p. 118.

5 John G. Stackhouse, 'Preface' in *Evangelical Ecclesiology: Reality or Illusion?*

6 Robert Webber, *Ancient-Future Evangelism: Making Your Church a Faith-Forming Community*, Grand Rapids: Baker Books, 2003, p. 73.

7 Phillip Richter and Leslie J. Francis, *Gone but not Forgotten: Church Leaving and Returning*, London: DLT, 1998.

8 Peter Brierley, *The Tide is Running Out: What the English Church Attendance Survey Reveals*, London: Christian Research, 2000.

9 See Robert Warren and Bob Jackson, *These are the Answers*, Abingdon: Springboard, no date; Alan Jamieson, *A Churchless Faith: Faith Journeys Beyond the Churches*, London: SPCK, 2002.

10 Digging deeply into the identity of the church was a favourite image of Michael Ramsey's ecclesiological method, which he borrowed from F. D. Maurice. See Ramsey, *The Gospel and the Catholic Church*, pp. 221–5; see also Rowan Williams' essay on Ramsey in his *Anglican Identities*, London: Darton, Longman & Todd, 2004, pp. 87–102.

11 *Lumen Gentium*, I.6; IV.36.

12 Dietrich Bonhoeffer, *Sanctorum Communio*, p. 143.

13 Daniel W. Hardy, *God's Ways with the World: Thinking and Practising the Christian Faith*, Edinburgh: T & T Clark, 1996.

14 See Howard A. Snyder, 'The Marks of Evangelical Ecclesiology' in Stackhouse (ed.), *Evangelical Ecclesiology*, pp. 77–103; and Howard A. Snyder and Daniel V. Runyon, *Decoding the Church: Mapping the DNA of Christ's Body*, Grand Rapids: Baker Books, 2002.

15 C. S. Lewis, *Mere Christianity*, London: Geoffrey Bles, 1952. For some fascinating background on Lewis' thinking before the publication of *Mere Christianity* and his inspiration of a contemporary – and very fruitful – series of 'explorations in Deep Church', see Andrew Walker, 'Recovering Deep Church: Theological and Spiritual Renewal' in Andrew Walker and Luke Bretherton (eds), *Remembering Our Future:*

Explorations in Deep Church, London: Paternoster, 1998, pp. 1–29.

16 See 'Observations of the Congregation for the Doctrine of Faith on the report of ARCIC-II: *Salvation and the Church*', *One in Christ* 24, no. 4, 1998, p. 385.

17 Henri de Lubac, *Splendour of the Church*, San Francisco: Ignatius Press, 1986, pp. 31–9, quoting Thomas Aquinas.

18 Second Helvetic Confession, chapter XVII.

19 Hunsberger, 'Evangelical Conversion toward a Missional Ecclesiology', p. 118.

20 John Webster, 'The Church and the Perfection of God' in *The Community of the Word: Toward an Evangelical Ecclesiology*, ed. Mark Husbands and Daniel J. Treier, Downers Grove: InterVarsity Press, 2005, p. 75. My italics.

21 Webster, 'The Church and the Perfection of God', p. 76.

22 De Lubac, *Splendour of the Church*, p. 175. My italics.

23 See 'The Blessed Sacrament of the Holy and True Body and Blood of Christ, and the Brotherhoods' in Martin Luther, *Word and Sacrament* 1, ed. E. Theodore Bachmann, *Luther's Works*, vol. 35, Philadelphia: Fortress Press, 1960, pp. 45–75.

24 Ramsey, *Gospel and the Catholic Church*, p. 185; Luther, 'The Blessed Sacrament of the Holy and True Body and Blood of Christ', p. 58.

25 Michael Ramsey puts well the connection between justification by faith and initiation into the Christian community: 'Similarly, justification by faith is never a solitary relationship with a solitary Christ. The man who is justified is an individual, but the Christ who justifies is one with His people as His Body; and the act of faith, in releasing a person from self, brings him into dependence upon his neighbours in Christ. Faith and justification are inseparable from initiation into his Body.' Ramsey, *Gospel and the Catholic Church*, p. 37.

26 Bonhoeffer, *Sanctorum Communio*, p. 165.

27 Bonhoeffer, *Sanctorum Communio*, p. 199.

28 Bonhoeffer, *Sanctorum Communio*, p. 184.

29 Bonhoeffer, *Sanctorum Communio*, p. 184.

30 Bonhoeffer, *Sanctorum Communio*, p. 188.

31 Bonhoeffer, *Sanctorum Communio*, p. 189.

32 Bonhoeffer, *Sanctorum Communio*, p. 181.

33 The most quoted example (including by Calvin) is Cyprian's assertion that 'You cannot have God for your Father if you no longer have the Church for your Mother', see Maurice Bèvenot (ed.), *Unity of the Catholic Church*, Oxford: Clarendon Press, 1971, p. 67. See also, among others, Augustine: 'Honour, love and praise the holy church, your mother, the heavenly Jerusalem, the holy City of God. It is she who, in this faith you have received, bears fruit and spreads throughout

the world. She is the "church of the living God, the pillar and mainstay of truth" (1 Timothy 3.15)' – 'Sermons 214.11' quoted in Peter Gorday (ed.), *Colossians, 1–2 Thessalonians, 1–2 Timothy, Titus, Philemon*, London: Fitzroy Dearborn, 2000, p. 4. For the Reformers' affirmation of the church as our mother, see John C. Olin (ed.), *A Reformation Debate: Sadoleto's Letter to the Genevans and Calvin's Reply*; Martin Luther, 'Lectures on Galatians 1535', ed. Jaroslav Pelikan, *Luther's Works*, vol. 26, Saint Louis: Concordia Publishing House, 1963, p. 441.

34 Bonhoeffer, *Sanctorum Communio*, p. 241.

35 Miroslav Volf, *After Our Likeness: The Church as the Image of the Trinity*, Grand Rapids: Eerdmans, 1998, p. 159.

36 Volf, *After Our Likeness*, see pp. 162–7 for a helpful discussion of the ecclesial mediation of faith.

37 Dietrich Bonhoeffer, *Discipleship*, ed. Geffrey B. Kelly and John D. Godsey, 'Dietrich Bonhoeffer Works', vol. 4, Minneapolis: Fortress Press, 2001, pp. 217–18; 220.

38 Bonhoeffer, *Discipleship*, p. 220.

39 Augustine, 'On Psalm 61', quoted in Ramsey, *Gospel and the Catholic Church*, pp. 157–8.

40 Augustine, 'On Psalm 61', quoted in Ramsey, *Gospel and the Catholic Church*, p. 157.

41 'The notion of *totus Christus* – of Christ's completeness as inclusive of the church as his body – will be impermissible if it elides the distinction between Christ and the objects of his mercy'. Webster, 'The Church and the Perfection of God', p. 95.

42 *Lumen Gentium*, I.1.

43 Eberhard Jüngel, *Theological Essays*, Edinburgh: T & T Clark, 1989, p. 206.

44 Bonhoeffer, *Discipleship*, p. 213.

45 Webster, 'The Church and the Perfection of God', p. 76.

46 De Lubac, *Splendour of the Church*, pp. 159–60.

47 Ramsey, *Gospel and the Catholic Church*, p. 57.

48 Dietrich Bonhoeffer, *Ethics*, London: SCM, 1963, p. 110.

49 Miroslav Volf traces the inter-relationality of the ecclesial life into the trinitarian realities of the divine life: 'Like the divine persons, so also ecclesial persons cannot live in isolation from one another; Christians are constituted as independently believing persons through their relations to other Christians, and they manifest and affirm their own ecclesial personhood in mutual giving and receiving . . . A Christian lives from and toward others.' Volf, *After Our Likeness*, p. 206.

50 I am grateful to Andrew Lord for this category of *the other beyond the church*.

51 Volf, *After Our Likeness*, p. 152.

52 Volf, *After Our Likeness*, p. 230.

53 Volf, *After Our Likeness*, p. 230.

54 Volf, *After Our Likeness*, p. 248.

55 Volf, *After Our Likeness*, pp. 247–8.

56 Ramsey, *Gospel and the Catholic Church*, p. 69.

57 Yves Congar, *I Believe in the Holy Spirit*, vol. 2, London: Geoffrey Chapman, 1983, p. 45.

58 Congar, *I Believe in the Holy Spirit*, p. 39.

59 Friedrich Schleiermacher, *The Christian Faith*, Edinburgh: T & T Clark, 1928, p. 603.

60 Irenaeus, *Adversus Haereses*, 4.26.5.

Chapter 5

1 Joseph Ratzinger, 'Homily of His Eminence Card', *Funeral Mass of the Roman Pontiff, John Paul II*, St Peter's Square, 8th April 2005. See the Vatican web pages for the full transcript.

2 François-Xavier Durrwell, *Mary: Icon of the Spirit and of the Church*, Slough: St Paul's Publications, 1991, p. 47.

3 For a recent and helpful evangelical study of Mary, see Scot McKnight, *The Real Mary: Why Evangelical Christians Can Embrace the Mother of Jesus*, London: SPCK, 2007. For a very different appraisal of Mary from a former Protestant pastor and theologian writing after his conversion to Roman Catholicism, see Scott Hahn, *Hail, Holy Queen: Mother of God in the Word of God*, London: Darton, Longman & Todd, 2001.

4 *Mary: Grace and Hope in Christ*, 'The Anglican–Roman Catholic International Commission', London: Morehouse, 2005, para. 6.

5 Quoted in Oberman, 'The Virgin Mary in Evangelical Perspective', p. 290.

6 Hans Asmussen, quoted in Oberman, 'The Virgin Mary in Evangelical Perspective', p. 295.

7 Raymond Brown, Karl P. Donfried and Joseph A. Fitzmyer, *Mary in the New Testament: A Collaborative Assessment by Protestant and Roman Catholic Scholars*, Philadelphia: Fortress Press, 1978, p. 290.

8 Quoted in Oberman, 'The Virgin Mary in Evangelical Perspective', p. 290.

9 'Common of the Saints: The Blessed Virgin Mary' in *Common Worship: Daily Prayer*, p. 492.

10 *Authority in the Church II* (1981), para. 30, quoted in *Mary: Grace and Hope in Christ*, para. 2.

11 Oberman, 'The Virgin Mary in Evangelical Perspective', p. 294.

12 John Donne, 'Annunciation', verse 2 in C. A. Patrides (ed.), *The*

Complete English Poems of John Donne, London: J. M. Dent & Sons Ltd, 1985, p. 430.

13 George Herbert, 'Anagram' in Ricks (ed.), *George Herbert: The Complete English Poems*, p. 71.

14 Oberman, 'The Virgin Mary in Evangelical Perspective', p. 281.

15 Quoted in *Mary: Grace and Hope in Christ*, para. 58.

16 Beverly Roberts Geventa, '"Nothing Will Be Impossible with God": Mary as the Mother of Believers' in *Mary Mother of God*, ed. Carl E. Braaten and Robert W. Jenson, Cambridge: William B. Eerdmans, 2004, p. 35.

17 I say '*seem* to distance himself from her' because I recognize that it may well not be quite as simple as it first appears. The significance of Jesus' address to Mary as 'woman' in John is a much debated and contested point. Commentators note that it is the same address used by Jesus to Mary at the foot of the cross, a scene full of tender closeness. Some commentators interpret the term symbolically, with Mary seen as representing womanhood, or even humanity itself, as a new covenant parallel to Eve.

18 From the title, Eugene H. Peterson, *A Long Obedience in the Same Direction: Discipleship in an Instant Society*, Downers Grove: InterVarsity Press, 2000.

19 Quoted in *Mary: Grace and Hope in Christ*, para.59.

20 Quoted in Richard Bauckham, 'The Origins and Growth of Western Mariology' in *Chosen by God: Mary in Evangelical Perspective*, ed. David E. Wright, London: Marshall, Morgan & Scott, 1989, p. 158.

21 For a very helpful and careful study of Mary from an Orthodox perspective drawing particularly on the theme of Mary as a symbol of the church, see John Behr, *The Mystery of Christ: Life in Death*, New York: St Vladimir's Seminary Press, 2006, pp. 115–40.

22 Luther, *LW* 41, p. 151.

23 'Sunday after the Ascension', *Common Worship*, London: Church House Publishing, 2000, p. 476.

24 Archimandrite Kallistos Ware and Colin Davey (eds), *Anglican–Orthodox Dialogue: The Moscow Statement Agreed by the Anglican–Orthodox Joint Doctrinal Commission 1976*, London: SPCK, 1977, para. 32.

25 'Common of the Saints: The Blessed Virgin Mary' in *Common Worship: Daily Prayer*, p. 492.

26 Jerusalem Bible.

27 John Donne, 'The Annunciation and Passion' in Patrides (ed.), *The Complete English Poems of John Donne*, p. 452.

28 Christina Rossetti, 'In the Bleak Mid-Winter' in William Michael Rossetti (ed.), *The Poetical Works of Christina Georgina Rossetti*, London: Macmillan, 1904, p. 246.

29 Quoted in David S. Yeago, 'The Presence of Mary in the Mystery of the Church' in Braaten and Jenson (eds), *Mary Mother of God*, p. 76.

30 Quoted in Timothy George, 'The Blessed Virgin Mary in Evangelical Perspective', in *Mary Mother of God*, p. 114.

31 Elizabeth A. Johnson, *Truly Our Sister: A Theology of Mary in the Communion of Saints*, London: Continuum, 2006, p. 286.

32 *Mary: Grace and Hope in Christ*, para.68.

33 Karl Barth, *Church Dogmatics*, Edinburgh: T & T Clark, 1956, I/II, p. 143.

34 Johnson, *Truly Our Sister*, p. 15.

35 Yves Congar, quoted in Johnson, *Truly Our Sister*, p. 127.

36 Behr, *The Mystery of Christ*, p. 138.

37 See Johnson's write-up of the aftermath of the Council of Ephesus in *Truly Our Sister*, p. 75.

38 Martin Luther, 'The Magnificat', ed. Jaroslav Pelikan, *Luther's Works*, vol. 21, Saint Louis: Concordia Publishing House, 1956, p. 314.

39 Bonhoeffer, *Discipleship*, p. 63.

40 Bonhoeffer, *Discipleship*, p. 66.

41 Bonhoeffer, *Discipleship*, p. 69.

42 Luther, 'The Magnificat', *LW* 21, p. 308.

43 Johnson, *Truly Our Sister*, pp. 270–1.

44 The expression 'Mary's pilgrimage of faith' comes from Vatican II's 'Dogmatic Constitution on the Church (*Lumen Gentium*) 1964', para. 58. It is significant that Vatican II chose to include its theology of Mary within its theology of the church rather than in a separate document.

45 Luther, 'The Magnificat', *LW* 21, p. 322.

Chapter 6

1 This chapter uses and adapts material previously published in my 'Holding Together: Catholic Evangelical Worship in the Spirit', *Anvil* 22, no. 1, 2005, and in a chapter with the same title in Andrew Walker and Luke Bretherton (eds), *Remembering Our Future: Explorations in Deep Church*.

2 See, for example, John 20.19; Acts 1.4, 4.23–31; 1 Corinthians 11.20, 14.23; Hebrews 10.25.

3 On the relationship between a life of worship and intensive expressions of worship in communal gatherings, it is interesting to compare Vaughan Roberts, *True Worship*, Carlisle: Authentic Worship,

2002, with Matt Redman, *Face Down*, Eastbourne: Kingsway, 2004. Despite very different emphases, they each acknowledge both dimensions of worship. See also David Peterson's detailed study (on which Vaughan Roberts draws), *Engaging with God: A Biblical Theology of Worship*, London: Apollos, 1992.

4 On the place of 'seeing the gospel' in evangelical worship, see Phillip Seddon, *Gospel and Sacrament: Reclaiming a Holistic Evangelical Spirituality*, Cambridge: Grove Books, 2004.

5 *Catechism of the Catholic Church*, Dublin: Veritas, 1994, pp. 273–4.

6 Calvin, *Institutes*, III.i.

7 Martin Luther, 'The Blessed Sacrament of the Holy and True Body and Blood of Christ and the Brotherhoods 18' in *Martin Luther's Basic Theological Writings*, ed. T. F. Lull, Minneapolis: Fortress Press, 1989.

8 Ralph P. Martin, 'Patterns of Worship in New Testament Churches', *International Journal for the Study of the New Testament* 37, 1989, p. 73, quoting Philipp Vielhauer, ed. Günter Klein, *Oikodome*, Munich: Kaiser, 1979, p. 433.

9 Luther, 'The Blessed Sacrament of the Holy and True Body and Blood of Christ'.

10 See further, David Ford, *Self and Salvation*, Cambridge: Cambridge University Press, 1999, especially chapter 4.

11 Christopher Irvine, *The Art of God: The Marking of Christians and the Meaning of Worship*, London: SPCK, p. xv; 17.

12 The potential of worship to shape the Christian mind and transform Christian action places a weight of responsibility, of course, on those who plan and lead worship 'to order worship so that it becomes a faithful representation of the kingdom of God'. James H. Steven, *Worship in the Spirit: Charismatic Worship in the Church of England*, Carlisle: Paternoster Press, 2002, p. 54, summarizing the thought of M. M. Kelleher.

13 Volf, *After Our Likeness*, p. 163. See pp. 162–7 for a helpful discussion of the ecclesial mediation of faith.

14 William Law, 'The Spirit of Love' in *William Law*, ed. P. G. Stanwood, 'The Classics of Western Spirituality', New York: Paulist Press, 1978, pp. 355–498 (p. 402). On Wesley, see chapter 3.

15 Quoted in Congar, *I Believe in the Holy Spirit*, p. 6.

16 John E. Colwell, *Promise and Presence: An Exploration of Sacramental Theology*, Milton Keynes: Paternoster, 2005, p. 186.

17 See, for example, Michael Vasey, *Reading the Bible at the Eucharist*, Bramcote: Grove Books, 1986; 'Scripture and Prayer: Enriching the Revised Roman Missal', *Liturgy* 19 (1994/5) and 'Scripture and Eucharist' in *Our Thanks and Praise: The Eucharist in Anglicanism*

Today, ed. David R. Holeton, Toronto Anglican Book Centre, 1998, pp. 147–61.

18 For very helpful advice on preaching systematically through scripture using the patterns and provision of *Common Worship*, see Phillip Tovey, *Preaching a Sermon Series with Common Worship*, Cambridge: Grove Books, 2004.

19 Martin, 'Patterns of Worship in New Testament Churches', p. 64.

20 An interesting example of this approach to liturgical worship can be found in Robert Webber, *Planning Blended Worship*, Nashville: Abingdon Press, 1998. For another good example from a more theological perspective, see the work of Simon Chan, *Liturgical Theology: The Church as a Worshipping Community*.

21 Cited in Martin, 'Patterns of Worship in New Testament Churches', p. 61, quoting John C. Lambert, *The Sacraments in the New Testament*, Edinburgh: T & T Clark, 1903.

22 Martin Stringer, *A Sociological History of Christian Worship*, Cambridge: Cambridge University Press, 2005, p. 238.

23 See Handley C. G. Moule, *The Pledges of His Love*, London: Seely & Co., 1907; and *At the Holy Communion*, London: Seeley & Co., 1914.

24 'Self-sharing' is a term borrowed from Rowan Williams. See his *Resurrection*, Harrisburg, PA: Morehouse, 1994, p. 108 and compare with David Ford's similar notion of the 'unlimited self-distribution of God' in 'Why Church?', *Scottish Journal of Theology* 53, 2000, pp. 50–71 (p. 59).

25 For a fuller account of evangelical eucharistic history, see my *Evangelical Eucharistic Thought in the Church of England*, Cambridge: Cambridge University Press, 1993.

26 Thomas Haweis, *The Communicant's Spiritual Companion*, London: Samuel Swift, 1812, p. 27.

27 Seddon, *Gospel and Sacrament*.

Chapter 7

1 For a helpful study of the natural relationship between liturgical worship and the functioning of the brain, including memory, see Peter Atkins, *Memory and Liturgy: The Place of Memory in the Composition and Practice of Liturgy*, Aldershot: Ashgate, 2004.

2 Monday 1 January 1739 in John Wesley, 'Journal and Diaries II: 1738–43', ed. W. Reginald Ward, *The Works of John Wesley*, vol. 19, Nashville: Abingdon Press, 1990, p. 29.

3 See further, Jeremy Fletcher and Christopher J. Cocksworth, *The Spirit and Liturgy*, Cambridge: Grove Books, 1998.

4 *The Entire Works of the Rev. Charles Simeon*, vol. 8, ed. Thomas Hartwell Horne, London: Holdsworth & Ball, 1832, p. 484.

5 Pius XII, *Mediator Dei*, London: Catholic Truth Society, 1983, 1.1.20, p. 14.

6 Augustine, 'On Psalm 37', quoted in Ramsey, *Gospel and the Catholic Church*, p. 157.

7 Rowan Williams, 'Angel Voices', *Church Music Quarterly*, December 2004, p. 8. This understanding of worship is probably closer to the actual etymology of *liturgy* in which the public work or service is a philanthropic gift of an individual for the benefit of the community; see James Barr, *Semantics of Biblical Language*, London: OUP, 1961, p. 149.

8 For a helpful study of Christian doctrine from the framework of the Christian year, see John E. Colwell, *The Rhythm of Doctrine: A Liturgical Sketch of Christian Faith and Faithlessness*, Milton Keynes: Paternoster, 2007.

9 Steven, *Worship in the Spirit*, p. 54, making use of Mary M. Kelleher, 'Liturgical Theology: A Task and a Method', *Worship* 62, no. 1, 1988.

10 From the Church of England's 'Collect of the First Sunday of Christmas' in *Common Worship*, p. 381.

11 Tom Smail, Andrew Walker and Nigel Wright, *Charismatic Renewal*, London: SPCK, 1995, pp. 76–7.

12 Although I am not seeking to assess Luther's views on Aquinas' theology in general or his baptismal theology in particular, it is worth noting that Luther's criticisms of Aquinas, while sharp at several points, are muted compared with his comments on other scholastic theologians. Moreover, his criticisms of Aquinas' theology of baptism are relatively minimal, and the most substantial of them is, according to Denis Janz, based on a misunderstanding of Aquinas' thought, exhibiting a failure to appreciate its nuances and qualifications: see Denis R. Janz, *Luther on Thomas Aquinas: The Angelic Doctor in the Thought of the Reformer*, Stuttgart: Franz Steiner Verlag Wiesbaden, 1989 – especially pp. 66–8.

13 Thomas Aquinas, *Summa Theologiae*, Cambridge: Cambridge University Press, 1975, volume 56, 3a. q.61.1; 3a. q.62.1. The basis of Aquinas' sacramental theology is found in volume 56. His baptismal theology is developed in volume 57 and his eucharistic theology in volumes 58–9.

14 Aquinas, *Summa Theologiae*, 3a. q.61.1.

15 Aquinas, *Summa Theologiae*, 3a. q.61.1.

16 Aquinas, *Summa Theologiae*, 3a. q.62.5.

17 It is worth noting that for Aquinas the minister of baptism does

not necessarily have to be ordained into a particular order of ministry. Indeed, in cases of extremity it is possible for the unbaptized to administer baptism, 'as long as they baptize in the form of the Church' (that is, using water and the trinitarian formulae). See *Summa Theologiae*, 3a. q.67, especially 67.5.

18 Aquinas, *Summa Theologiae*, 3a. q. 63.3.

19 Aquinas, *Summa Theologiae*, 3a. q. 63.6.

20 Aquinas, *Summa Theologiae*, 3a. q. 60.3.

21 'The Babylonian Captivity of the Church' in Martin Luther, 'Word and Sacrament 2', ed. Abdel Ross Wentz, *Luther's Works*, vol. 36, Philadelphia: Fortress Press, 1959, p. 61.

22 Luther was critical of the *Sentences* (essentially an anthology of theological opinion that operated as a primary theological source in the medieval church), claiming that they misunderstood the relationship between sacraments and faith: Luther, *LW 36*, p. 67.

23 Luther, *LW 36*, p. 74.

24 Luther, *LW 36*, p. 62.

25 For example, 'Luther's Larger Catechism' (1529) in Martin Luther, *Luther's Primary Works*, ed. Henry Wace and C. A. Buchheim, London: Hodder & Stoughton, 1898, p. 133.

26 Luther, *LW 36*, p. 49.

27 See, for example, Luther, *Luther's Primary Works*, p. 130.

28 'The Holy and Blessed Sacrament of Baptism (1519)' in Luther, *LW 35*, p. 38.

29 Aquinas, *Summa Theologiae*, 3a. q.66.5. Here Aquinas is quoting Augustine.

30 Aquinas, *Summa Theologiae*, 3a. q.62.6.

31 Aquinas, *Summa Theologiae*, 3a. q.62.5. For Luther's caution see Luther, *LW 36*, p. 74.

32 Luther, *Luther's Primary Works*, p. 138.

33 Aquinas, *Summa Theologiae*, 3a. q.66.11.

34 Aquinas, *Summa Theologiae*, 3a. q.68.2.

35 Aquinas, *Summa Theologiae*, 3a. q.68.2.

36 Aquinas, *Summa Theologiae*, 3a. q.68.2.

37 Aquinas, *Summa Theologiae*, 3a. q.68.4.

38 Luther, *LW 36*, p. 69.

39 Luther, *LW 36*, p. 69.

40 It is worth saying that by the end of his training for ordination he came to see me to say that he had got it!

41 Luther, *LW 41*, p. 151.

42 Luther, *LW 41*, p. 172.

43 Luther, *Luther's Primary Works*, p. 134.

44 Luther, *Luther's Primary Works*, p. 134.

45 Luther, *Luther's Primary Works*, p. 134.

46 Luther, *Luther's Primary Works*, p. 134.

47 Luther, *Luther's Primary Works*, p. 134.

48 'The Holy and Blessed Sacrament of Baptism (1519)' in Luther, *LW 35*, p. 37.

49 Aquinas, *Summa Theologiae*, 3a. q.61.1.

50 Aquinas, *Summa Theologiae*, 3a. q.68.1.

51 The English word 'symbol' is derived from the Greek words *sum*, meaning 'with' and *ballo*, meaning 'I throw'. Hence the verb *symballein* literally means 'to throw together'. It is where two very different realities meet, engage and interact – where they come and are held together.

52 Aquinas, *Summa Theologiae*, 3a. q.62.1.

53 See the Church of England's 25th Article of Religion, 'Of the Sacraments'.

54 Luther, *Luther's Primary Works*, p. 138.

55 See, for example, Luther, *LW 41*, p. 171.

56 Graham Hughes demonstrates how 'physicality is a condition of our intellectuality' in his *Worship as Meaning: A Liturgical Theology for Late Modernity*, Cambridge: Cambridge University Press, 2003, see especially pp. 21–5.

57 Oliver Davies, *The Creativity of God: World, Eucharist and Reason*, Cambridge: Cambridge University Press, 2004, p. 195.

58 *UK Focus*, June 2003, pp. 4–5.

59 Quoted in Hindmarsh, 'Is Evangelical Ecclesiology an Oxymoron?', p. 30.

Chapter 8

1 The Preface can be found in Rattenbury, *Eucharistic Hymns*, pp. 145–63. The Hymns can also be found in Rattenbury, pp. H1–55. Where 'Preface' is cited in the following notes, it refers to Wesley's re-worked version of the Brevint text. Where reference is made to Brevint's original text it is cited as 'original text'.

2 Rattenbury, *Eucharistic Hymns*, p. 12.

3 Daniel Waterland, 'The Christian Sacrifice Explained' in *A Review of the Doctrine of the Eucharist*, Oxford: Oxford University Press, 1880, p. 435.

4 Preface, I.1–2, his italics.

5 See Aquinas, *Summa Theologiae*, 60, 3: 'It is at once commemorative of that which has gone before, namely the Passion of Christ, and demonstrative of that which is brought about in us through the Passion of Christ, namely grace, and prognostic, i.e. a foretaste of future glory.'

6 The numbers following each hymn refer to their number in the hymnbook.

7 Preface, II.4.

8 Preface, II.7.

9 Quoted by Hywel W. Roberts, 'Puritan and Separatist Sacramental Discourses' in *Union and Communion 1529–1979*, London: Westminster Conference, 1979, p. 66.

10 Quoted by Stephen Mayor, *The Lord's Supper in Early English Dissent*, London: Epworth, 1972, p. 98.

11 On Matthew Henry, see his *The Communicant's Companion*, 1704; see Daniel B. Stevick, *The Altar's Fire: Charles Wesley's Hymns on the Lord's Supper, 1745 Introduction and Exposition*, Peterborough: Epworth, 2004, p. 65. On Newton and other nineteenth-century evangelicals, see Seddon, *Gospel and Sacrament*.

12 See Hymns 2.1, 22.2, 2.4, 8.2.

13 Hymn 21.8.

14 Seddon, *Gospel and Sacrament*, p. 20. I am grateful to Philip Seddon for introducing me to the sacramental hymns of John Newton and William Cowper and particularly to his unpublished article on the same written in 2004.

15 See, for example, John Wesley's entry in his journal, 'Ye are witnesses. For many now present know, the very beginning of your conversion to God (perhaps, in some, the first deep conviction) was wrought at the Lord's Supper.' Journal, 27 June 1740.

16 William Carus (ed.), *Memoirs of the Life of the Rev. Charles Simeon*, London: J. Hatchard, 1847, p. 9.

17 Josiah Bateman, *The Life of the Right Rev. Daniel Wilson*, vol. 1, London: Murray, 1860, p. 25.

18 The quotations in order are from Hymns 23, 5, 6 and 21, all of which speak of the suffering and death of God. For a complete catalogue of the hymns on this theme, see Stevick, *Altar's Fire*, pp. 80–3.

19 Preface, II.8.

20 Hymn 21.1, 3.

21 Preface, III.1.

22 Preface, III.1.

23 Brevint's original text, IV.1.

24 Preface, III.2.

25 Hymn 73.2.

26 Preface IV.5; Hymn 66.1.

27 Hymn 58.4; 93.6.

28 'Gospel Holiness' in *The Works of Thomas Goodwin*, vol. 12, Edinburgh: J. Nichol, 1680, p. 312.

29 See Davey (ed.), *Anglican–Orthodox Dialogue: The Moscow Statement*.

30 *The Final Report*, 'The Anglican–Roman Catholic International Commission', London: SPCK, 1981, para. 8, p. 15. It is worth noting that Pope Benedict uses the dynamic language of gift to describe the transformative effect of the Eucharistic Prayer. 'The new prayer – which the Church calls the "Eucharistic Prayer" – brings the Eucharist into being. It is the word of power which transforms the gifts of the earth in an entirely new way into God's gift of himself, and it draws us into this process of transformation. That is why we call this action "Eucharist", which is a translation of the Hebrew word *beracha* – thanksgiving, praise, blessing, and a transformation worked by the Lord: the presence of his "hour". Jesus' hour is the hour in which love triumphs. In other words; it is God who has triumphed, because he is Love.' The full text of this homily, preached at Marienfeld, Cologne on 21 August 2005, can be found on the Vatican website.

31 Preface, IV.6.

32 John Owen, 'The Chamber of Imagery in the Church of Rome Laid Open' in William H. Goold (ed.), *Works*, Edinburgh: T & T Clark, 1862, vol. 16, p. 62.

33 Charles Simeon, *The Works of the Late Rev. Charles Simeon*, London: Cadell & Davies, 1819, vol. 11, p. 556.

34 Daniel Wilson (ed.), 'A Practical Address to the Communicant Previous to his Receiving the Holy Sacrament of the Lord's Supper' in *Sermons and Tracts*, vol. 2, London: George Wilson, 1825, pp. 387–8.

35 Edward Bickersteth, *A Treatise on the Lord's Supper*, London: L. B. Seely & Son, 1824, p. 119.

36 John Charles Ryle, *Knots United*, eleventh edn, London: William Hunt, 1886, p. 390.

37 See my *Evangelical Eucharistic Thought*.

38 Hymn 90.1.

39 Darwell Stone, *A History of the Doctrine of the Holy Eucharist*, vol. 2, London: Longmans, 1909, p. 223.

40 See my *Evangelical Eucharistic Thought*, p. 191, quoting Robert Bruce, 'First Sermon on the Sacrament in General' in *The Mystery of the Lord's Supper*, ed. T. F. Torrance, London: James Clarke, 1958, pp. 63–4.

41 Calvin, *Institutes*, IV.xvii.32.

42 Hymn 100.

43 Hymn 124.1, 4.

44 See the Prayer of Consecration in the 'Order for Communion' in the Book of Common Prayer (1662).

45 Preface, VI.2.

46 See Stevick, *Altar's Fire*, p. 152.

47 Preface, IV.2.

48 See my *Evangelical Eucharistic Thought*, pp. 211–66.

49 Preface, VI.2.

50 Hymn 22.3; see also 125.2.

51 See my *Evangelical Eucharistic Thought*, p. 211.

52 Preface, IV.2.

53 N. T. Wright, 'The Cross and the Caricatures', <www.fulcrum-anglican.org.uk>.

54 Stevick, *Altar's Fire*, p. 183.

55 Preface, VII.1.

56 Donald Baille, *The Theology of the Sacraments*, New York: Scribner, 1957, p. 122, quoted in Stevick, *Altar's Fire*, pp. 194–5.

57 Bonhoeffer, *Discipleship*, p. 63.

58 'Sermon 19: The Great Privilege of those that are Born of God' in Wesley, *Works 1*, pp. 413–32.

59 Preface, VII.5.

60 Hymn 141.6.

61 Hymn 131.4.

62 Preface, VII.7.

63 Preface, VII.9.

64 From Augustus Toplady's classic hymn 'Rock of Ages, cleft for me'. (I have pluralized the line.)

65 Hymn 137.5.

66 Hymn 133.3.

67 Hymn 135.4.

68 Ronald C. D. Jasper and Geoffrey J. Cuming, *Prayers of the Eucharist Early and Reformed*, second edn, New York: SCM, 1980, p. 23.

Chapter 9

1 I am grateful to Ian Stackhouse's book, *The Gospel-Driven Church: Retrieving Classical Ministries for Contemporary Revivalism*, Milton Keynes: Paternoster, 2004, for the term 'gospel-driven'.

2 Lesslie Newbigin, *The Gospel in a Pluralist Society*, London: SPCK, 1992, p. 33.

3 P. T. Forsyth, *Positive Preaching and the Modern Mind*, London: Independent Press Ltd, 1953, p. 3.

4 Stackhouse, *The Gospel-Driven Church*, pp. 107–8.

5 Forsyth, *Positive Preaching and the Modern Mind*, p. 3.

6 For a very helpful summary of Aristotle's teaching on communication, see George G. Hunter, *The Celtic Way of Evangelism*, Nashville: Abingdon Press, 2000, pp. 56–75.

7 Thomas Traherne, *Centuries*, London: The Faith Press, 1969,

1.8, p. 5. For a recent study of Traherne, see Denise Inge, *Traherne, Happiness and Holiness: Selected Readings from Thomas Traherne*, Norwich, Canterbury Press, 2007.

8 Stackhouse, *The Gospel-Driven Church*, pp. 101–2.

9 See Paul's argument in 1 Corinthians 1.18—2.16.

10 Martyn Percy, *Engaging with Contemporary Culture: Christianity, Theology and the Concrete Church*, Aldershot: Ashgate, 2005, pp. 223–6.

11 Hunter, *The Celtic Way of Evangelism*, p. 57.

12 It is fitting that John Stott's final public address, delivered at the 2007 Keswick Convention, concluded with an encouragement to be Christlike.

13 Nikitas Stihatos, 'On Spiritual Knowledge, Love and the Perfection of Living' in *The Philokalia*, ed. G. E. H. Palmer, Philip Sherrard and Kallistos Ware, vol. 4, London: Faber & Faber, 1995, p. 149.

14 The conclusion to the Declarations in *Common Worship Ordination Services*, London: Church House Publishing, 2007. Prayer for the candidates follows in the form of the singing of *Veni Creator* invoking the Holy Spirit, the Litany, as the prayer of the people and then the ordination prayer itself.

15 Newbigin, *The Gospel in a Pluralist Society*, p. 227.

16 Bede, *Ecclesiastical History of the English People*, London: Penguin Books, 1990, p. 166.

17 Bede, *Ecclesiastical History of the English People*, p. 147.

18 Michelle P. Brown, *How Christianity Came to Britain and Ireland*, Oxford: Lion Hudson, 2006, p. 95.

19 An interesting example is written up by George Lings in *Northumbria Community: Matching Monastery and Mission*, Encounters on the Edge No. 29, Sheffield: Church Army, no date.

20 Brown, *How Christianity Came to Britain and Ireland*, pp. 144, 95.

21 See, for example, Robert E. Webber, *Ancient-Future Evangelism: Making Your Church a Faith-Forming Community*, Grand Rapids: Baker Books, 2003; and Webber, *Ancient-Future Evangelism*.

22 Oswald Chambers, *So I Send You: A Series of Missionary Studies*, second edn, London: Simpkin, Marshall, 1934, p. 165.

23 See *Being a Priest Today*, with Rosalind Brown, 2nd edn, Norwich: Canterbury Press, 2006.

24 Christopher J. H. Wright, *The Mission of God*, Downers Grove: InterVarsity Press, 2006, p. 309.

25 The monastery was revived under Matthew the Poor, which has had a lasting effect on the community. The essence of this thought can be found in Matthew the Poor, *The Communion of Love*, New York: St Vladimir's Seminary Press, 1984.

26 *The Confession of Saint Patrick*, trans. by John Skinner, London: Doubleday, 1998.

27 For the influence of the Irish mission, see Thomas Cahill, *How the Irish Saved Christianity*, London: Hodder & Stoughton, 1995, p. 194.

28 James Bruce, *Prophecy, Miracles, Angels, and Heavenly Light?*, Milton Keynes: Paternoster, 2004, p. 239.

29 *The Revised Catechism of the Church of England.*

30 Adapted from *Being a Priest Today*, p. 216.

31 See John de Reeper, *A Missionary Companion: A Commentary on the Apostolic Faculties*, Dublin: Browne & Nolan, 1952, p. 1.

32 Dioceses, Pastoral and Mission Measure of the General Synod of the Church of England. See <http://www.cofe.anglican.org/about/gensynod/agendas/feb2007.html>.

33 The strict answer to the question according to the traditions of the church is Peter, who founded the European church in Rome.

Epilogue

1 For a helpful introduction to the Lindisfarne Gospels, see Michelle Brown, *Painted Labyrinth: The World of the Lindisfarne Gospels*, London: British Library, no date.

2 Joseph Lightfoot, *Epistles to the Colossians and to Philemon*, p. 154.

3 I am very grateful to Simon Barrington-Ward and my conversations with him for some of these insights and, even more, for all he has taught me about using the Jesus Prayer. For an excellent introduction, see his *The Jesus Prayer*, London: BRF, 2007.

Index of Names

251 n.1, 284 n.11

Warfield, B. B. 40

Warner, Pauline 130

Waterland, Daniel 189

Watts, Isaac 194–5

Webber, Robert 17–18, 85, 244, 283 n.20

Webster, John 26–9, 82, 93, 99

Wesley, Charles 14, 19, 74–5, 154, 159, 188–227

Wesley, John 14, 15, 19, 52, 54–5, 64–9, 70–71, 73–6, 78–9, 80–83, 148, 154, 159, 178, 187–227

Westminster Directory 160

Whitefield, George 14, 154

Wilkinson, George 15

Williams, D. H. 51

Williams, Rowan 283 n.24, 284 n.7

Wilson, Daniel 154, 196, 209

Wolterstorff, Nicholas 270 n.52

Wright, Chris 250

Wright, N. T. (Tom) 26–9, 80, 221, 231

Yeago, David 22, 267 n.23, 281 n.29

Yong, Amos xi

Zwingli, Huldrych 38, 110